LECTIONARY PREACHING RESOURCES

Series C

Edited by
Francis Rossow and Gerhard Aho

Publishing House
St. Louis

Copyright © 1988 by Concordia Publishing House
3558 South Jefferson Avenue, St. Louis, MO 63118-3968
Manufactured in the United States of America

Library of Congress Cataloging in Publication Data
(Revised for Series C)

Lectionary preaching resources.

    Contains sermonic studies for the Gospel and Epistle readings from Series A–C of the three-year-lectionary. The primary source for these studies is previous issues of the Concordia journal and the Concordia theological quarterly.
    Includes indexes.
    Contents: [v. 1] Series A—[v. 2] Series B—[v. 3] Series C.
    1. Bible. N.T.—Homiletical use. 2. Bible. N.T.—Liturgical lessons, English. I. Rossow, Francis C., 1925–   II. Aho, Gerhard. III. Concordia journal. IV. Concordia theological quarterly.
BS2392.L43 1986   251   85-28000
ISBN 0-570-03991-6 (pbk. : v. 1)

1 2 3 4 5 6 7 8 9 10   96 95 94 93 92 91 90 89 88

CONTENTS

PREFACE

The sermon studies in *Lectionary Preaching Resources: Series C,* for the most part, originally appeared in the *Concordia Journal* (Concordia Seminary, St. Louis, Mo.) and the *Concordia Theological Quarterly* (Concordia Theological Seminary, Fort Wayne, Ind.). A few new sermon studies were prepared to provide a comprehensive resource.

In a joint meeting the editors selected those they regarded as most likely to help the pastor in his weekly sermon preparation. These studies were edited to conform to a uniform length and style for the present volume. The Three-Year Lectionary as presented in *Lutheran Worship* was used for text selection.

These sermon studies provide a practical resource to the pastor in his weekly sermon preparation. The "Sermon Notes/ Introduction—Sermon Outline" format provides the pastor with helpful suggestions for both the content and the structure of his sermon. By working through the notes, one can quickly grasp the thrust of the text; the outline suggests one possible sermonic approach to the text. Studies have been included for every Sunday and major festival in the church year, thus making this an ongoing resource for every iteration of Series C.

It is our hope that, under God, these studies will prove to be a blessing not only to the pastor who consults them but ultimately to his hearers as well.

THE EDITORS

First Sunday in Advent

EPISTLE   1 Thessalonians 3:9–13 (KJV)

Sermon Notes/Introduction

Paul does two things at once. He thanks God for the Thessalonians and offers petitions to God on their behalf. Paul's thanks arise from the news from Timothy that the Thessalonian Christians are continuing in faith and love (3:6). Paul makes these petitions because he has spent only a short time in Thessalonica and wants to complete what is lacking in the faith of his friends. Furthermore, his efforts have been cut short by persecutors of the faith (2:14–16), and so he is uncertain about the Thessalonians' spiritual health. Paul uses the word "tribulation" to describe his present woes as he, torn from the Thessalonians, waits alone and impatiently while Timothy travels north to ascertain the Thessalonian situation. The tribulation is not merely some future trouble for the church but present difficulties faced by Paul and by all Christians.

Christians today need to see the Biblical response to tribulations as God's message of hope in their often difficult lives. God's answer to the tribulation is twofold. Ultimately He will deliver us by the parousia (coming or appearing) of our Lord Jesus. In the meantime He comforts, strengthens, and prepares us today with the ministry of the apostolic Word. Since no one knows the day of the parousia (5:2), Paul is more anxious to prepare and strengthen his people than to discern any divine secrets. Since he knows the health of the Thessalonians' faith, Paul's petitions for them are really more of a blessing or benediction than pious wishful thinking. His words also provide us an excellent summary of what Paul's ministry was to accomplish and what the ministry of the apostolic Word can accomplish today, especially in terms of preparing for the coming of the Lord.

Thanksgiving and Christmas are times when people either visit loved ones or are visited by them. Thanksgiving was just three days ago, and perhaps visitors may still be in the worship service this morning. In our visits we tend to talk about sports, food, family, church, and almost anything under the sun. Paul wanted to visit his friends and talk about something more important and to prepare them for an even more important visit. He wanted to talk about Jesus Christ and prepare the people for Christ's coming. When we listen to Paul's words, not only shall we know how to be prepared, but listening will prepare us.

Sermon Outline
WHEN CHRISTIANS LISTEN TO GOD
THEY BECOME PREPARED FOR CHRIST

I. When Christians listen to God, their faith is completed.
  A. The content of our faith (what we believe) grows through hearing the Word.
    1. For example, one may know Jesus as Savior but be confused about His Supper. Listening will help.
    2. For example, one may know God's love but not be certain of the events surrounding the second coming. Listening will help.
  B. The more information that we have from the Bible, the stronger we will be.
    1. We are so sinful and blind by nature.
    2. As Christians, we suffer tribulation.
    3. So many false teachings confront us.
II. When Christians listen to God, they increase in love.
  A. God in Christ causes us to love.
  B. We especially love other Christians.
    1. We are one with them.
    2. We share not only attitudes but also actions.
  C. We also love all people.
    1. Our love is a witness.
    2. We are constrained to love.
  D. Paul is a good example of this love.
    1. He sacrificed himself for his people.
    2. He gave himself to serve others.
III. When Christians hear the Word of God, their hearts are established.
  A. We are established to live blameless lives (cf. Phil. 2:15).
    1. "Blameless" describes our conduct.
    2. Even this blamelessness comes from Christ.
  B. We are established in a state of holiness.
    1. This state is Christ's gracious doing.
    2. It is not a gradual accomplishment.
    3. It is the cause of blamelessness, not its effect.
  C. We are prepared to stand at the coming of Christ.

Hearing God's Word prepares us because it completes our faith, increases our love, and establishes our hearts. We prepare for any visitor on holidays and special occasions. Since Christ is coming at any time, we must be prepared at any time. We prepare ourselves in the same way as the Thessalonians almost two thousand years ago—by hearing the message of Christ.

KLEMET PREUS

First Sunday in Advent

GOSPEL   Luke 21:25–36

Sermon Notes/Introduction

At the start of a new church year it is useful to be reminded of the sobering fact that some day soon the world, with all its history, will be brought to a sudden halt by the return of our Lord in glory. At that point the future will no longer be an extension of the present. Instead, it will offer us a glorious alternative to all the sorrow and anguish of this existence. With that prospect before us we shall do well to take up a portion of Scripture that deals with the signs that immediately precede the end of all things. The burden of Jesus' own words on this subject may well be subsumed under the general heading "Remain Ready to Stand."

Sermon Outline
REMAIN READY TO STAND

I. Amid growing chaos (vv. 25–26).
   A. Sun, moon, and stars were set by the Creator to rule the day and the night (Gen. 1:17–18). As "powers of the heavens" they keep reminding us of the order and stability that God built into the universe.
      1. But just before the Lord's return to bring the course of history to its end, even these steady elements in our cosmos will begin to show signs of breaking up. (See Is. 13:10; Ezek. 32:7–8; and Joel 2:10 and 3:15 for earlier references to phenomena of this kind that mark the approach of the Day of the Lord.)
      2. The sea is a symbol in Scripture of nations churning in turmoil (cf. Dan. 7:2) but kept under control by God's providence and power (Ps. 65:7). But there,

too, forces and events will be allowed to become unhinged, as it were.

B. People exhibit a twofold reaction to these awesome signs.

1. Panic, anxiety, and dismay grip those who do not know the Son of Man.

2. New courage and a fresh heart characterize those who recognize the signs as the prelude to God's mighty act of deliverance.

C. The followers of Jesus Christ will recognize the signs as heralding the "summer" of God's kingdom coming in glory.

1. After these cosmic disturbances (cf. the *tote* of Luke 21:27), people everywhere will see the Son of Man returning by way of the kind of cloud with which He was taken up into glory (Acts 1:9; note the use of the singular in each case).

2. He will come in power and great splendor (Luke 21:27). The era of His "veiled" activities in grace will end.

D. Jesus' description of this growing chaos in the universe summarily dismisses false dreams.

1. Rejected are people's dreams of creating their own utopias here on earth. This text is a reminder that no new social or political structures will bring in a perfect setting, as liberation theology and Marxism proclaim.

2. Equally unacceptable is every type of expectation that a millennium will precede the parousia. (Rev. 20:1–7 is a description of the age in which the church is now at work.)

II. In the presence of the Son of Man (Luke 21:36).

A. Knowledge of Jesus Christ as the Son of Man prepares us to stand in His presence. Jesus Himself preferred to use this title during His earthly ministry, a ministry in which He demonstrated its meaning.

1. The Son of Man has authority to do what is the prerogative of God alone: to forgive sins (cf. Mark 2:10).

2. The Son of Man is the Suffering Servant (Is. 53) ready to go into death (cf. Mark 10:33–34).

3. The Son of Man is the celestial figure of Dan. 8:23, who has received power and dominion to rule for

His church as its Head (cf. Mark 14:62 and Eph.
1:22–23).
B. Christians are called to live a life that readies them for
the return of the Son of Man.
   1. We cling to Jesus' words because they will never
      pass away; they remain steady and sure amid all
      chaos and disruption (Luke 21:33).
   2. We stay alert in prayer always (v. 36), asking for a
      way to escape when "the skies fall in."
   3. We avoid hangovers from yesterday's debauchery,
      the drunkenness that is expected to drown today's
      sorrows, and the worries dealing with tomorrow's
      problems (v. 34).
   4. We recognize the announced cosmic disasters as
      ushering in the time of release from the oppression
      and affliction that often beset God's children (v. 28).

The First Sunday in Advent serves us well as an occasion
to recall the why and the how of being ready always to stand
up straight amid the debris of history and in the face of the
coming judgment. For "that day" will be hard on those who
"sit on the face of the earth" (v. 35) in pursuit of their own
comfort and convenience. Therefore, be ready to stand!

MARTIN H. SCHARLEMANN

Second Sunday in Advent

EPISTLE   Philippians 1:3–11

Sermon Notes/Introduction

As in the Epistle for the First Sunday in Advent, in this
text Paul deals with sanctification in the wider sense. He is not
so much concerned with our specific good works as he is with
God's working in us. Paul again is thanking God for fellow
Christians. His prayer for them offers a description of the sanctified Christian. The prayer, begun in verse 4, is not expressed
until verse 9. Verses 5–8 are the basis for his prayer. Verses
5–7 describe the Philippians' condition. Verses 9–11 present
the natural expression of this gracious condition. Both sections
begin with an expression of Paul's affection (vv. 3–4, 8), and
both sections refer to the "day of Christ Jesus." Incidentally,
the expression "fellowship in the Gospel" (v. 5) seems most
naturally understood as a close equivalent to "common faith"

or the "fellowship of grace" in verse 7. Some commentators take the expression to mean a monetary gift or sharing in mission work. Although these activities would spring from "fellowship in the Gospel," such a definition tends unnecessarily to narrow the term.

Today the world is full of gloom and doom preachers and all sorts of bizarre claims about the end times. People often are more concerned about determining the impossible than preparing for the inevitable. The beauty of Christianity is that it is a religion not of conjecture but of comfort. The Word gives us confidence not only that Christ will come but that God has prepared and continues to prepare us for this coming. So a Christian is not just someone who anticipates and waits for Christ but one who is ready and prepared for Him.

Sermon Outline
GOD PREPARES US FOR THE DAY OF CHRIST

I. God prepares us for the day of Christ by giving us the Gospel.
   A. God alone is responsible for the creation of my faith.
      1. I am too sinful to create faith or cooperate with God.
      2. The idea of grace excludes my efforts.
      3. This creation is through the Gospel.
   B. God also preserves and perfects my faith.
      1. He does so by the Gospel.
      2. He does so alone.
   C. God's work in me enables me to stand confidently on the last day.
      1. I am standing in Christ.
      2. My standing depends not on me but on God's grace.

While God prepares us for the day of Christ by the giving of the Gospel, this Gospel also produces something in us.

II. God prepares us for the day of Christ by bringing forth fruits in us.
   A. These fruits spring from our righteousness in Christ.
      1. They have value because we are in Christ.
      2. And so by them God is glorified.
   B. These fruits are produced gradually.
      1. They develop as we grow in our relationship to Christ (knowledge).
      2. They develop as we grow in moral experience (insight).

C. The works done in us will stand when Christ comes.
   1. They will be pointed out publicly (Matt. 25:34–36).
   2. But our sins, being forgiven, will not be mentioned.

God prepares us for the day of Christ (1) by giving us the Gospel and faith, which gives us our standing before Him, and (2) by bringing forth fruits in us that will be publicly praised as glorifying God when He comes. Why should we be distraught and disquieted over all the confusing and silly theories about Christ's coming? Let us look to the Gospel instead. Thereby we are prepared, perfected, and made ready. This way is far better.

KLEMET PREUS

Second Sunday in Advent

GOSPEL   Luke 3:1–6 (RSV)

Sermon Notes/Introduction

The person and activities of John the Baptist are part and parcel of the "gospel of Jesus Christ, the Son of God" (Mark 1:1). He is the Advent figure par excellence, serving as a paradigm of the church's responsibility at the start of a new church year; namely, to concentrate on preparing the hearts and minds of its members for the approach of their Lord. We shall, therefore, celebrate this season of Advent with our ears attuned to Luke's account of the public appearance of John as marking a signal moment in God's dealings with us who are His people.

Sermon Outline
A SIGNAL MOMENT

I. The setting.
   A. Political institutions are decaying.
      1. In 9 B.C. the political leaders of Asia Minor had issued a decree expressing their conviction that the great Augustus (cf. Luke 2:1) had inaugurated a new era of hope for all humanity. But Augustus was followed by Tiberius (3:1), who managed to ascend the throne by way of the machinations of Livia and soon turned into a madman. All five political personages named by Luke in 3:1 not only fix the moment of John's prophetic activity but also remind us of the disintegration of Roman power.

   2. We have begun a new church year amid the debris
      of many familiar political structures, on some of
      which we had come to depend for a measure of
      stability and integrity. The world we had become
      accustomed to is coming apart at the seams.
B. Religious corruption is rampant.
   1. Luke speaks of one high-priestly office but lists two
      names: Annas and Caiaphas. This is the evangelist's
      way of indicating to what depths that office had
      fallen. (By political intrigue Annas was able to get
      five of his sons and Caiaphas, his son-in-law, into
      an office established by God to be occupied by the
      successors of Aaron for the lifetime of each one.)
   2. We live in a day of brash blasphemy. Many have
      fallen prey to the occult, to various cults, to the
      worship of Satan, and to Eastern religions of all
      kinds. Doctrinal disarray prevails almost every-
      where in mainline Christian churches.
C. Yet it is into such conditions of decay and darkness
   that God sends His prophetic Word. The Lord of the
   church asks us to take on the world as it is to prepare
   people for the coming of Jesus Christ. We are asked
   to serve as a light to the world.
   1. In the days of John there was a yearning for lib-
      eration (cf. v. 15).
   2. Many sheep today, in the words of Milton, "look
      up but are not fed." They need to hear the pro-
      phetic Word.
II. Its significance.
A. It is an example of recapitulation.
   1. As the old Israel was turned into God's special peo-
      ple by water (Red Sea), in the desert, and by the
      Voice from Mount Sinai, so John was called into
      the desert as a prophetic voice to baptize with water.
   2. Advent serves to remind us that the church (as the
      new Israel) lives, as it were, in a desert, sustained
      by water and the voice of prophet and apostle (cf.
      1 Cor. 10:1–6).
B. It is a call to repentance.
   1. John called on Jews to repent even though by de-
      scent they were children of Abraham.
      a. "Repentance" was a familiar term in that day,
         but Judaism put it like this: "Repent; then the
         kingdom of God will come."

b. John turned the formula around. Said he: "Repent; for the kingdom of God is upon you" (cf. Matt. 3:2).

2. We who are God's children are to repent because God, in Baptism, has appropriated to us the forgiveness of sins.

C. It is a call to administer the Sacrament of Baptism.

1. John baptized for the remission of sins (Luke 3:3).

2. Christian Baptism has even greater significance; it takes us back into the crucifixion and resurrection of our Lord (Rom. 6:3–5). By Baptism we become members of Christ's body, which is the church (cf. 1 Cor. 12:13).

III. Its sequel.

A. "Fruits" worthy of repentance are called for (Luke 3:8).

1. John spoke in harsh words of judgment over the Israel of his day (cf. especially Matt. 3:5–12) and uttered words promising salvation (Luke 3:6).

2. In the same way Advent invites us to examine ourselves in light of God's Law so that we may fully understand the measure of His grace.

B. By the Spirit's power, changes take place in people's lives.

1. John's proclamation changed the life-style of many persons so radically that his work could be likened to leveling the mountains (of pride) and filling in the valleys (of humility). The words of Is. 40:3–5 were fulfilled in John as the voice in the desert.

2. The church's Advent message aims to move us to bring forth more bountifully than ever what Paul calls "the fruit of the Spirit" (Gal. 5:22).

What today's Gospel tells us of God's signal moment in history, the season of Advent addresses to us in terms of our personal life with God. Before our baptisms we belonged to the realm of darkness. Now we belong to the kingdom of light. Amid the growing darkness of the moment in which we live, let us, like John, testify to the true Light that came into this world to "enlighten every man" (John 1:9).

MARTIN H. SCHARLEMANN

Third Sunday in Advent

EPISTLE   Philippians 4:4–9 (RSV)

Sermon Notes/Introduction

The theme of Advent takes a different shape this Sunday, and the readings help with this mood. The strong tone of judgment, characteristic of the first two Sundays in Advent, now makes room for a burst of joy and the "peace of God which passes all understanding" (Phil. 4:7). The Epistle from Philippians is the old Introit for this Sunday and serves to bind together the three readings around the theme "Rejoice!"—a most appropriate choice for this "Gaudete" Sunday. The theme of joy is dominant in Philippians (1:4, 18, 25; 2:2, 17, 18, 28, 29; 3:1; 4:1, 4, 10) and is always juxtaposed with suffering, for Paul always characterizes the Christian life-style in Philippians as joy in the midst of suffering. In his captivity Paul is preoccupied with communicating to the Philippian community that his sufferings for Christ are not a negation of the Gospel but an affirmation of his authenticity as an apostle of Christ.

Thus, the theme of joy in the midst of suffering dominates this letter from beginning to end, giving it an eschatological flavor that reaches a climax in this pericope. Joy is the stance of the Christian in the midst of suffering because the parousia is near. By prayer and supplication the Christian may petition God to ease the anxiety of a life lived in imitation of Christ so that, through forbearance, he may have the peace of Christ. These are lofty goals for the Philippians and for our communities. But every Christian community receives them as part of the apostolic tradition that is handed down generation after generation through the Word: "what you have learned and received and heard and seen in me" (v. 9). Paul sets himself up as a model of joy in the midst of persecution but calls all Christians to imitate Christ in the qualities of His life and His attitude in suffering. So Paul encourages the Philippians to have the same mind of Christ as portrayed in the great hymn of Christ's humiliation and exaltation (2:6–11). Most commentators take verse 8 of our pericope as a list of Hellenistic virtues, but they are more likely the attributes of Jesus Christ, the perfect gift from above. These are the same attributes used to describe Christ and the Christians in the Beatitudes of the Sermon on the Mount (Matt. 5:1–12).

For the suffering church that is anxiously preparing for the celebration of the incarnation, when the Savior is born in a manger in Bethlehem, these are sumptuous themes on which to dine on the Third Sunday in Advent. Our anxiety over life in a broken universe gives way to joy inside our tears. We truly expect and actually prepare for the inbreak of God's peace in the Christ Child, a peace that passes all understanding. The paradox is that joyful tears yield lives of peace with God. Zephaniah announces the joy and demonstrates God's presence in our midst, while Luke shows us how the Holy Spirit helps us prepare by cleansing the way and anticipating the consummation of all things.

The mood of this pericope is the imperative to live in the theology of the cross. Consider the following internal structure of this pericope (imperatives italicized):

(v. 4) *Rejoice* in the Lord always; . . . *Rejoice!*

(v. 5) *Let all men know* your forbearance.

(v. 6) *Have no anxiety* about anything.

(v. 6) *Let your requests be made known* to God. And the peace of God . . . will keep. . . .

(v. 8) *Think about* these things.

(v. 9) What you have learned and received and heard and seen in me, *do.*

With this internal structure in mind, the following outline recognizes the theme of the Third Sunday in Advent and the general theme of Philippians that finds its climax in this pericope.

Sermon Outline
JOY INSIDE OUR TEARS

I. Joyful tears make known our forbearance before people (v. 5).

    A. Forbearance recognizes that the Lord is near (v. 5).

    B. Forbearance petitions God (v. 6).

        1. We offer prayer and supplication.

        2. We offer it with thanksgiving.

    C. Forbearance keeps our hearts and minds in the peace of God (v. 7).

II. Joyful tears show our imitation of Christ.

    A. We imitate His qualities (v. 8).

        1. We received these qualities in Baptism, when we became "Christ's."

        2. They are detailed in the Beatitudes of the Sermon on the Mount (Matt. 5:1–12).

B. We imitate His suffering for the Kingdom (Phil. 3:10).
  1. We suffer in our fight against opponents of the Gospel (1:27–30).
  2. We suffer with the same mind of Christ detailed in the incarnational poem of 2:6–11.
C. We imitate the apostolic tradition, which assures us that the God of peace will be with us (4:9).
  1. We recount what we have learned, received, heard, and seen from the apostles (v. 9).
  2. We proclaim the incarnate Word, whose birth we celebrate at Christmas.
  3. We celebrate God's peace in the Eucharist.

ARTHUR JUST

Third Sunday in Advent

GOSPEL   Luke 3:7–18 (RSV)

Sermon Notes/Introduction

The season of Advent is a time of preparation not only for Christmas but also for receiving the Lord Jesus Christ in our daily lives and at His parousia. The Lord Christ wants to come into our lives and remain with us to deliver us from sin and the power of death, to strengthen us in our faith, and to motivate and empower us for service in His kingdom. We need to prepare to receive Him, because without such preparation we will not be ready for His coming.

Sermon Outline
PREPARATION BY REPENTANCE

I. Godly preparation leads first to a repentance that recognizes one's sins (vv. 7–9).
  A. Self-satisfaction with one's life may hide sins and the need for contrition even from the Christian.
    1. Many Jews did not come to John to repent and receive the mercy of God. They came instead for approval and commendation, because they thought they were good children of Abraham. Such an attitude of pride hid from them their true condition, that of being under the judgment of God because of their sins.
    2. Christians today are also beset by the sin of pride,

which, if left unreproved, leads to a self-satisfaction that covers over sins and the need for contrition before God.

B. Such self-satisfaction prepares the Christian not for Jesus Christ but for a life of self-gratification and death.

    1. John saw through the lack of repentance fostered by the attitude of pride. He saw how barren of good works his audience was, how dead in faith. The Jews that were coming to John in this state of unrepentance were not the true children of Abraham (cf. Rom. 4:1–12; 9:6–8). No appeal to their outward status of being the fleshly children of Abraham would avail before God (cf. John 8:39–40). They thus warranted the indictment "brood of vipers." When the stubble is set on fire in the harvest in preparation for the winter sowing, serpents of all sorts try to flee. In like manner John's audience in the face of God's judgment would try to flee. Because of their hardhearted state of unrepentance, displayed by their lack of good works (fruits of repentance), God could more easily raise up children to Abraham from stones.

    2. Before God we Christians can claim no status or good conduct by which we can hope to have a place in His kingdom. Our sins and lack of good works testify against us. To make such a self-righteous claim before God on the basis of a Christian reputation will only result in a fearful flight from God's judgment and in the end eternal death.

C. The first purpose of preparation is to strip away everything that would lead to self-satisfaction by recognizing our sins in godly fear and sorrow. Daily contrition over sins, together with a realization of our unfruitfulness before God, will be brought about by the Holy Spirit through our reading and meditating on the Word of God. It isn't easy or pleasant to recognize oneself as the object of the ax of God's judgment, to realize that the ax could possibly hit us. But such a realization is a necessary part of our contrition (cf. Matt. 7:19; Luke 13:6–9; and John 15:5–6).

II. Godly preparation also leads to a repentance that in faith clings to the promise of God's grace and forgiveness in Jesus Christ (Luke 3:15–18).

A. The message of Advent points us to Jesus Christ as

the Savior. John was not the Messiah. He was the herald of the Messiah's coming. His message and baptism were means of preparing the people for the One coming after him, the Mightier One (cf. John 1:26–31). John's baptism in water cannot be separated from his message of judgment and hope that urged the people to turn from their sins and disobedience and to look to the Mightier One who was coming to deliver them. In John's message the Messiah had a dual purpose—deliverance and judgment (Luke 3:17). Jesus, in contrast to John, would "baptize with the Holy Spirit and with fire." This description of Jesus' baptism in verse 16 tells us the difference between the ministries of John and Jesus. While John's ministry was one of preparation, Jesus' ministry would be to purify the people from their sins. Whether we are to understand the description "baptize with the Holy Spirit and with fire" only as an illustration of the purifying role of the Messiah (cf. Is. 61:1–2; Mal. 3:1–4; Luke 4:16–21; and especially Acts 10:38 and its context) and that role only as one of deliverance or judgment or both, or whether we are also to understand this description as a promise that Jesus would actually confer on people the power of the Spirit as He purified them from their sins has been debated by commentators. Most likely it is both. Some opt for the latter by pointing to the event of Pentecost in Acts 2 (cf. Acts 10:34–48 and 11:15–16, where Peter seems to do this).

B. The Advent message is of a Mighty One who has come to deliver His people. Jesus Christ in Luke 3:15–18 is pictured as both Judge and Savior (v. 17), but the emphasis is on the latter. For His role as Judge in separating the wheat from the chaff has the purpose of gathering in the wheat. The imagery of winnowing and gathering in the harvest is often used to illustrate the judgment (Is. 41:15–16; Jer. 15:7; Matt. 13:30; Rev. 14:14–20).

C. The Advent message brings assurance of hope and everlasting peace through faith.

III. Godly preparation results in a Christian life befitting repentance, a life that honors Jesus Christ as Savior and Lord (Luke 3:8a, 16, 10–14).

A. In response to the message of Advent we ask, "What then shall we do?" (vv. 10, 12, 14). We ask this question because we have been delivered by the Mighty One, and we desire to serve Him. Notice how the examples given in verses 10–14 are taken from daily life. Godly preparation touches everything we do and results in a daily renewal of service to God. Living for others instead of self-gratification is now the goal.

B. We desire to serve Jesus Christ for the sake of the Gospel so that others might be directed to Him.

LOUIS A. BRIGHTON

Fourth Sunday in Advent

EPISTLE   Hebrews 10:5–10 (RSV)

Sermon Notes/Introduction

On this Fourth Sunday in Advent the church now hunkers down and focuses on the essence of the holy season. The theme of this Sunday is Christological. There is a conscious attempt in the readings to see God's incarnational purpose riveted in the crucified body of the Messiah. Micah announces the ancestry of the Son of David born in Bethlehem; Mary proclaims that the child in her womb is the Messiah-Christ; and the author of Hebrews uses Psalm 40 to declare that the incarnate Lord is the one to be offered on the cross as the final sacrifice for the world's sins.

Thus, this last Sunday before the Nativity of our Lord is dominated by a theme that inextricably binds together the incarnation and the atonement. As we stand on the holy ground of Christmas, this is a fine theme for us to consider. And the Epistle from Hebrews is a marvelous vehicle by which to proclaim this message. Our pericope immediately precedes the climax of Hebrews in 10:11–18, in which Christ is proclaimed as the exalted High Priest. But today's reading is seminal in understanding Hebrews, for it presents the basic idea that in Christ the old becomes new, that "He [Christ] abolishes the first in order to establish the second" (v. 9). He does so by sacrificing Himself "once for all." The distance between the atonement and Christmas is only temporal, for when the child is born in Bethlehem, His death is already seen as the climax of His incarnation.

It is fair to say, therefore, that Jesus Christ is born to die. And it is also fair to say that with the birth of Jesus Christ, the old becomes new, the old covenant of sacrificial offerings giving

way to the new covenant of the once-for-all sacrifice of God's
Son for the sins of the world. The author of Hebrews sees
Psalm 40 as a prophetic statement in which the Messiah does
"the will of God" by His self-sacrifice. The eyes of the people
of God who gather to celebrate the incarnation and the atonement on this Fourth Sunday in Advent should be focused on
the sanctifying power of Christ's offering, which cleanses them
from all their sin. Here God's people are declared holy; here
they are set apart as the body of Christ; here they see themselves as new creatures in the new creation. The shift from old
to new unleashes a spiritual power that rocks the universe. One
does not usually associate power with Christmas, but if this
season is what our Epistle says it is, there is a power breaking
into the world that changes the world forever. One cannot
preach in this holy season of our Lord's birth without recognizing that the incarnation, the atonement, and the resurrection
of Jesus Christ are power-laden events.

As one considers the following outline, an introduction
might discuss how God cloaks His power in humble images:
The Savior is born in the sleepy village of Bethlehem, not in
Rome; shepherds, not Pharisees, come to worship the child;
the birth takes place in a stable, not a palace. How strange for
our God to use His power not for the glory of humanity but
for the saving of humanity. God's powerful kingdom comes
through abject humility, for in humility and weakness His power
is released, an understanding that unlocks the mystery of the
incarnation and the atonement. Christmas is the season of
power because of the reason for the birth of the child—Jesus
Christ was born to die.

Sermon Outline
BORN TO DIE

I. Christ's death abolishes the sacrificial cult.
  A. The old covenant sacrifices are not desired (v. 5).
    1. They were to be a reminder of sin (v. 3).
    2. The blood of bulls and goats does not take away
       sin (v. 4).
  B. The old covenant of the Law is but a shadow of things
     to come (v. 1).
    1. In Christ, the Law is fulfilled, as is written in the roll
       of the book (v. 7).
    2. In Christ, the will of God is fulfilled, as is written in
       the roll of the book (v. 7).

II. His death is an offering up of Himself.
  A. The body of Christ has been prepared in the new covenant (v. 5).
    1. The atonement reveals the mystery of the incarnation (v. 5).
    2. The atonement unleashes the power of a new age.
  B. The body of Christ (the church) has been sanctified through the offering of the body of Christ once for all (v. 10).
    1. To be sanctified is to be part of the new creation.
    2. To be sanctified involves participation in the death of Christ.
      a. In our Baptism we die and rise with Christ.
      b. We partake of His body and blood in the Eucharist.

ARTHUR JUST

Fourth Sunday in Advent

GOSPEL   Luke 1:39–45 (KJV)

Sermon Notes/Introduction

We often imagine the joy of sharing Christmas in a family setting. But the ideal is rarely attained, for the outward activities of the season can so easily rob the family of the true gift of Christmas. Of course, to the secular world the ideal of a beautiful family celebration is a mirage that is impossible to realize because people do not seek it in Jesus Christ. Christians can show how a family can celebrate the festival in a real, genuine, and lasting way.

Sermon Outline
THE CHRISTIAN FAMILY
CELEBRATES CHRISTMAS

I. Hearts and lives that have not been touched with the joy of the news of Jesus Christ ultimately have nothing to celebrate and nothing to share.
  A. Mary was deeply moved and convinced by the announcement that the Savior was coming (Luke 1:28–38). The message that the Messiah was coming overshadowed all else, even her forthcoming marriage. She dropped everything to share the news with her cousin

Elizabeth. Mary had something of great importance to tell.

B. When we do not have uppermost in our family celebration of Christmas the sharing of the news of the Savior, Jesus Christ, it shows that we are not moved by or convinced of its importance. Given this state of mind, the Word of God unveiling before the eyes of our hearts the glory of Jesus Christ may no longer stir us to repentance and faith. Instead, we seek in other things the purpose and joy of celebration and of life—but to no avail (cf. Luke 12:13–21). The ideal of a beautiful and significant family celebration of Christmas remains but a fleeting and unattainable mirage that leaves in its wake an empty, even bitter taste (cf. 10:38–42). This happens because the meaning of Christmas and its celebration are sought in things that are passing away and not in the truth of God's Word.

C. As a result, we will have nothing to share that will bring true joy and meaning. We will share only worldly activities and hopelessness, and in the end, death. The house, the family, that is not built on the foundation of Jesus Christ and His Word will perish (cf. Matt. 7:24–27; Luke 19:41–44).

II. In sharing the news of Jesus Christ we celebrate the presence of God and receive His blessings.

A. As Christians share with one another the message of the birth, life, death, and resurrection of Jesus Christ, God the Holy Spirit through that Word brings spiritual blessings of life and salvation.

1. Mary and Elizabeth were chosen by God to play different roles in the Christmas story, but each had an important part. Through the role that each played, they shared with the other the news and joy and hope of what God was bringing about in sending the Savior.

2. So we Christians today, through whatever role or ministry we have, are to share with our families and our fellow Christians the Gospel message of Jesus Christ. As Mary and Elizabeth, through the Word of God that they shared, received blessings of confirmation, inspiration, joy, and hope from the Holy Spirit (Luke 1:41, 42, 44, 45), so today, as we share the Word of God, we receive blessings to sustain,

encourage, and empower us in our Christian faith and life.

3. That the Holy Spirit and not a person's emotional will is the author of such joy and hope through the Word is witnessed by the miraculous movement of the child in the womb of Elizabeth (vv. 41–42). Although we are told that an emotional experience of a mother can cause movement of the fetus, here the miraculous expression of the emotion of the unborn child produced by the Spirit is meant. This in turn moves and motivates Elizabeth by the same Spirit to joyful reflection and response (cf. Gen. 25:22).

B. Through the Gospel message of Christ incarnate, crucified, and risen, God establishes fellowship within a Christian family and among Christians that endures in the hope of the Christmas promise.

1. Mary and Elizabeth received from God a beautiful fellowship that was expressed in the Magnificat. Mary's hymn of praise attests to the fellowship that existed between the two women during the three months of Mary's stay (Luke 1:56). It also indicates to us how Mary and Elizabeth prepared for the events that were soon to happen. Their preparation was founded on the Word of God and guided by the Holy Spirit. Resulting from such fellowship and preparation was a joyful confirmation of their faith and hope that God would keep His promise of a Savior. Such a celebrating preparation in the presence of God would remain with them forever (cf. Matt. 1:23—Emmanuel, "God with us").

2. Such a fellowship of joyful preparation will also result today as Christian families share and believe the Word of God. This fellowship is built on the promise of God's Word and celebrates the presence of God in Jesus Christ.

As Mary responded to the angel with the words "Behold the handmaid of the Lord; be it unto me according to Thy word" (Luke 1:38), we too respond in faith to the Gospel promise of God. Our response will move us to share the news of Jesus Christ with our families and our fellow Christians. The fellowship that will result will motivate us to love each Christian with an awe and respect for the way that God can use people touched by His love (vv. 42–45).

LOUIS A. BRIGHTON

The Nativity of Our Lord:
The Third Service (Christmas Day)

EPISTLE   Titus 3:4–7 (RSV)

Sermon Notes/Introduction

Titus was a Gentile, a companion of St. Paul. The apostle, after a brief stint of service on the island of Crete, left Titus in charge. It was his task and ministry to bring stability to newborn Christians and infant churches there. The writing of the letter falls around A.D. 63 while Paul may have been in Macedonia. Titus 3:4–7, the Christmas Day Epistle, is a profound statement of grace by St. Paul. God's *philanthropia* (love for humanity) prompted Him to send the gift of His Son into the world at the nativity of our Lord. Paul defines grace simply by stating that God's love is given to us not because we deserved it but as a free gift.

The power of God's grace in Christ is brought to us by the "washing of regeneration," which clearly refers to Baptism and not to an outpouring of the Spirit at Pentecost. Although Paul does not mention the part that faith plays in this drama in which God is clearly the actor and initiator of His love, it is implied when he says that those who are recipients of God's grace in Christ are made heirs, the inheritors of eternal life. In faith a person appropriates God's gift of grace and receives its blessings now and into eternity.

Introduction: I have before you a nicely wrapped present, and on the box it says, "Open at Christmas." I wonder what it might be. A special gift for the pastor? A sum of money for the church to pay the mortgage or to buy a new organ? Well, we shall never know what is in this gaily wrapped box unless we open it. So let us open the gift! There, it is open, but all that is inside is a slip of paper. What does it say? "A gift to the congregation—the gift of My grace in Jesus Christ." Signed: "God the Father." Amidst all the gifts that you have received this Christmas, I trust you will treasure this gift above all others, the gift of God's love and grace in Jesus Christ. This Christmas let us open the gift of God's grace.

Sermon Outline
THE GIFT OF GOD'S GRACE

I. The Savior of the World (v. 4).
   A. He is presented to us out of love.
   B. We are undeserving of such love (v. 5).
II. The Gracious Act of Baptism (vv. 5–6).
   A. Baptism regenerates and saves by grace.
   B. The Holy Spirit is poured into our lives through Baptism.
III. The Assurance of an Eternal Inheritance (v. 7).
   A. In faith we make the blessings of grace our own.
   B. In faith we lay hold of eternal life as God's heirs.

Some gifts are treasured for a lifetime because of the sentiment behind the gift. The greatest gift giver is God. Deep sentiment lies behind His most precious Christmas gift—the gift of His grace in Christ Jesus. Shall we treasure this gift or despise and cast it aside as we do the wrappings from a gift we have received? Not only would God have you open His gift, but also He would have you receive it in faith and treasure it to all eternity.

EDMOND E. AHO

The Nativity of Our Lord:
The Third Service (Christmas Day)

GOSPEL   John 1:1–18 (NKJV)

Sermon Notes/Introduction

Verses 1–5 are a profound statement regarding the Person of Christ. "The Word" (v. 1): Jesus is one with the being and mind of God and also the expression of the intelligence, will, and power of God. His person is identified with God. His office is to reveal God. The eternity, personality, and deity of Christ are affirmed. "Darkness" (v. 5): People are unable by their own reason or strength to understand Christ. John is called "a man" (v. 6) to contrast him with Christ, who is God. "Children" (v. 12) is distinct from the term "sons" more commonly used by Paul. The latter suggests a position and legal rights secured by adoption; the former implies likeness, nature, and life resulting from birth. Believers are "born" (v. 13) by the supernatural exercise of divine power. Christian life is imparted by the Spirit of God. "Only begotten" (v. 18) draws an absolute distinction between Christ and those who are called "children of God" by faith in Him.

The text stresses the reality of the incarnation. The goal of the sermon is that the hearers would grasp more fully the implications of God's becoming a man.

Introductory thought: We are celebrating an uncommon birthday today. Without Jesus' birth, no birthday could give promise of future good. The Gospel gives the reason for the joy to all people of which the angels sang.

Sermon Outline
THE WORD BECAME FLESH

I. What a profound mystery!
   A. Jesus is God (vv. 1–2).
      1. He is not merely in God or an emanation from God.
      2. He reveals God so that no one can know God except through Jesus (v. 18).
   B. Jesus is the Creator (v. 3).
      1. His wisdom and might are displayed in the depths of the seas, in the heights of outer space, in the way in which we hear and see and think.
      2. He is Lord of the universe.
   C. Yet Jesus is also a man (v. 14).
      1. He was a helpless infant who developed and grew up in human fashion.
      2. He was a friend of sinners who was numbered with the transgressors. He was confronted with temptations, acquainted with sorrow. He suffered and died. He became like us, except that He was without sin. He partook of our humanity in the fullest sense. It is a mystery indeed: The Word became flesh.

Through this incarnate Word God has something of eternal import to say to us. Here in the incarnation is God's own testimony.

II. What a unique testimony!
   A. God uses human beings to bring His testimony to the world.
      1. He used John the Baptist (vv. 6–8).
         a. John was a fine witness.
         b. But many nevertheless rejected his testimony (vv. 9–11).
      2. Today God uses pastors as well as lay Christians.
      3. Are our ears open to God's testimony?

    B. The testimony is that Jesus Christ is full of grace and truth.
      1. He is full of grace toward you. You can leave your sins and burdens with Him.
      2. He is full of truth toward you. In a deceitful world you can still rely on Him.
    C. God enables us to receive the testimony.
      1. We cannot receive it by our own powers (vv. 5a, 10).
      2. The Spirit creates faith through the testimony about Jesus (vv. 9, 13).
      3. To believe in Jesus is to be born of God.

The Word becoming flesh is an unparalleled event; in the assuming of our humanity by the Son of God we see a mighty wonder and receive a saving testimony. Our birthday was the prelude to our rebirth in Baptism, through which we have the joy of salvation. That joy is a reality because the Word became flesh.

GERHARD AHO

First Sunday After Christmas

EPISTLE   Hebrews 2:10–18 (RSV)

Sermon Notes/Introduction

The late Lord Haldane of England had a remarkable mother. In the foreword to her book of reminiscences, the Archbishop of Canterbury wrote of this unusual woman, "She taught me the greatness of life, the littleness of death, and the nearness of God."

As we turn our eyes to today's Epistle in this sacred season, one thing that strikes us most forcibly is the presence of God among humanity in the person of Jesus Christ. The prophetic word was fulfilled: " 'And His name shall be called Emmanuel' (which means, God with us)" (Matt. 1:23). We sing:

O Lord, we welcome Thee,
Our hearts for joy are leaping.
Thou, Jesus, dearest Child,
Thy precious promise keeping,
Art come from heav'n to earth
To be our Brother dear;
Thou, gracious Son of God,
Wilt banish all our fear. (TLH 93)

The One we welcome as our Brother has perfectly identified Himself with humanity. He has not only become *like* a
man; He has *become* man. This did not happen by chance or
without significance. It was purposeful; it was fraught with
meaning; it brought great blessings for the brothers and sisters
with whom He became one and for whom He would ultimately
die. His coming and particularly His death for us all enable
Him to be the source of much for which we should be grateful
on this sacred day.

Sermon Outline
JESUS, OUR SOURCE OF GRATITUDE

I. First of all, through His death He destroyed "him who has
the power of death, that is, the devil" (v. 14). Our Lord's
death set at naught the power of Satan. His death has
utterly destroyed death.

II. Second, our Lord is able to deliver us from the fear (*phobos*) of death (v. 15). When philosophers speak of "existential anxiety," they mean the "pointlessness" of life and
our sense of mortality. We do not have what Big Daddy
in *Cat on a Hot Tin Roof* calls the "pig's advantage," that
is, ignorance of death. For many people over 50, their
major concern is their own demise. From this *phobia*
(v. 15) Christ our Lord delivers us.

III. Third, our Lord became a faithful and merciful High Priest
to make expiation for the sins of the people (v. 17). See
2:9: ". . . so that by the grace of God He might taste death
for everyone." On "expiation," see also 1 John 2:2; 4:10.
It was for sin (Law) that He came (Gospel). "The Son of
Man came . . . to give His life as a ransom for many" (Matt.
20:28; Mark 10:45). In the words of the hymn:
Come, O long-expected Jesus,
Born to set your people free. (*LW* 22:1)

IV. Fourth, He is able to help those who are tempted (Heb.
2:18). See 1 Cor. 10:13. He indeed answers our prayer,
"Lead us not into temptation, but deliver us from evil."

Christ, our dear Lord and Savior, the One who is not
ashamed to call us His brothers and sisters (Heb. 2:11), is
certainly with us this day. By virtue of His death He has redeemed us, paid the penalty for our sins, and made us children
of the heavenly Father. By virtue of His resurrection He is
present with us in His church today and has made it possible
for us, who have been claimed by Him, to be certain of life

everlasting with Him. He said, "I am the resurrection and the life; he who believes in Me, though he die, yet shall he live, and whoever lives and believes in Me shall never die" (John 11:25–26).

We who trust in Him know that His death has destroyed death and that His resurrection has assured us of our own. He has preeminently taught us "the greatness of life, the littleness of death, and the nearness of God." Such a One is the Christ of Bethlehem. Knowing His grace and mercy to us, we say with Luther:

O dearest Jesus, holy child
Prepare a bed, soft, undefiled,
A holy shrine, within my heart,
That you and I need never part. Amen. (*LW* 38:5)
RUDOLPH H. HARM

First Sunday After Christmas

GOSPEL   Luke 2:41–52 (RSV)

Sermon Notes/Introduction

Have you ever complained about going to church every Sunday? Have you ever insisted that such worship is routine and therefore not worth the time and effort you devote to it? Preachers and preachers' families are not above such complaints, so it is not surprising that we hear them also from the laity. It is easy to gather a whole series of horror stories on the lack of benefits from routine worship. It is easy to point to the value of spontaneous, creative programs of worship in other congregations and church bodies and to envy them. It is even easy to point out that God does not tell us that we are to worship on Sunday or have daily devotions, though even critics must admit that He does call on us to worship Him regularly.

Sermon Outline
ROUTINE WORSHIP—NONROUTINE RESULTS

I. Routine worship: It has advantages and dangers.
   A. Regular routine worship is easy. There is no question of where the family is to be on Sunday morning. It is not necessary to decide where to go on the day off or whether to shop. The pattern is set: The family is going to spend Sunday morning at church.
   B. Routine worship may become mechanical. This was

true for many of the Jews in Jesus' day. It is also true
for those who follow a liturgical order of worship without being aware of its meaning. To appreciate the
beauty and significance of liturgical worship requires
familiarity with its meaning.

C. Routine worship may become legalistic. This was the
case with the Pharisees (Matt. 23:1–12). Note in this
passage that Christ told His disciples to follow their
directives. But note also His judgment on their legalism
and routine in 5:20.

Sometimes routine worship leads to nonroutine results.
The Gospel tells us that Mary and Joseph went up to Jerusalem
"according to custom." Jesus at age 12 was now a "son of
the Law" and was expected to go along. It was a routine trip
in fulfillment of the Law; His active obedience also was a
shadow of things to come. Subsequently, He who created
heaven and earth was subject to His parents—another instance
of His active obedience in keeping the Fourth Commandment.

Mary's presence was not required at the feast, but she
loved the habitation of God's house and the place where His
glory dwells (Ps. 26:8). This was a close-knit, model family.
Joseph had a high regard for Mary and loved her. They worshiped together. They did not want to be separated even
though the journey was an arduous one.

II. Nonroutine results.

A. *For temple teachers and hearers.* It was an unusual
experience for them to meet a young child of 12 who
was so knowledgeable. This same amazing privilege
extended to the hearers in the temple court (Luke
2:47).

B. *For Mary and Joseph.* Note that Mary and Joseph
cared for the Lord not only physically but also spiritually by arranging for Him to go to Jerusalem as required by the Law. They experienced surprise but also
amazement at this wonder Child of theirs. Mary and
Joseph trusted Jesus and therefore were not unduly
alarmed at first (v. 44). Note that even good children
may at times cause grief to their parents.

C. *For other members of the party.* No doubt they were
aware of the alarm of Mary and Joseph and subsequently of His wonderful testimony in the temple court.

III. Why such nonroutine results from routine worship? Christ
was present.

A. Jesus made the difference between what might have
been a routine trip to Jerusalem for the Passover and
a never-to-be-forgotten experience. His presence
brought about the fulfillment of Hag. 2:9.

B. Today Jesus is present in His Word. He comes to us
if we are open to His testimony. Just as this first word
of Jesus was too deep for His mother to comprehend,
so we must patiently await His enlightenment and the
enlightenment of the Spirit.

C. This Messiah brings temporal blessings, but more important, He brings the spiritual blessing of forgiveness
(Luke 2:52). By His life, death, and resurrection He
has brought us "into favor with God."

Maybe the routine of coming to church every Sunday
morning is not so bad after all. Yes, Satan will have his share
of success in convincing us that it is routine and that we can
afford to daydream or to plan for the week ahead. We can
shut out the preacher and shut out the Lord. If we open our
ears, though, Christ is present and the power of the Word is
present. We may gain important insights from routine church
attendance, instances when the Word is directed to us as individuals. So also today even routine worship can have nonroutine results.

JOHN W. KLOTZ

Second Sunday After Christmas

EPISTLE   Ephesians 1:3–6, 15–18 (RSV)

Sermon Notes/Introduction

In order that Christians might fulfill the purpose in this life
that God intended (to live to the praise of His glory, vv. 6, 12),
the apostle Paul reminds the Ephesians (and us) that reasons
for praising God reach back much further than Jesus' coming
to earth on the first Christmas. God's love and grace toward
us were evident "before the foundation of the world" (v. 4)
was laid.

Sermon Outline
THE CHURCH IS BORN

1. The church was born in the mind and will of God before
creation.

A. God chose us to be His long ago.
   1. He would not endure the estrangement of the crown of His creation caused by sin.
   2. His choice was prompted by His great love and undeserved kindness toward us (v. 6).
   3. His choice was meant to stir us to praise.
B. God carried out in time what He chose in eternity to do.

II. Jesus' birth is the key to the birth of the church.
A. Through Jesus we are made holy and blameless (v. 4).
   1. We receive the benefit of Jesus' righteousness by faith. In God's eyes we are righteous.
   2. Jesus earned this righteousness for us by His holy life.
   3. This righteousness frees us from the guilt of sin. To feel guilt when we have been freed of it is unnecessary and an insult to the grace of God and the Savior who freed us.
B. Jesus in His suffering and death endured the punishment for our sin.
   1. Through faith we are free of the punishment of our sin.
   2. We need not live in fear of this punishment.
   3. God means for us to serve Him and praise Him.
C. Through Jesus and the working of the Holy Spirit we become God's sons and daughters (v. 5).

III. Faith-filled Christians are evidence that the church is alive (v. 15).
A. Faith shows itself in love.
   1. Faith shows itself in the love of God.
   2. Faith shows itself in the love of one's neighbor.
B. Faith shows itself enlightening the eyes of the heart (v. 18).
   1. We know God and Jesus Christ.
   2. We know a glorious hope for this life and for heavenly life.
   3. We talk to God in prayer, thus maintaining the relationship.

Reflect on these blessings from God and praise Him always!

RUDOLPH A. HAAK

Second Sunday After Christmas

GOSPEL   John 1:1–18

Sermon Notes/Introduction

At the beginning of his gospel John tells us what Jesus meant to him and what He can mean to us. He uses comparisons. John points to the best, the greatest of mere human beings, among whom he also has a rightful place, and gives full recognition to what they accomplished with power from on high. Then he puts Christ alongside them and shows Him towering over them as the Himalayas would tower over the Mount of Olives. Note how ably John introduces each of these men. First, there was a man sent from God whose name was John. He was the forerunner of the Christ. Second, he alludes to himself, who in the company of others beheld Christ's glory, as he did especially on the Mount of Transfiguration. Then John the Baptist comes in again. Finally, there is Moses, the great lawgiver. These were great men. Jesus Himself said of the Baptist that he was the greatest of the Old Testament prophets. John the evangelist speaks of himself as the one whom Jesus loved. Moses long ago had said that the Lord would raise up a prophet like himself.

Yet great as these men were, the Lord was far greater than any. The Law came by Moses, but grace and truth came by Jesus Christ. John the Baptist was the greatest of the Old Testament prophets, but he said of Christ, "I am not worthy to untie his sandals." The evangelist John gives us the reason. Christ already existed in the beginning. He created the world. As Creator, he also made Moses and John the Baptist and John the evangelist. Moreover, in Him was life, and the life was the light for all people. Whoever heard Moses was actually hearing the Word, the Son of God. He also enlightened John the Baptist for his work through His Holy Spirit. He prepared John the evangelist for his important work. He is truly the greatest. That is why even unbelievers, in a sense at least, observe His birthday. That is why Christians teach their children to think of Christmas as Jesus' birthday. He is the greatest.

Sermon Outline

OF CHRIST'S FULLNESS WE HAVE RECEIVED AND MUST EVER RECEIVE

I. He gives us His truth.

    A. He was able to give it because He was with the Father from the beginning.
    B. Our human power, without His help, would never be able to grasp it.
    C. It clearly portrays the life we can live in Him.
II. He gives us His grace.
    A. Moses helps us to see our need of it.
    B. John the Baptist preached repentance that we might see the greatness of Christ.
    C. That will be our message until the end of time.

DO NOT BLAME OTHERS IF YOU CANNOT CLEARLY SEE YOUR LOVING GOD

I. The enemies of the truth try to hide Christ from our view.
    A. Darkness is all about us in the world.
    B. Most people have not yet come to Christ.
    C. The devil will do his best to try to draw us away.
II. But Christ is greater than any power of darkness.
    A. He is Himself the Light.
    B. He has revealed God from the beginning of time, having been with God.
    C. His message shines bright and clear.
    D. Keep your eyes on Christ the Light, and no one can lead you into darkness again.

THE TRUE GLORY OF THE SAVIOR WHOSE BIRTH WE CELEBRATE

I. He is the only-begotten Son of God.
    A. Moses pointed to His glory long ago.
    B. John the Baptist showed His greatness in comparison with himself.
    C. John, the one whom Jesus loved, is an eyewitness of His glory.
II. He is the everlasting fountain of the love of God.
    A. He has brought us out of darkness into His marvelous light.
    B. In that marvelous light we see God.
       1. He is not full of wrath toward us, as we would deserve.
       2. He is full of forgiving love in His Son.
       3. He gives us all the blessings that He has created for us.

MARK J. STEEGE

The Epiphany of Our Lord

EPISTLE   Ephesians 3:2–12 (RSV)

Sermon Notes/Introduction

If the text is read from KJV or RSV rather than from a lectionary, be sure to omit the opening "if" or "assuming that." The conditional or participle serves only to confuse the oral interpretation. Most translations begin verse 2 with an independent sentence.

The Epistle, Gospel, and Old Testament readings for the Epiphany festival are the same for each year of the three-year cycle. Both the Epistle and the Gospel make clear that the designers of the three-year lectionary sought to emphasize the universality of salvation in the newborn King on this day.

"Bringing Christ to the nations" is a well-known phrase to 20th-century radio audiences. It identifies well the Christian church's call to share its wealth with all on our globe, and many have thrilled to hear the message of salvation reach out to far corners of the earth.

Centuries before radio became a Gospel medium, another man found joy in his call to preach to people far and wide. Paul was his name, and his own exciting description of this ministry to the nations of his day provides the opportunity to speak about "Riches for All."

Sermon Outline
RICHES FOR ALL

I. The riches are given in Christ (v. 8).

Paul inscribed a large *Chi Rho* over the first three chapters of his Letter to the Ephesians. Note how often he links thought after thought to Jesus Christ. In the pericope of the day, the apostle reaches a climax with the phrase "the unsearchable riches of Christ." "Unfathomable" and "incomprehensible" are other translations for the Greek word rendered "unsearchable" in the RSV. There are spiritual riches for all people, spiritual riches that boggle the mind. But let there be no mistake. These riches are only in Christ Jesus. For in Him they glorify, magnify, and worship the newborn King in company with those who brought gifts of gold, frankincense, and myrrh.

II. The riches are shared through preaching (vv. 3–11).

It is to the sharing of these riches, however, that Paul addresses himself most thoroughly. The riches are shared through what the apostle called elsewhere "the foolishness of preaching." His own preaching ministry to Gentiles occupied Paul especially in this pericope. That ministry is called the stewardship of God's grace and the mystery made known by revelation.

Paul uses the term "mystery" several times in his writing. It refers to something at one time hidden but now disclosed. The word should not always be interpreted to mean the same thing. For example, the mystery of Eph. 1:9 is different from that in the text in hand. In the latter, the mystery revealed is that the Gentiles are fellow heirs of the Gospel blessings in Christ. The mystery is also that the Lord appoints messengers to bring such wealth in Christ to Gentiles. This was a mystery revealed even to heavenly creatures in Paul's day as it had never been made known before.

Old Testament revelation, of course, spoke about the universality of the salvation blessings of God. The Old Testament Reading for the day makes a point of that. Just how this was to be fulfilled, however, was not as clear in times past as it was in Paul's day. His ministry to the Gentiles showed clearly God's intention and plan, an aggressive effort to reach the uttermost parts of the earth with the Gospel news.

The call to worldwide mission work is the obvious application of this second part of the sermon outline.

III. The riches effect access to the eternal God (v. 12).

It remains to ask what are the special benefits that accrue to anyone who grasps the unsearchable riches of Christ. Nothing less than boldness and confidence of access to approach an eternal God. The beauty of this access becomes most apparent when we analyze ourselves. Sin has separated us from God. No amount of effort by the sinner will bridge the chasm. But riches in Christ accomplish that bridging. We have no more right to come with gifts of gold and frankincense than the Magi had. And yet, like those men of old, we may approach the eternal God boldly and confidently. We will not be cast away even as they were not cast away in their worship of the Child. There is, therefore, no condemnation to those who are in Christ Jesus. That is the benefit of grasping riches in Christ.

Citizens of the world have many things to share with each other. The rich do well to share of their bounty with the poor. The well-fed have an obligation to feed the hungry. The expertise of one might be of great use to another. But spiritual riches in Christ are the choicest gifts to share with all people.

May the church continue to feel keenly its responsibility to bring Christ to the nations. That is bringing riches to the world.

WAYNE E. SCHMIDT

The Epiphany of Our Lord

GOSPEL   Matthew 2:1–12 (RSV)

Sermon Notes/Introduction

The account of the visit of the Magi to pay homage to the Christ Child has called forth many questions. Who were the Magi? Where did they come from? How many Magi were there? What were their names? Many of the questions are interesting and intriguing, but they are not significant to the Christian faith. Today's pericope invites the inquirer to ask the right questions, to seek correct answers, and to make the proper responses.

Sermon Outline

RIGHT QUESTIONS, CORRECT ANSWERS, AND PROPER RESPONSES

I. There are questions that have been asked and need to be asked.
   A. The Magi came to Jerusalem and to Herod with the question "Where is He who has been born king of the Jews?" The Magi had already asked and answered for themselves the prior question *"Who is He* who has been born king of the Jews?"
   B. Herod asked the chief priests and the scribes where the Christ/the Messiah was to be born. He asked the Magi when the star appeared. As the last part of Matt. 2 shows, he was asking these questions for the wrong reasons.
   C. Who is He that came? Why did He come? For whom did He come? These are some of the important questions that need to be asked today.
II. In His holy Word God has provided all the correct answers to all the proper questions.
   A. *Where?* The Christ/the Messiah was to be born and was born in Bethlehem.
   B. *When?* He was born in the fullness of time (Gal. 4:4),

according to God's schedule. Knowing the exact time and date is not essential to the Christian faith.

C. *Who is He?* The Magi identified Him as the King of the Jews. They had obviously read or heard one or more of the Messianic promises in the Old Testament. Such promises include Gen. 3:15; 12:3; 2 Sam. 7; Ps. 2; 110; and Num. 24:17. The Magi's reference to Jesus as "the King of the Jews" anticipates Pilate's reference to Him as the King of the Jews during the trial on Good Friday and again in the inscription placed above His head on the cross. The Magi understood that the Child of Bethlehem was the King and Supreme Ruler over all people.

D. *Why did He come?* He came because all people are by nature sinners and under the wrath of the holy God. He came to minister to people and to save them from sin, death, and eternal separation from God. He came to rule and to reign as King and Lord in the hearts of people in whom the Holy Spirit would work new life through the Gospel. Ultimately, God will put all things under His feet (Ps. 110; Eph. 1).

III. God expects proper responses from His people.

A. Herod and the chief priests and scribes did not respond properly.

1. The chief priests and the scribes knew where to find the correct answers to the proper questions. But their knowledge appears to have been merely an intellectual knowledge.

2. Herod knew where and about when the Christ/the Messiah, the King of the Jews, was born. He apparently feared for his job and sought to kill the Child.

B. Led by the Holy Spirit to believe and to understand that God's Good News in Jesus Christ was meant for them, the Magi rejoiced at God's manifestation of His Son. They worshiped the Child of Bethlehem as their King and offered Him tokens of their love, after which they returned home by "another way."

C. God the Holy Spirit enlightens and empowers us through Word and Sacrament to rejoice at God's revelation of His love and forgiveness in Jesus Christ; to worship Jesus Christ, King from eternity, with our lives, time, efforts, and treasures; and to go "another way."

The Gospel for the day suggests many interesting and intriguing questions. Christians need and welcome the guidance of God the Holy Spirit as they seek to ask the right questions of God's holy Word, as they search for the correct answers God has provided, and as they pray that the Holy Spirit will so enlighten and empower them through the Gospel that they make the proper responses.

ARTHUR G. GRAUDIN

The Baptism of Our Lord: First Sunday After the Epiphany

EPISTLE   Acts 10:34–38 (RSV)

Sermon Notes/Introduction

The ILCW three-year lectionary series highlights a highly significant event in the life of our Lord on the Sunday after the Epiphany. It is known as the Sunday of the Baptism of Our Lord. The absence in most congregations of midweek Epiphany services may well tempt some to substitute the Epiphany pericopes for those of the First Sunday After the Epiphany, but to do that every year would be unfortunate. The Baptism of Our Lord deserves a regular place in the liturgical calendar.

Nationally and internationally, racism looms as a major human concern. Large cities in the United States must address themselves periodically to the problem of segregated schools and the explosive issue of school busing. Distant South Africa rages from time to time because of the policies of apartheid. Sinful human beings of all races and classes have lurking within their bosoms embryonic or fully matured cases of racism. But God is no racist, and this is evident not only from His creation of all people but also from the monumental act of His love in providing salvation for all of fallen humanity. The apostle Peter drew attention to this nonracist attitude of God when he preached on "Jesus—Chosen Savior of All Races."

Sermon Outline
JESUS—CHOSEN SAVIOR OF ALL RACES

I. The Baptism of Jesus (vv. 37–38a).

The account of the baptism of our Lord is taken from a different Gospel for each year of the three-year lectionary cycle. The reading from Acts 10:34–38, however, is appointed to be read each year, an indication that the designers of the lectionary considered it an especially appropriate reading to complement the day's Gospel. Peter's reference to the baptism of the Lord should, therefore, receive adequate homiletical treatment. The annual repetition of the Old Testament Reading is a similar call to draw on its references to Yahweh's selection of His servant.

The emphasis in this part of the sermon outline rests on the Father's choosing and appointing activity as this was manifested at Jordan's stream when John the Baptist, forerunner of the Savior and preacher of repentance, baptized Him who stepped forward to fulfill all righteousness.

II. The Ministry of Jesus (vv. 36, 38b).

Jesus' baptism marks the beginning of His public ministry. But Peter did not stop in his sermon with this first ministerial event. He proceeded to sketch in bold lines some other essentials of our Lord's ministry. Christ went about doing good, just as the Old Testament Reading foretold. Chief testimony to His choice as the Savior of all races was the manifestation of power in the miracles of His ministry. The Emmaus disciples summarized it well when they called Him "a prophet mighty (*dunatos*) in deed and word."

Jesus' power was also not without an object. He exercised lordship over the consequences of sin and so brought into subjection the devil himself. The words "oppressed by the devil" (v. 38) begin the homiletical trajectory that sends the preacher into the context of the pericope, verses 39–40, which speaks of the final victory over Satan, the Savior's resurrection from the dead.

The sixth, seventh, and eighth Sundays after Epiphany bring Epistle readings from the classic resurrection chapter, 1 Cor. 15. Note in particular the triumphant tone of verses 51–58, the reading appointed for the Eighth Sunday After the Epiphany: "Death is swallowed up in victory." Christ had power over the devil indeed. This is the ministry of the Savior of the world, chosen by God for this purpose.

III. The Mission of Jesus (vv. 34–37).

Jesus' ministry itself took place in the land of Israel, but the blessings are for the entire world. That was the specific message that God inspired the apostle Peter to emphasize in his sermon. At this point the Cornelius context of the pericope might be reviewed.

A caveat is in order here. The phrase "anyone . . . who does what is right is acceptable" (v. 35) can be easily misunderstood. *Dikaiosunē* is the word used for "what is right." One dare not, of course, read the fullness of Paul's *dikaiosunē theou* into the *dikaiosunē* of Peter's sermon. But it would be equally incorrect to leave hearers with the idea that a religiosity toward some vague God is adequate for salvation. Cornelius prayed at the ninth hour. He engaged, in other words, in Jewish prayer practices in Caesarea. He was acquainted with the Old Testament Lord of Messianic prophecy. But more than that, Peter was able to refer to a knowledge of at least some of the things that he was declaring—*oidate*. Cornelius, a Gentile, walked in the tradition of Zechariah and Elizabeth (Luke 1:6) and in the way of Simeon (2:25)—*dikaios*. That was the starting point of Peter's encounter with Cornelius the Gentile.

The baptism and ministry of Jesus culminate in a world mission. All colors, all classes, both Jews and Gentiles, receive the blessings of God in Christ Jesus. God is no racist. His Son is Savior of all.

WAYNE E. SCHMIDT

The Baptism of Our Lord:
First Sunday After the Epiphany

GOSPEL   Luke 3:15–17, 21–22 (RSV)

Sermon Notes/Introduction

The account of the baptism of our Lord in the Gospel according to St. Luke offers a clear contrast between the person and work of John the Baptist and that of Jesus. The narrative is striking in that the arrest of John the Baptist is interposed (vv. 18–20), although these verses are not a part of the pericope. John the Baptist is here taken out of the action so that our Lord can be the only figure on the scene. The baptism account therefore does exactly what John would have wished: "He must increase, but I must decrease" (John 3:30). John's words in the pericope emphasize that he is preparing the way for the chosen One, who will work in the power of the Holy Spirit and whose deeds will make those of the Baptist fade in significance. The Gospel is the ministry of Jesus Christ, and He alone must be the center of our preaching and the only justification for our ministry.

A soft drink company once advertised its product as "the real thing." Our society is often concerned about natural products. We will not accept a substitute. The Gospel for today points us to a "real thing" of far greater importance—our Lord Jesus Christ.

Sermon Outline
THE REAL THING

I. The Forerunner.
  A. John the Baptist's ministry had people asking whether he might be the Christ (v. 15).
    1. They were in expectation.
    2. John's preaching had accomplished its purpose (vv. 7–14).
  B. John's response to their question: "Not I!"
    1. A mightier one is coming; in comparison to Him, John is unworthy (v. 16).
    2. His work will be greater than John's.
      a. He will baptize with the Holy Spirit and fire.
      b. He will bring in the harvest and separate the wheat from the chaff. The harvest will be in His hands.
II. The Real Thing—the Christ.
  A. Jesus' baptism is a public proclamation of His ministry.
    1. John the Baptist is not even mentioned here. Jesus is the central figure.
    2. The witness of the Spirit is shown in His descent as a dove.
    3. The blessing of the Father is on His "beloved Son" (see Is. 42).
  B. Jesus' work begins for us as the beloved Son.
    1. He is the real thing.
    2. In this first act of His ministry Jesus publicly receives His commission.
    3. He must be the center of our lives as our Redeemer.

In the final analysis, nothing matters except this One who was baptized in the waters of the Jordan. He was not an impostor or traveling preacher. He was the One to whom all the prophets pointed. John the Baptist could also only direct the attention of the people to Him, for He is the Beloved Son of the Father. He is the Real Thing.

MARK E. WANGERIN

Second Sunday After the Epiphany

EPISTLE   1 Corinthians 12:1–11

Sermon Notes/Introduction

We hear much today about the charismatic gifts of the Spirit. One is sometimes asked, "Are you charismatic?" or "Have you received the baptism of the Spirit?" The questioner often implies that unless one has the gifts of the Spirit—and the gift of tongues is usually stressed—one is a lesser Christian. On the other hand—and sometimes in reaction—the Holy Spirit's activity of giving gifts for the Christian's life is ignored, belittled, or even denied. Today's Epistle encourages us to avoid both of these errors as the apostle Paul discusses the role of the Spirit in our lives as Christians. In particular, Paul instructs us as God's people always to be aware of the Spirit's work of enabling the sinner to acknowledge and confess Jesus Christ as Lord. Resulting from this confession is a Christian life empowered by the Holy Spirit and enriched by the gifts He bestows. This Christian life is to be lived under the lordship of Christ. This is the central thought of the text. Whatever gifts the Spirit gives to His Christians are to show forth the lordship of Christ as Savior of the world.

Sermon Outline

THE LORDSHIP OF JESUS CHRIST
EXHIBITED BY THE GIFTS OF THE SPIRIT

I. The gifts of the Spirit (cf. Rom. 12:1–8; Eph. 4:11–16).
   A. Two words in the Epistle describe the gifts of the Spirit: *pneumatikos* and *charisma* (vv. 1, 4). The former means "of the Spirit"; the latter means "a gift of grace." From these two words we can say immediately that the gifts come from the Spirit as gifts of God's grace, gifts for spiritual purposes within the sphere of the grace of God. A word study of *charisma* shows that the whole Christian life is touched by the Spirit in the bestowal of these gifts. No part of the Christian life is without them; that is, there is no Christianity apart from the Spirit's bestowal of gifts. It therefore is a false and unscriptural dichotomy to suggest that some Christians have gifts and others do not.
   B. Gifts are given by the same Spirit to all Christians

(v. 7), but not all have the same gifts (vv. 8–11; also vv. 4–6; cf. vv. 27–31).

C. The purpose of the gifts is not to evaluate the Christianity of oneself or others (cf. vv. 12–26) but to enable the mutual service of all Christians as each shares the benefits of his or her gifts with others (v. 7).

D. The controlling purpose and interest of the gifts is the lordship of Jesus Christ (v. 3). It is for the service in the kingdom of God that the gifts are given, and in this service they glorify God.

II. The gifts of the Spirit are for the glory of Christ in the proclamation of the Gospel.

A. The misuse of the gifts is a denial of the lordship of Christ and a distortion, even a destruction, of the proclamation of the Gospel (vv. 4–6; 14:1–5, 23–25).

   1. Misuse causes divisions in the body of Christ.

   2. It hinders the proclamation of the Gospel by shifting the center of the Christian proclamation to sanctification or even enthusiasm and works-righteousness.

   3. It glorifies human beings and belittles Christ.

   4. Misuse is anything that does not ring true with the Scriptures—elevating one gift above another, boasting about gifts, categorizing Christians as Spirit-filled and not-Spirit-filled, judging a Christian's faith and life by the awareness of gifts, serving self rather than others, glorifying the Spirit above Jesus Christ in Christian proclamation.

   5. Such misuse destroys the doctrine of salvation by faith.

B. The gifts of the Spirit are properly used in repentance and faith.

   1. A repentance born of the Word is the corrective that opens the heart to humble awareness and use of the gifts.

   2. A faith rekindled each day by the Word of the forgiveness of sins in Christ receives and motivates holy and joyful use of the gifts of the Spirit.

C. The Christian then uses whatever gifts are given by the Spirit to show forth the love of Christ and to proclaim the Gospel.

Because of the lordship of Christ by right of His work of salvation, the Holy Spirit comes to us with His blessings.

Through the Word the Spirit motivates the Christian to use these blessings under the lordship of Christ for the sake of the Gospel and to the glory of God.

LOUIS A. BRIGHTON

Second Sunday After the Epiphany

GOSPEL   John 2:1–11 (NIV)

Sermon Notes/Introduction

Just as the word "Epiphany" (which means "manifestation") implies, the Epiphany season manifests the power of the deity of Jesus Christ for the good of all kinds of people. These manifestations in Scripture continue to be signs to us, just as they were to the first disciples, of Jesus' power.

These signs display that power not simply to show it off but to demonstrate what His power accomplishes for people whom He loves. Certainly one big lesson in Jesus' first miraculous sign, the turning of water into wine at the wedding feast in Cana, is that He brings about remarkable changes in the lives of sinful human beings. This is something urgent for us to know about Jesus: "Jesus Makes Radical Changes." This is important for us to know because as Christians we are deeply aware of the need for change.

Sermon Outline
JESUS MAKES RADICAL CHANGES

I. Jesus made a radical change at Cana in Galilee.
   A. There was a real need at Cana. During the wedding feast, the wine ran out, and that was upsetting for the couple celebrating their marriage. Wine was so important for such a celebration in that day that the lack of it meant that the party was over before it was scheduled to end (vv. 1–2).
   B. In a miraculous way Jesus turned 20–30 gallons of water into wine—not just ordinary wine but wine so good that the master of the banquet called it "the best" (vv. 6–10). Jesus made a radical change in water.
   C. This action of Jesus had a powerful influence on the disciples. John comments that it was the first of Jesus' miraculous signs and that it revealed His glory (His deity, His ability, His love) so powerfully that "his dis-

ciples put their faith in him." If they hadn't believed in Him as Messiah before, they did now. If they hadn't believed firmly before, they did now (v. 11). Jesus made a radical change in the lives of His disciples. He brought them from unbelief to faith.

II. Jesus' most radical change was His change from death to life.

   A. The miracle at Cana in Galilee was a sign of Jesus' power to make radical changes.

   B. As a sign of His power to make changes, the miracle certainly points to His most miraculous change—that most radical of all radical changes—His coming to life after His death on the cross and all that it means in terms of victory over sin, death, every evil, and every evil one (1 Cor. 15:20–28).

   C. Because of His radical change from death to life, by which He brought defeat to all that is opposed to God, He can make radical changes in our world and in our lives.

III. Jesus makes radical changes in our lives.

   A. The first radical change that He makes is to bring us, as He did the disciples, from unbelief to faith in Him as the One sent by God to save us from sin and every evil. He does this through His Word as He manifests to us His death and resurrection for our salvation (Rom. 10:5–17). Then He follows up by making other radical changes in our lives.

   B. Through His gift of faith He restores us to God as His own forever through the forgiveness of sins (Col. 1:13–14).

   C. In connection with this new faith relationship with God, Jesus begins radically to change the way we act. We begin to become new creatures and to live for Him who died for us and rose again, as St. Paul writes so clearly in 2 Cor. 5.

   D. Jesus does not stop making radical changes in our lives. Because we are His disciples, He is continually turning the water of our lives into excellent wine. He stays close to us in Word and Sacrament so that we move continually from unbelief to faith, from selfishness to love, from despair to hope. He enables us to learn from our sins and mistakes. He works in the evil that touches our lives to produce good (Rom. 8:28–39). We experience the insipid water of our lives being radically changed into the best wine.

E. Jesus also changes the ordinary circumstances of our lives for us as we turn to Him for guidance from day to day. He may order and radically alter our affairs and the affairs of people around us for our benefit. He bids us to look to Him for His intervention in every time of need (Luke 11:9–10).

F. Happily for us, the most radical change that Jesus will make for us is at the time of our death. That change is surely previewed by what followed His death. He will transform us through death from this life into the larger life of heaven, and at the last day He will raise up our bodies and change them to be like His glorious body. He truly saves the best wine until last (Phil. 3:20–21).

Today we rejoice with a bride and a groom of long ago that Jesus turned water into wine. It reminds us that He has made and does make radical changes that affect our lives. This is a time not only to recognize what He has done and to thank Him but also to look to Him today and every day for the radical changes that we so desperately need, especially for His gifts of faith and hope and love. We are bold to do this not simply because He turned water into wine but because "he died for all, that those who live should no longer live for themselves but for him who died for them and was raised again" (2 Cor. 5:15). We have beheld His glory, and we have put our faith in Him.

CHARLES T. KNIPPEL

Third Sunday After the Epiphany

EPISTLE   1 Corinthians 12:12–21, 26–27 (RSV)

Sermon Notes/Introduction

Whereas the emphasis in 12:1–11 is on the individual and the diversity of spiritual gifts that God bestows on "each one" (vv. 7, 11), this Epistle reading, which incorporates most of the remainder of chapter 12, is Paul's instruction about the unity of these varied individual gifts in the body of Christ. This body, the church in its broadest sense, is to be a well-organized and smooth-running operation. Paul illustrates this by the analogy of the human body. Individual members are to use their divinely ordained and bestowed gifts so that the body may function as intended.

Like the Corinthians, many Christians within the church today are individualists who (1) want to work independently and thereby often work counterproductively in the church, (2) try to acquire spiritual gifts that God never intended them to have, (3) look down on those with less dramatic gifts, (4) feel inferior or even worthless because their gifts are less "showy" or contribute in a less apparent way than others. The goal of the sermon outlined below is to remind Christians that our spiritual gifts, no matter what they may be, are valuable. But they find value only as they are used in concert with the whole body of Christ.

When it comes to joining with others in accomplishing a goal, everybody seems to want to be or dreams about being the proverbial quarterback. We like the glory of being able to stand out. But as any employer or coach will tell you, it is the multitude of people doing their tasks well behind the scenes that makes success possible. St. Paul uses the same principle for our life together in the church. He motivates us to success with body language.

Sermon Outline
BODY LANGUAGE

I. Christ is the body.
   A. Through His body, Christ has reconciled us.
      1. He has reconciled us first to God.
      2. He has reconciled us also to one another as we "drink of one Spirit" (v. 13).
   B. We, though many and diverse, find identity and unity only in His body.
      1. We were baptized into Him by the one Spirit (v. 13).
      2. Through this action we have become one with Christ (cf. John 17:21; Rom. 6; and other Pauline references to the mystical union of believers "in Christ").
II. We are the individual members.
   A. Each has singular gifts and intended functions.
      1. These gifts are determined by God (1 Cor. 12:18).
      2. There is no room in the body for criticism, envy,

or feelings of inferiority and uselessness (vv. 15–17, 21).

B. We have a vested interest in each other.
  1. We care about each other. The pain and suffering of one member affects us all adversely. Likewise, the honor of one member makes all members feel good (v. 26).
  2. Working together, the body functions and accomplishes its goal.

In the heat of the Revolutionary War, Benjamin Franklin is credited with saying, "We must all hang together, or assuredly we shall all hang separately." By virtue of our calling as Christians, we each have an important part in the general working of Christ's church. The body of Christ is no place for individualists. By hanging together and exercising our gifts to the fullest, the body flourishes to the honor of its members and to the glory of Christ.

PAUL E. CLOETER

Third Sunday After the Epiphany

GOSPEL   Luke 4:14–21 (NIV)

Sermon Notes/Introduction

In the power of the Holy Spirit poured out on Him at His baptism, Jesus begins His ministry. By word and act Jesus proclaims that God indeed has intervened in our world, wresting control of humanity and its destiny from the grip of Satan. It was on the Sabbath that Jesus arrived in Nazareth. In accord with His regular practice He went to the synagogue. This was the first of two visits that Jesus made to Nazareth (cf. Matt. 13:54–55 and Mark 6:1–2). Customarily, the synagogue worship was divided into three parts. In the worship part prayers were offered. The reading of the Scriptures consisted of lessons from the Law, usually read verse by verse by seven persons, and lessons from the prophets read three verses at a time. Teaching formed the third part of the service. On this occasion Jesus was both reader and preacher. We do not know whether the selection that Jesus read and that formed the basis of His sermon was the pericope for that day. In any event, the quotation from Isaiah is a beautiful Messianic prophecy. Jesus speaks of His endowment and of the purpose for which He

came. "Because" He was anointed by God with the Holy
Spirit, He is filled with the Spirit and thus set apart for His holy
office. The ancient synagogue regarded Is. 61:1–2 as one of
three passages in which the mention of the Holy Spirit was
connected with the promised Messiah. "To the poor" (those
in utter spiritual destitution, the consciousness that precedes
entrance into the kingdom of God and that cannot be relieved
by one's own efforts but only by the free mercy of God) He
preaches the good news of that free mercy. "To the prisoners"
(properly, prisoners of war [cf. Is. 42:7]; to Israel both as captive
and as exile, as prisoners of Satan's spiritual bondage) He
proclaims release. To "the oppressed" (literally, to those "broken in pieces"; cf. Is. 42:3) He proclaims freedom. To one and
all in spiritual bondage, blindness, poverty, and oppression He
announces the arrival of an era in human history that God
regards with favor and in which He grants His blessings in
abundance, when salvation and the free favor of God abound.
It is the first day of the "year" of Jubilee, a fixed period of time
wherein liberty is proclaimed throughout the whole land.

Sermon Outline
GOD'S NEW YEAR OF JUBILEE

I. In the Person of His Son Jesus Christ.
  A. The Spirit of the Lord was on Him (Luke 4:18).
  B. At His baptism He was set apart and endowed for His
      work in ministry (3:21–22).
  C. He was sent by God in fulfillment of promise (Is. 61:1–
      3).
  D. He came with power and compassion.
      1. The power and compassion are seen in His healing
         signs (Luke 4:23).
      2. They are seen above all in His atoning death and
         resurrection.
II. God heralds the dawn of the new Year of Jubilee (Lev.
    25:8–17).
  A. It is the acceptable time of the Lord (Luke 4:19).
      1. The Year of Jubilee originated with the people of
         Israel (Lev. 25:8–17).
      2. In the New Testament it becomes a fixed time in
         the life of Jesus—Incarnation to the Second
         Coming.
  B. In it God's grace and love abound (Luke 4:18).

       1. To the poor He proclaims the good news, God's
         free mercy.
       2. To the "prisoner of war" He proclaims release.
       3. To the oppressed He proclaims freedom.
    C. This promise is fulfilled today in your hearing (v. 21).
       1. All promises find their focus in Jesus Christ.
       2. This is the day of opportunity for us.
       3. Rejoice in our "Year of Jubilee."

NORBERT H. MUELLER

Fourth Sunday After the Epiphany

EPISTLE   1 Corinthians 12:27–13:13 (RSV)

Sermon Notes/Introduction

The way in which this text has been sentimentalized and even trivialized by careless readers is well known. Genuine love is an easily misunderstood concept. Letting the Word speak in its proper context is the means of illuminating the profound truth that Paul is seeking to teach.

Clearly, love is a "still more excellent way" (12:31). All spiritual gifts have a purpose, but genuine love (*agapē*) binds them all together. Its value is understood by the repeated use of conditionals ("if") in the early verses of chapter 13. The frequent use of the negative ("not") in verses 4–7 proves that love is not easily defined by human language, which can often describe only what something is not instead of what it truly is. Love in truth is the premier divine quality that gives significance to every other valued Christian gift, including faith and hope (13:13). The goal of the sermon is to lead the hearers to begin to understand the surprising value of love as God bestows it and they practice it. The problem is that we tend to emotionalize love, which makes it subject to our unreliable feelings. The means to the goal is the carefully considered understanding of the fullness of love and how we love because He first loved us.

The words of this "Love Chapter" are both amazing and surprising, worthy of more than an inscription on a wall plaque or a reading at a wedding. Love is part of God's nature and the enduring quality that is most to typify His people. If we by the Spirit's guiding truly let Him speak to us in this text, we will learn "The Surprising Value of Love."

Sermon Outline
THE SURPRISING VALUE OF LOVE

I. It gives meaning to the Christian life.
  A. No spiritual gift has any purpose without love (vv. 1–2).
    1. The ability to speak in tongues is a useless gift without love.
    2. The gifts of prophecy and understanding have no point without love.
  B. No heroic act of service does any good without love (v. 7).
    1. Giving away everything, as commendable as it may seem, accomplishes nothing without love.
    2. Surrendering oneself in martyrdom does not mean anything without love.
II. It defines the Christian faith.
  A. Believing in Jesus has no lasting value without love (v. 2).
  B. Believing in Jesus is defined in a visible, dramatic way by Christians who love as the Savior loved.
III. It completes the Christian hope.
  A. Spiritual maturity increases as genuine love increases and leads to hope for the life to come (vv. 9–12).
    1. In love we grow in confidence.
    2. In love we "see" more clearly (v. 12).
  B. Full understanding based on abiding love is our sure hope that will not disappoint us.

Perhaps it seems surprising that Paul would rank love above the essential qualities of faith and hope. Yet the value of love is always surprising as it lends meaning to the Christian life, faith, and hope. It is the "tie that binds," the divine quality that lasts forever.

DAVID E. SEYBOLD

Fourth Sunday After the Epiphany

GOSPEL   Luke 4:21–32

Sermon Notes/Introduction

1. *Verse 22*—The acceptance and rejection of Jesus in one verse leads some critics to conclude that Luke is really combining two separate incidents. Among other inadequacies,

such a theory betrays a naiveté over against the perverse ways of unbelief. It is, indeed, interesting that the verb *martureō,* meaning "to bear witness," should be used here to describe the reaction to Jesus of those who finally reject Him. *Martureō* is variously translated here, for example, "to speak well of," "to approve of," or "to be well impressed with." All these renderings suggest a positive reaction. (The hostile connotations sometimes associated with the verb—cf. Matt. 23:31; John 7:7; 18:23—are hardly to be assumed here.) The lesson is obvious. One can be ever so close to the truth and be initially impressed (*ethaumazon;* cf. Mark 6:2: *exeplēssonto*) and yet miss the saving significance of Christ.

2. *Verse 23*—"What we have *heard* you did at Capernaum." There is no need, and it is exegetically suspect (cf. Matt. 13:54; Mark 6:5), to conclude that this phrase intimates that the people had only *heard* but did not actually *believe* that Jesus had performed miracles. One can believe that Jesus performed—and performs—miracles and yet be an enemy of the universal Christ.

3. *Verse 28*—Human nature likes to be impressed; it does not especially like to be reminded of the need for instruction, and it positively froths with fury when flattering exclusivity is shattered. Those who "witnessed" and were amazed finally flared up in rage with murder on their minds (*katakrēmnizō—* to hurl down a precipice). Note the recurrence of *plēroō* (v. 21); Scripture has been fulfilled. This ought to fill the hearers with joy. Instead, they are filled with rage (v. 28).

4. The nuance of the present participle *akouontes* (v. 28) should not escape notice. Even as they are listening, the people begin to fume. The hostility did not need to build itself up over a longer period of time. When Jesus' Messianic claims are rejected, wrath is instantaneous and violent.

5. *Verse 30*—Whether Jesus' escape is miraculous or not is not clear. At all events it is majestically sovereign.

6. To rescue the sermon from fruitless negativism, the preacher will need to keep in mind that as he identifies the enemies of the universal Christ, he does not do it just to denounce but to identify and eliminate. As each part of the sermon is developed, the hearers must be helped to understand why and how enmity toward the universal Christ, which threatens also them, is to be overcome.

You will not be surprised when I say, "We must fight the enemies of the universal Christ." Perhaps you will be surprised when I say, "This means that we must fight ourselves." No, this does not mean that we must fight our total selves. After all, the Spirit of God rules within us. But those old enemies of the universal Christ have a way of slipping back into our lives and trying to control us. And those enemies can look pious despite their hostility. We must resist their return, and if they have taken up illegal residence, we must dislodge them. Following leads in today's Gospel, we will be concerned to identify and describe the various hostilities so that we can recognize and deal with them.

Sermon Outline
DON'T BE A PIOUS ENEMY
OF THE UNIVERSAL CHRIST

I. Note the textual emphasis that Christ is universal, the Savior for all (vv. 25–27).
   A. The widow of Zarephath.
   B. Naaman the Syrian.
II. Beware of the delusions of perverse piety.
   A. One may be initially impressed with Jesus and yet be offended at His claims to be the universal Christ.
   B. Beware of the perverse exclusivity that flatters human pride (cf. Acts 13:46, 50; 22:21–22). Exclusivity, claiming Christ for our select group, can acknowledge that Christ is the Messiah but not that He is the universal Christ. It flatters our sinful pride if this great figure, Jesus, the Savior, the Son of God, is our private possession instead of God's gift to all.
   C. Beware of confusing the thrill of faith with the delight of titillation. There is the allure of the theology of glory in any of its forms (Luke 4:23b). The hometown people wanted something more spectacular than proclamation (cf. v. 18). So does our flesh.
   D. Pious excuses for rejection are always at hand. Can it be that the mighty God, Yahweh, should be mightily at work in a hometown lad who has made something of a splash elsewhere? Not unless He can bring spectacular proof. Why, we know His carpenter father and His family (cf. Matt. 13:55; Mark 6:3).
III. The universal Christ will triumph; triumph with Him.
   A. He died for all and rose again. The hostility arising here will swell up until it explodes in the hatred of the crucifixion. But the lifting up on the cross will also mean exaltation that will draw like a magnet. Sinners will

come from all nations. Triumph with the universal
Christ. Get the Good News out.

B. All who reject Him will have to live with that rejection—
eternally.

C. All who believe in Him will be vindicated—eternally.

"Today!" (Luke 4:21). To delay is to court disaster. There
must be decisive action *now!*

H. ARMIN MOELLERING

Fifth Sunday After the Epiphany

EPISTLE   1 Corinthians 14:12b–20 (RSV)

Sermon Notes/Introduction

This text compels reckoning with the phenomenon of glossolalia. In these days of rampant Neo-Pentecostalism, dealing
with glossolalia in the pulpit would too easily be heard only as
a polemic—and wrongly heard. The subject can be treated
more constructively in the dialog of the Bible class. The decision
to preach on this text ought to include the decision for con-
current (or better yet, preceding) correlated Bible studies in the
parish. Then pulpit use of the text should be limited to a recognition of its originally intended thrust, an identification of the
contrast that was drawn for the sake of making that thrust, and
an exposition of the contrasting phenomenon of plain speech.

Introductory thoughts ought not to be generalized through
prescription from the outside but should reflect the parish in
which the specific sermon is to be preached. This much of the
caveat might best be understood as urging most pastors in most
parishes to choose a different text for the Fifth Sunday After
the Epiphany.

If the decision is to use the text for the sake of its positive
thrust, the ILCW Series C propers that are companions to the
Epistle offer potentially useful correlation with an emphasis on
plain speech. The Prayer for the Day (in Contemporary Worship 6: *The Church Year: Calendar and Lectionary,* p. 61)
acknowledges Jesus as the new light of the Word with whom
we have been filled. The opening verse of the Psalm (Ps. 85:8–
13—also in CW6) stresses the desire to "hear what God the
Lord will speak." The Old Testament Reading emphasizes ver-
bal communication in the quotation of the worshipful words
of the seraphim and by the cleansing of Isaiah's lips to enable

him to volunteer as God's spokesman. Finally, the Gospel begins with the note that "the people pressed upon Him to hear the Word of God" (Luke 5:1). Such correlations provide ready material for leading into the body of a sermon on "The Power of Positive Speaking."

Sermon Outline
THE POWER OF POSITIVE SPEAKING

I. Positive speaking of the plain Word builds the church by constructing it.
   A. Paul advocated positive speech because the church at Corinth was under construction. The presence of an outsider or a stranger in the gathering of the congregation shows that there were gradually being added to the church those people who came to believe in Jesus. The way in which such people would be brought to the faith could be well illustrated by reference to the first three chapters of Romans. After declaring the Gospel to be the power of God for salvation, Paul proceeds to preach the Law to plow the ground of the heart and prepare it to receive the precious seed of the Gospel. In Rom. 3:21–26 he makes a clear statement of the Gospel. When the stranger hears thanksgiving for such cause, and the Holy Spirit works faith in the heart through such hearing, he or she becomes able to say "Amen" (verily, truly) to the thanksgiving, and another precious person is added to the church.
   B. The perpetual "under construction" state of the church requires continuous application of Paul's direction to the Corinthians. The church, commissioned collectively and distributively to preach the Gospel of Him in whom alone salvation is to be found, can accomplish its constructive purpose only by speaking the Gospel plainly to prepared hearts, as illustrated in Rom. 1–3. For "faith comes from what is heard, and what is heard comes by the preaching of Christ" (10:17).
II. Positive speaking of the plain Word builds the church by strengthening it.
   A. Paul advocated positive speech because the church at Corinth needed strengthening by inner growth through instruction. The need for inner growth is illustrated by the catalog of subjects with which Paul deals in this Epistle: factions in the church, failures in church dis-

cipline, misunderstandings about marriage, abuses of the Lord's Supper, and denial of the resurrection of the dead. The answer to such need was to be found in positive speech, words spoken with the mind, so that through instruction (being informed, being taught, being led to understand) the people of God could be led by His power in His Word toward mature adulthood in Christ. In this connection it is interesting to note that the material from Romans 1–3, basic as it is, was addressed not to people who did not yet believe but "to all God's beloved in Rome, who are called to be saints" (1:7).

B. The ideal perpetual maturing of the church in our day as well requires constant instruction in the Word. To build a current catalog of need as compelling as that to which Paul ministered through his letter to the Corinthians is an easy task for the person who observes life in his or her own church setting. The rich dwelling of the Word of Christ in the people of God through the plain and positive speaking of that Word in their midst, as well as through their own study of it, constitutes the means by which people of God individually and collectively in the church will be strengthened by growing in Christ.

The Epistle begins with the exhortation to "strive to excel in building up the church" (1 Cor. 14:12). It continues with a "therefore" that urges readers toward positive speaking of the Word for the sake of "building up," both in the sense of construction by adding those who believe and in the sense of strengthening those who already believe through inner growth by instruction.

The Epistle ends with a plea for Christians to be mature in their thinking. It points the way to one form of maturity in thinking: positive speaking of the plain Word. May that pointing be matched, by the grace of God, with our going in the indicated way.

ROLAND A. HOPMANN

Fifth Sunday After the Epiphany

GOSPEL   Luke 5:1–11

Sermon Notes/Introduction

This is a familiar pericope, and that familiarity confronts the preacher with a challenge. How will he prepare a sermon that is fresh and vigorous but not cheapened by cute novelty? The history of preaching on this Gospel brings some lessons and cautions. Since the Reformation, Lutheran preaching has tended to use it as the occasion to describe a work ethic, the Christian performance in one's calling. Although Luther's sermons on this text touch on other themes (one is even wildly allegorical; cf. WA 27:253–59), he also dwells on the work ethic. Likewise, C. F. W. Walther develops the theme "Our Work a Test of our Christianity" in this way: I. Our work reveals who is Christian, or how and why a Christian works. II. Our work reveals who is a non-Christian, or how and why a non-Christian works. Although Walther has many helpful and interesting things to say, this is probably not the best approach to the pericope. If one does not take this theme, which route shall he go? The attempt has been made to psychologize the text: How can one escape resignation, surrender, and apathy in the face of failure after the expenditure of so much effort? Although it is conceivable that a good Law-Gospel sermon could be developed on a theme like "After the Night of Frustration the Day of Success" (cf. 2 Cor. 4:7), there should be a safer route to go.

As usual, the critics are of no help. Some scholars suggest that this passage is only a variant of John 21. Bultmann contends that the story is "spun out" of the word about fishers of men (Mark 1:17). Dibelius disagrees and argues that it is by no means an elaboration of the Marcan passage but an independent narrative, a "legend." There is not much help available here.

These notes will suggest that the pericope can be homiletically ignited by a striking word from Gottfried Keller: "If you are going to be a fisher of men, you will have to bait the hook with your heart." The preacher need not shy away from the threat of being corny by asking somewhere along the line: "Does your heart belong to Jesus? If it does, you will be willing to use it for bait. Nothing else will substitute for your heart, not even what is all too often so close to our hearts—money! If you are going to be a fisher of men, you will have to bait the hook with your heart."

Lukewarm faith can hardly make one a fervent witness for Christ. But how does one arrive at and continue in that state of fervent discipleship that makes it possible to bait the hook with one's heart? What happened to Peter is illustrative. He passed through a shattering experience that threatened to reduce him to a collapsed, quivering blob. But he also found forgiveness here and restitution to discipleship later in a way that set him back solidly on his feet (John 21).

Sermon Outline
BAIT THE HOOK WITH YOUR HEART

I. There are other kinds of bait that we use in trying to attract the desired catch. (Consider the gospel of success, etc.)
   A. We can be fishing and catching nothing because we are using the wrong bait. Or perhaps we are using the right bait in the wrong way (loveless witnessing, arrogance, or self-righteousness).
   B. But we can also be hauling them in and still not be using the right bait.
II. Only the reconstituted heart makes good bait.
   A. Heretical movements make catches, too. (Give examples of the zeal of errorists.)
   B. The reconstituted heart has been shattered by the awareness of sin and reassembled and revived by the forgiving Christ.
      1. This is more than mere confrontation with Rudolf Otto's *mysterium tremendum*. There is also the emphasis on the confession "I am a sinful man" (Luke 5:8).
      2. Jesus does not prettify sin. He does not deny that Peter is a sinner. The church is *ecclesia peccatorum* and *ecclesia peccatrix*. That is good reason to be terrified but the poorest of reasons to flee from Christ, who came into the world to save sinners. Luther says, "The more you feel that you are a sinner, and the more you want to run away from God, just so much more you should press forward to him." Luther also describes Peter's words as a disgrace: "But that is how a miserable conscience carries on; it flees from the One who wants to confer grace on him and to whom it ought to run barefoot from the end of the world. Now it has Him in the

boot and says to Him, 'Go away, go away.' " Alexander MacLaren writes, "The departure of the physician does not tend to cure the disease. . . . The superficial knowledge of my evil may drive me away from Jesus Christ; the deepest conviction of it will send me right into His arms. . . . 'Against thee, thee only have I sinned'; and therefore to thee, thee only will I go."

C. When the bait is our heart, we catch for life, not for death (zōgreō, v. 10).
D. Do not confuse the bait with the hook. The hook is the Good News. The bait is only the winsome way you present the Gospel. If you confuse the bait with the hook, you may win followers for yourself but not for Jesus. The heart as bait does not take over for the Holy Spirit, but it is taken over by the Holy Spirit. Do not trust programs, competency, or even the sincerity of your own heart, but trust the directive of Jesus. Your heart in your witnessing will, to be sure, make you more impressive, more appealing, and more convincing. But it is still the Holy Spirit who converts where and when it pleases Him. But for you to continue in witnessing despite difficulties, frustrations, and setbacks, your heart will have to be in it. And if your witness is to contain Law and Gospel, that twofold experience of Peter will help put conviction in your voice.

To the trembling sinner Jesus says, "Do not be afraid" (mē phobou, v. 10; the present imperative indicates that an existing condition should end. I. Howard Marshal suggests that mē phobou functions here as a declaration of forgiveness). It takes courage, and there are risks in using your heart to bait the hook. But those who are forgiven can do it. Mē phobou— "Stop being afraid!" Bait the hook with your heart.

H. ARMIN MOELLERING

Sixth Sunday After the Epiphany

EPISTLE   1 Corinthians 15:12, 16–20 (RSV)

Sermon Notes/Introduction

Coming from Paul's great resurrection chapter and dealing directly with the chief article of Christian doctrine, Christ's resurrection from the dead, this text is to be handled with all the reverential awe due to our great and gracious God of salvation. Yet it ought not to be treated as a preempting of Easter during Epiphany with a rude bypassing of the blessings of Lent. It should be seen in the spirit of the early Christians as a recognition that every Sunday is a resurrection celebration and every day is a living of the resurrected life. That approach binds the thought of the Epistle with that of the other propers to sound a loud warning that denial of the resurrection or any other God-given doctrine can threaten the Christian's fruitfulness as a tree continuously prospering because it is planted and nourished by the stream of living water. For the Sixth Sunday After the Epiphany this great resurrection passage suggests a message on "The Misery and Blessing of Resurrection Faith."

Sermon Outline
THE MISERY AND BLESSING
OF RESURRECTION FAITH

I. The fact of Christ's resurrection.
   A. Christ's resurrection is declared truth (vv. 12, 20) supported by much evidence (e.g., vv. 3–11). But there is misery for our human natures because God, though He gives us reason, does not make it possible for us to use reason in a scientific investigation that proves Christ's resurrection. In this respect even the declaration of this central doctrine of the resurrection calls on us to humble ourselves under the mighty hand of God.
   B. Christ's resurrection is paradoxical truth, contrary to human opinion or expectation, received only by the gift of faith. We are saved only by grace through faith, which is the gift of God. A person can say that Jesus Christ is Lord only by the Holy Spirit. And we are blessed that God's gift of faith imparts so perfect a conviction. "Now faith is the assurance of things hoped for, the conviction of things not seen" (Heb. 11:1).
II. The meaning of Christ's resurrection for our life now.
   A. Christ's resurrection subjects us to the misery of anxiety because our conviction of the resurrection compels our constant recognition of the prior fact of death. Unable to do the unbeliever's whistling in the dark, the Christian's daily remembrance of the resurrection is at the same time a daily remembrance of death. By one man

sin came into the world, and death by sin. We are confronted daily with the terrible reminder that we are by nature sinful and unclean, deserving death and eternal damnation.

B. Christ's resurrection gives us the blessing of freeing us from the inhibitions of anxiety to abound in the work of the Lord (1 Cor. 15:58). Though death remains the result of sin even for the believer, it ceases to be punishment for sin to him. "For our sake He made Him to be sin who knew no sin, so that in Him we might become the righteousness of God" (2 Cor. 5:21). God's gift of faith in the resurrected Christ "will be reckoned to us who believe in Him that raised from the dead Jesus our Lord, who was put to death for our trespasses and raised for our justification" (Rom. 4:24–25). Freed by the gift of righteousness, we can work at being the righteous people whom Christ has made us by being lovingly obedient to Him who has said, "If you love Me, you will keep My commandments" (John 14:15). Acting out of our Lord's gift of faith, through the study of His Word we keep our roots bathed in the water of life, by which God also works in us to see and understand the things we ought to do and to give us grace and power to do them.

III. The meaning of Christ's resurrection for the life to come.

A. Christ's resurrection forces us to recognize that our conscious, personal existence persists through eternity. Far from letting us think that death could mean an absolute passing out of existence, the resurrection gives misery to the child of God, who is still beset by the old man of sin during this earthly life. It compels us to stare God's judgment and the pit of hell in the face.

B. Christ's resurrection assures us that our persistent existence shall be blissful eternal life with Christ. By His resurrection He leads us to know death as a sleep from which we shall awaken. By causing Paul to label Him as the first fruits of those who have fallen asleep, Christ lets us see ourselves in our awakening as fruit that will be like Him. We shall be like Him, for we shall see Him as He is. Together with all saints and angels we shall adore Him. Together with Him we shall rule over all things.

Christ's resurrection is fact. Having become fact to us by

God's gift of faith, it has elements of both misery and blessing for us. But it is a misery to us only in its negation of the old man of sin in us. To the newborn person of faith it is blessing beyond description and a sure hope. By God's continuing gifts to us through His Word, we receive endurance to withstand the direct threats and the hardest tests and living power to do the works of Him who has called us out of the darkness of death into the marvelous light of eternal life.

ROLAND A. HOPMANN

Sixth Sunday After the Epiphany

GOSPEL   Luke 6:17–26 (KJV)

Sermon Notes/Introduction

Vv. 17–19: The popularity of Jesus had reached its height. Throngs came from Jordan and Tyre and Sidon. Matt. 4:25 adds Galilee, Decapolis, and the region beyond Jordan. Christ performed many miracles, and power kept going out of Him. Jesus spoke the Sermon on the Mount from a plateau in the mountains between the horns of Hattin in Galilee. *V. 20:* The theme of the sermon is the blessedness of the children of the kingdom. "Blessed" reflects Ps. 1. "Oh, the blessedness of the man who is poor." Matthew adds "in spirit." "The poor," "the hungry," and "the weeping" all describe the penitent sinner. "The kingdom of God" is the gracious rule of God in the heart, bringing the forgiveness of sins and eternal life. *V. 21* (Matt. 5:6): The hungry are those who hunger and thirst after righteousness. Note the durative present: "are hungering." The hungry will be filled with the righteousness of Christ. The weeping ones shall laugh for joy in the Redeemer. *V. 22:* Because of their allegiance to Christ, they would be separated from the Jewish synagogues, reviled, and rejected for bearing the name of Christian (cf. Acts 11:26; 24:15). *V. 23:* The reward is always one of grace (Matt. 19:29). Prophets were persecuted (1 Kings 19:14; Matt. 19:29). *V. 24:* The rich, the full, and the laughing ones are impenitent sinners who feel no need for God's grace. The impenitent rich now have the only consolation they will ever have. *V. 25:* The full will experience hunger, and the laughing ones will weep in the judgment of God. *V. 26:* The world loves its own (cf. 1 Kings 18:19; Jer. 5:31).

Happiness eludes so many people. Many look for it in the wrong places. Some despair of finding it.

Sermon Outline
GOD'S PRESCRIPTION FOR HAPPINESS

I. Know yourself.
   A. Children of the world are described.
      1. The rich feel they lack nothing (the Pharisee, Luke 5:31; the rich young ruler, Matt. 19:20).
      2. They are full of their own imagined righteousness (Luke 5:31; Matt. 9:13).
      3. They laugh (Ps. 73:8).
      4. All people speak well of them; the world loves its own.
   B. Children of Christ's kingdom are described.
      1. They are poor in spirit (Ps. 32:5).
      2. They hunger after a righteousness that they do not have (Luther, the dying thief, the prodigal son).
      3. They weep (Peter, Matt. 26:75).
      4. They bear the cross (Matt. 23:34, 37; Acts 4; 7; 12:1–2).

The road of happiness begins with unhappiness over ourselves and our waywardness. The Law condemns us all. In its mirror we are daily to see our sin and to turn to God in repentance. God responds in grace (Is. 66:2; Ps. 51:17; 1 John 1:9).

II. Know God's grace.
   A. Unbelievers do not find it.
      1. The rich become paupers (Dives, Luke 16:23).
      2. The full end up hungry (Matt. 19:22).
      3. Those who deny Christ are denied (Matt. 10:34).
   B. Children of the kingdom know God's grace.
      1. The poor have the riches of the kingdom (Luke 12:32).
      2. The hungry are filled with the righteousness of Christ.
         a. Christ won righteousness for all (Is. 53).
         b. God gives righteousness to all who believe (Rom. 3:21–22; 4:5, 16; Gal. 2:16).
      3. Those who weep will laugh (Ps. 126:5; Is. 61:2–3; Matt. 25:21; John 15:11; 1 John 1:4).
      4. Those who bear the cross will be glorified (Ps. 17:15; Matt. 10:32; 1 Cor. 15:49; 1 Peter 1:3–5).

"Rejoice in the Lord always, and again I say, Rejoice" (Phil. 4:4). God's grace turns your poverty into riches, your hunger into satisfaction, your weeping into laughter, your suffering into a crown of glory that does not fade away.

HENRY J. EGGOLD

Seventh Sunday After the Epiphany

EPISTLE   1 Corinthians 15:35–38a, 42–50 (NKJV)

Sermon Notes/Introduction

1. Verse 35 poses two questions Paul deals with in this text. The first is "How are the dead raised up?" In other words, how can life be given to a body that is dead, buried, and decayed? Given those circumstances, resurrection seems to be a non sequitur—it doesn't follow. What fellowship does life have with death, resurrection with decay? The second question is "With what body do they [the resurrected] come?" In other words, what will our resurrected bodies be like?

2. Verses 36–38 are Paul's answer to the first question. He calls attention to an analog in nature. We plant a seed in the ground; we bury it out of sight and more or less forget about it. It decays. Yet that isn't the end of it. From that decayed seed there soon springs up a plant, a new life, the same and yet different. The seed, in effect, has been resurrected. "God gives it a body as He pleases" (v. 38).

From this everyday phenomenon we are to infer a "death and resurrection principle," a principle so obvious that one is a fool (v. 36) not to see it. And that principle has two aspects: (1) Burial and decomposition must precede the new life—they're prerequisites for it. (2) The new life, in God's design, invariably follows such burial and decomposition—if there's death, there's also resurrection.

What we do to a dead person is much like what we do to a seed—we plant the corpse in the ground ("it is sown," vv. 42–44). We bury it out of sight and in the course of time forget about it. Eventually it decays. But all this, strange as it may seem, is only a prerequisite for new life. Who would ever think that the way to the resurrected and heavenly life should be through stifling confinement and nauseating decay in a six-foot-deep plot of ground in a cemetery? To all appearances, that's the end of it all. Yet the day will come (Judgment Day) when the body will rise, the same and yet different, and live more gloriously and abundantly than ever before. The resurrection, in God's design, invariably follows the burial and decomposition. That's the way it works with a seed. That's the way it works with a human body. It's a key principle. ("Foolish one, what you sow is not made alive unless it dies," v. 36.)

3. Verses 42–50 are Paul's answer to the second question. As indicated earlier, our resurrected body will be the same and yet different. To begin with, of course, it will be a body. ("Body" is the antecedent of each "it" in verses 42–44.) As one writer has reminded us: given the circumstances, a resurrected body will cast a shadow in the sunlight and make a noise as it tramps across the floor. But it will be a different body, with an immortality, glory, and power staggering our imagination (vv. 42–44). Perhaps our Lord's transfigured body (Matt. 17:2) or, better yet, His resurrected body (John 20:26–27; Luke 24:31) gives us some indication of what our resurrected bodies will be like: recognizable yet possessing abilities and splendors not evidenced in the body's present state on earth.

4. To a modern reader verses 44 and 50 may seem problematic to the answers of Paul described in the two preceding notes. The expression "a spiritual body" in verse 44 may sound like a contradiction in terms. That's because for us today the word "spiritual" usually suggests something ethereal and non-substantial, leading us perhaps to conclude that the resurrected person doesn't really have a body, after all. That such is not Paul's meaning is clear because he still calls it a body, "a spiritual *body*" ("body" is the noun modified; "spiritual" is merely the modifying adjective), and from the fact that the *incarnate* Jesus is called "a life-giving *spirit*" in verse 45. What Paul means by "a spiritual body" is a body that is no longer both bad *and* good, both flesh *and* spirit, but a body that is altogether good, altogether spirit(ual) because it is, after the resurrection, completely under the sway of God the Holy Spirit.

The same is true of verse 50. Paul doesn't mean that bodies won't go to heaven. He means that bodies *in their present condition*—lustful, sinful, flesh (body) riddled with flesh (sinful nature)—will not enter heaven. Instead, "spiritual" bodies will enter heaven, that is, bodies altogether good (spiritual), altogether governed by God the Holy Spirit and consequently minus certain limitations like mortality, fatigue, hunger, thirst, etc. These are the kinds of bodies that will inherit the kingdom of God. But—they will be bodies!

In short, we must be careful not to read into verses 44 and 50, positioned in a chapter designed to establish the resurrection of the body, a conclusion that is the reverse of that doctrine.

5. What Paul means by "a spiritual body" is further evidenced by the contrast he details in verses 45–49 between the first Adam of Genesis 2 and 3 and the last Adam, the God-Man Jesus of Nazareth. Please note that the contrast is between two men, people with *bodies*. The first Adam is just "soul"—*psyche;* the last Adam is "spirit"—*pneuma* (v. 45). The first Adam merely receives—passive; the last Adam is *"life-giving"*—active (v. 45). The first Adam's origin is earth (dust); the second Adam's origin is heaven (v. 47). Then follows, climactically, the fabulous promise of verses 48–49: we, now with bodies like that of the first Adam, will, at the resurrection, have bodies like that of the last Adam—as surely as second follows first (vv. 44, 46). See Phil. 3:21.

Sermon Outline
PAUL'S ANSWERS TO TWO RESURRECTION QUESTIONS

I. Will we have a body at all? (Here use appropriate materials from notes 1 and 2.)
II. What kind of body will it be? (Here use appropriate materials from notes 3–5.)

Paul can give us these glorious assurances because—and only because—Jesus lived, died, *and rose* again in our behalf.

FRANCIS C. ROSSOW

Seventh Sunday After the Epiphany

GOSPEL   Luke 6:27–38 (KJV)

Sermon Notes/Introduction

The Gospel accents the idea that the lives of the children of the Kingdom should shine with distinctive love. *Vv. 27–28:* The imperatives here are all in the durative present tense: "Keep on loving," etc. The demands overturn all popular notions. *V. 29:* Behind this verse is the law of criminal justice: "An eye for an eye and a tooth for a tooth" (Ex. 21:24; Lev. 24:19–21). The Pharisees concluded that this principle could be applied also in private morality. Jesus enunciates another principle: Rather suffer injustice than take justice into your own hands. If applied carelessly, these words would only encourage the ruffian and the thief. The cloak is the outer garment; the coat, the inner. *V. 30:* Indiscriminate giving would foster shift-lessness. But it is better to suffer in body and goods than to let passions rule. *V. 31* is the Golden Rule. *Vv. 32–34:* These verses inveigh against popular selfish morality. *V. 35:* Love does not make us children of the Highest, but it does show that we are such. *V. 36:* Here is the principle found already in the covenant of the Old Testament. *V. 37:* Jesus says: "Do not pass judgment without sufficient evidence. Do not condemn by voicing your judgment to others. Rather, forgive." *V. 38:* "Your bosom": the loose part of the Oriental garment just above the belt. "It shall be measured to you again": This is both judgment and mercy—judgment against the niggardly, grace to the generous.

"Be merciful as your Father is merciful." It is impossible for us to attain to God's perfection, but we should strive to be imitators of Him (Eph. 5:1). Furthermore, the mercy of God that we experience ought to motivate us to practice mercy.

Sermon Outline
BE MERCIFUL AS OUR FATHER IS MERCIFUL

I. Love your enemies.
  A. That is what God does.
    1. Humanity is at enmity with God because of sin (Rom. 8:7).
    2. God loved this world in Christ (John 3:16; Rom. 5:8; 2 Cor. 5:19; 1 John 4:9–10).
  B. Like God, we are to love our enemies.
    1. Popular attitudes:
      a. An eye for an eye and a tooth for a tooth (Rom. 12:19).
      b. Love those who love you (Luke 6:32).
    2. Jesus' ethic: Love as God loves.
      a. Do good to those who hate you (Prov. 25:21–22; Luke 10:30–37; Rom. 12:20–21).
      b. Bless those who curse you (1 Cor. 4:12; 1 Peter 2:23).
      c. Pray for those who despitefully use you and persecute you (Luke 23:34; Acts 7:60).
      d. Suffer wrong rather than do wrong (Is. 53:7; Luke 6:29).
    3. Then you will show yourselves to be children of the Highest (Luke 6:35; John 15:9; Eph. 5:1).
II. Give.

A. God gives liberally to all (Ps. 65:11; 103; Matt. 5:4–5; James 1:17; Explanation of the First Article).
B. Be like God in your giving.
  1. Do not give selfishly (Matt. 19:27; Luke 6:34).
  2. Give generously (Luke 6:30, 35).
  3. God promises to bless the cheerful giver (Mal. 3:10; Luke 6:38; 2 Cor. 9:7; Heb. 13:16).
III. Forgive.
  A. God forgives.
    1. He does this for Jesus' sake (Is. 53:6; 2 Cor. 5:21).
    2. He forgives all penitent sinners (Ps. 51:17; 130:4; Matt. 9:2; Luke 7:47; 15:21–24; Rom. 8:33).
  B. We are to forgive.
    1. Guard against judging and condemning (Luke 15:25–32; John 8:7).
    2. Forgive (Matt. 18:21–35; Eph. 4:32).

Motivated by the great mercy of our heavenly Father, let us show mercy by loving our enemies, by giving, and by forgiving.

HENRY J. EGGOLD

Eighth Sunday After the Epiphany

EPISTLE   1 Corinthians 15:51–58 (KJV)

Sermon Notes/Introduction

1. Verse 55 is a classic instance of a rhetorical device called apostrophe, that is, turning away from one's audience to address an absent or imaginary person. As the climax to his discussion of Christ's bodily resurrection and its implication for the hope of our own bodily resurrection, Paul suddenly turns away from his addressees (the Corinthians and us) and talks to Death, conversing with it as if it were a real person. It is a one-way conversation, to be sure, a phenomenon not only implicit in the device but also here in the fact that Death has been destroyed (v. 26); it *can't* talk back. That is, Paul does all the talking not only because monolog is characteristic of the rhetorical device called apostrophe but, above all, because Death is incapable of a reply—there can be no dialog. What Paul does, of course, in this one-way conversation with Death is chortle over it, chuckle over its defeat, "rub it in." "O death, where is thy sting? O grave, where is thy victory?" Death is

one enemy toward whom we never turn the other cheek and to whom we are never gracious in its hour of defeat. Sin-originated, Death deserves all the derision we can give it.

2. Verses 56 and 57 are cryptic and economical, implying thoughts not actually stated (but stated elsewhere: in this chapter, in this letter, in the entire Scriptures). The completed thought might go like this: (1) "the sting of death is sin"; (2) "the strength of sin is the Law"; (3) Christ has abolished the threat of the Law; (4) therefore, sin has lost its strength; (5) therefore, death has lost its sting. (Steps 3 through 5 are implied, not expressed.) But Paul's logic is inexorable: The terror of death has been eliminated because Christ has dealt with this enemy thoroughly rather than superficially, going back to its fundamental causes, removing not only its sting but also the supply, the power source, for that sting.

3. Note how the appeal to be "steadfast, immovable" (RSV)—the central thrust of this text—is sandwiched between a "therefore" and a "forasmuch" (KJV). There is a "because" statement before the exhortation, and there is a "because" statement after the exhortation. Paul provides a reason before he issues his imperative, and he provides a reason after he issues his imperative. The fact of our resurrection hope precedes his appeal ("therefore") and the meaning of that fact ("forasmuch as . . . your labor is not in vain in the Lord") follows his appeal. A similar example from everyday life might go like this: *Since the doctor has given you a clean bill of health,* return to your office *with the confidence that you can successfully carry on your work.* Notice in this example how the part not italicized, the imperative, is not only preceded by a declarative (italicized) but also followed by a declarative (italicized), declaratives that together provide a basis for the imperative—providing the courage to issue the imperative and providing the hope of obeying the imperative successfully. So it is in our text. Paul, as it were, floods, immerses, surrounds the reader with motivation. Law is wrapped, even smothered, in Gospel. If the reader should happen to miss the reason he can be steadfast and immovable before he reads that appeal, Paul makes sure he gets exposed to that reason immediately after he reads that appeal. Paul takes no chances. He makes assurance doubly sure. He saturates his reader with the Gospel.

4. In fact, there is Gospel within Gospel in the last part of verse 58: the expression "in the Lord" not only defines the Christian's work (Lord's work) but also brings to bear on him the power, the energy, for that work (Lord's power). The point

is that the Christian's work *for the Lord* is done *by the Lord*. Paul seems to arrange Gospel in this pericope as we might arrange berry boxes: there's always room to stack one more inside the one just placed.

Although I spent a childhood constantly confusing the two, I believe I can safely assume that most of us know the difference between deciduous and coniferous trees. Deciduous trees lose their leaves when winter comes, but coniferous trees (more accurately called evergreen) retain them—at least, most coniferous trees do. There are also two kinds of Christians: deciduous and coniferous. There are those who drop their leaves when the temperature cools, and there are those who stay green no matter what happens.

Sermon Outline
CONIFEROUS CHRISTIANS

I. The problem described.
  A. Institutionally (congregation, student body, group, etc.).
  B. Individually.
II. The solution provided.
  A. External: Eliminate or reduce causes of depression and instability.
  B. Internal: Acquire a faith that can cope with untoward circumstances.

This part of the solution is the more crucial. No life, not even life in our great country, can be without trial and fiery affliction. Nor is it meant to be. God intends that we be put to the test. Anybody can hang on to his leaves when he is wafted by balmy spring breezes, but how about when the gales and storms and frosts start coming? What then? Can we then be coniferous? What is needed, in short, is a man for all seasons, one who in the language of the Epistle is "steadfast, immovable, always abounding in the work of the Lord." What is needed, in brief, is a coniferous Christian.

Merely wishing it will not make it so, not even wishing it from a pulpit. Only Christ can make it so, that Jesus Christ who is "the same yesterday and today and forever," whose love is coniferous, evergreen. What He achieved for us on Good Friday and Easter has opened up a whole new world for us, a world of heaven and a world of new creaturehood. If you can pardon my getting all the mileage I can out of my analogy, "If any man be in Christ, he is a new tree; he puts off deciduous and puts on coniferous."

FRANCIS C. ROSSOW

Eighth Sunday After the Epiphany

GOSPEL   Luke 6:39–49 (RSV)

Sermon Notes/Introduction

1. This pericope is lifted from our Lord's "Sermon on the Plain" and must be examined in that context. Christ enjoins His disciples to extend the Messianic ministry through the apostolic mission. The sermon first declares the Good News of the Kingdom, the Messianic message of God's free grace, His loving favor to the poor (Luke 6:20–26). There follows the directive to live as "sons of the Most High" (v. 35), to respond to God's giving and forgiving love with lives marked by the response of love (see 1 John 4:19: "We love, because He first loved us"). This love expresses itself in mercy (Luke 6:36), mercy such as the Father has displayed, which has on it "the mark of its divine origin" (*Concordia Self-Study Commentary,* New Testament, p. 65).

2. Loving mercy does not invade the divine prerogative of judgment (see Rom. 14:10) but is extended without concern or valuation of its object's worthiness. In the person of the Christ, the disciple discovers that the Judge is a merciful God who gives and forgives. As forgiven sons of the forgiving and giving One, they, too, are to be forgiving and giving. (Note the assurance of reward in Luke 6:38.) Disciples who serve in the spirit of love make no calculation on returns but are amply repaid, not by the persons benefited but by God's gracious bounty. The verb is almost impersonal: "There shall be given . . . His unmerited, generous reward." Arndt has "God Himself will be our paymaster."

3. The discourse changes at verse 39. As representatives of their Lord, as "sons of the Most High," the disciples are called to "lead" the blind. This can be done only by those who have clarity of vision, or the result is disastrous. A blind leader of the blind destroys both himself and others. Nor will a pupil obtain a clearer vision than the teacher. Therefore, the teacher must beware of being blind and uninstructed. The striking illustration of splinter and beam drives the message home (as does the good and the rotten tree metaphor that follows). As those called to lead others to repentance, the disciples must

first have a clear vision of themselves as forgiven. Thus the call to beam-removing repentance is a prerequisite to leadership of others. Without such preparation, the leader's activity is presumptuous rather than loving.

Sermon Outline
LIKE FATHER, LIKE SON

"Like father, like son" is a familiar adage suggesting cause and effect in parent-offspring relationships. On the lips of Jesus, it reminds us of the gracious perception belonging to the Father wrought by the sacrificial ransom offered on Calvary's cross. There one receives the merciful "adoption of sons" by the obedience of the Son of the Most High, whose "ransom for us life obtained." We stand *before* the judgment seat, not *on* it, and we stand acquitted. At Calvary we need judge no longer, for we are no longer judged. The One who "sees and knows us" sharpens our perception. God's forgiving love has removed the beam from our eye and directs our attention to our brother. As the Father has displayed mercy, so His forgiven children are called to reflect and proclaim that mercy as those who themselves first have taken seriously God's call to repentance. Remember, it was Paul who took this injunction seriously, whose vision was constantly Christ-corrected, who could boldly exhort the Corinthians, "Be imitators of me, as I am of Christ" (1 Cor. 11:1).

LEROY E. VOGEL

The Transfiguration of Our Lord:
Last Sunday After the Epiphany

EPISTLE   2 Corinthians 4:3–6 (RSV)

Sermon Notes/Introduction

1. The frequent light image in this text calls to mind the light so prominent in the Transfiguration of our Lord, recorded in the Gospel for this Sunday, Luke 9:28–36.

2. But this same light image is a "reflection" also of other passages in the Scriptures: God's creation of light (see 2 Cor. 4:6), Christ as the Light of the world (Epiphany emphasis), perhaps even the blinding light of Paul's Damascus experience.

3. Actually, light is more than a metaphor. In respect to God it is in some incomprehensible way *literal* as well. "God

is light." According to verse 4 Christ is "the likeness of God"; hence He is light (a truth brought to our attention by the testimony of the Bible, not only by the demands of logic). Since we are in the likeness of Christ, it follows that we Christians too are in some blessed way "light" (3:18). Light is more than an image; it can be a wonderful fact of life, a sharing in the life of God.

4. The parallel between the light of creation and the light of salvation alluded to in the Epistle turns out to be ultimately a climactic contrast rather than a mere parallel. At creation the accent was on God's spoken Word—God's power; in salvation the accent is on God's incarnate Word, Jesus—God's grace.

5. The blindness and sin mentioned in verses 3–4, penetrated and overcome by the light of the Gospel, are parallel to the chaos that prevailed at the time of creation, a chaos overpowered by God's creation of light.

6. Moses, who appeared with Christ and Elijah on the Mount of Transfiguration, is shown on another mountain in the Old Testament Reading for this Sunday (Deut. 34:1–12), the mountain from which he saw the promised land just before his death. Paul discusses this same Moses in 3:7–16, a section introducing an elaborate parallel between the light on his face—and the consequent veil—and the light "in the face of Christ" mentioned in 4:6, as well as the veil image of verses 3–4.

7. The veil that appears to cover the Gospel (v. 3) is really over the eyes of the unbelievers, as verse 4 makes clear, even as the sun is invisible to the blind not because the sun is veiled but because the eyes of the blind are "veiled."

8. Even as a small object immediately in front of the eye, like a coin, for instance, can shut out the sun, so some trifle of the "world" mentioned in verse 4 can shut out the light of the Gospel, making it appear to be veiled when it is our vision that is veiled.

9. Satan is called "the god of this world" in verse 4, not because he is in truth deity, but because people mistakenly pay him homage as if he were deity.

10. The "perishing" of verse 3 are more precisely identified by the term "the unbelievers" in verse 4.

11. Note that the movement of thought from Christ to God in verse 4 is reversed from God to Christ in verse 6:

Christ, who is the likeness of God. (v. 4)
The light of the knowledge of the glory of God in the face of Christ. (v. 6)

Might this be an indirect reinforcement of their equal God-hood made so explicit in the text?

12. Verse 5 contains a paradox. First, Paul claims that he and other Gospel preachers don't proclaim themselves (but rather Christ); then he adds that in a sense they do proclaim themselves—but only as slaves for their hearers on account of Jesus. In this connection note the obvious contrast (an idea fully developed in the following verses) between Christ as *Lord* and self as *slave*.

13. The context that follows shows that we enjoy a trans-figuration privilege that even the disciples present at our Lord's Transfiguration did not enjoy. While Jesus did not dwell in the booths proposed by Peter, He does "tent" in the tabernacle of our body (4:7–10).

All of us know of instances in which light can illuminate or light can blind, depending on our relationship to that light, whether we use it properly or misuse it.

Sermon Outline
THE RELATIONSHIP OF THE GOSPEL TO THE PEOPLE EXPOSED TO IT

I. Where the Gospel does not bear fruit, it may seem to be the fault of the Gospel.
  A. The Gospel appears to be veiled (v. 3).
  B. Actually, the veil is over the eyes of the unbeliever, not over the Gospel (v. 4).
    1. Inherent spiritual blindness or some trifle of the world shuts out the light of the Gospel.
    2. Satan, "the god of this world" (v. 4), is responsible for this condition.
II. Where the Gospel does bear fruit, it may seem to be to the credit of the hearer.
  A. The fruit: We preach Christ, not ourselves (v. 5).
    1. We proclaim Christ as Lord.
    2. If we do proclaim ourselves, it is only ourselves as slaves of people on account of Jesus (v. 5).
  B. The reason: We do this only because the same God who created light at the beginning of time has shined into our hearts through the Gospel of Jesus Christ and overcome our sin and blindness.
    1. "God is light." Christ is "the likeness of God" (v. 4); hence He is light. The Gospel "contains" Christ (v. 4); hence the Gospel is light.

2. This Gospel light creates new life in us, even as
   God's Word at creation brought light out of darkness, order out of chaos, life out of nothing.

Since our bodies are the temple of God, we can share in
that light and life so characteristic of our God.

FRANCIS C. ROSSOW

The Transfiguration of Our Lord:
Last Sunday After the Epiphany

GOSPEL   Luke 9:28–36 (KJV)

Sermon Notes/Introduction

In a way, the message of the Lenten season, which begins
this week, is disturbing: The Son of God dies! This doesn't add
up. How can the Son of God possibly die? Or how can one
who dies possibly be the Son of God? Death and deity just
don't go together.

In the face of this incompatibility, people are tempted to
do one of two things, both of them equally bad. Either they
admit Jesus to be the Son of God but look on His crucifixion
as an unfortunate accident, as an unpleasant interruption just
when everything was going so nicely, or they accept the crucifixion but regard the one crucified as nothing more than a
man—an exceptional man, to be sure, but still just a man. To
put it more simply: either people accept the deity but reject
the death, or they accept the death but reject the deity.

The transfiguration of Jesus corrects both of these mis-
taken notions. It shows that the Son of God must die. And it
shows that He who dies is the Son of God. In short, it har-
monizes death and deity.

Sermon Outline
DEATH AND DEITY—THEY GO TOGETHER

I. The Transfiguration shows that the Son of God must die.
   A. The disciples—and especially Peter—readily accepted
      that Jesus was the Son of God (9:20), but they couldn't
      stomach the idea that He was to suffer and die. (See
      Matt. 16:22, where Peter blurts out, "Be it far from
      thee, Lord; this shall not be unto thee.")
      1. Jesus responded to Peter's outburst with a solemn
         warning (v. 23).

2. He responded to the disciples' problem with the Transfiguration. Although both Jesus' miraculous transformation (Luke 9:29) and the witness of the Father (v. 35) reaffirm Christ's deity, please note that Moses and Elijah, representing respectively the Law and the Prophets, speak of Christ's "*decease which he should accomplish at Jerusalem.*" Significance? The crucifixion wasn't an unfortunate accident. Even the Law and the Prophets said that it had to happen. It was an essential part of God's eternal plan for the salvation of the world. It belonged.

B. The Christian church, throughout its history, has had within its pale people who rejected the fitness, value, or necessity of Christ's crucifixion. They may have conceded His deity, and they may have regarded His crucifixion as a historical fact. But they did not believe that crucifixion to be an essential part of God's saving plan. To them the crucifixion was at worst a vulgar finale to a brilliant career and at best a heroic example of how to cling to one's convictions and have the courage to die for them. But they wrote off as "crude" or "bloody" theology any claim that Jesus' crucifixion was supposed to happen and that it does things for people (like saving them or making them good).

C. Christians today may still commit this error in a modified or diluted form.

   1. Our problem: We may grant the worth of the crucifixion but fail to see its full worth (for example, seeing only an execution occurring on Calvary but not a damnation). Or we may emphasize the sadness and injustice of the crucifixion at the expense of its joy and value; we may mourn the event rather than celebrate it.

   2. Jesus' solution: the Transfiguration. It demonstrates that His decease is "meet, right, and salutary"; that it is a decease in the fullest sense of the word, a decease including damnation as well as execution; and that it is a decease giving joy, not sorrow.

II. The Transfiguration shows that He who dies is the Son of God.

A. Throughout its history the Christian church has had to cope with the error of accepting Christ's death but rejecting His deity. (Some who have entertained this error have even called themselves Christians!)

1. These errorists may have believed that there was a Jesus of Nazareth and that He was a wise man, a good man, a man way ahead of His times. They may have regarded His crucifixion as important; they may have accepted His death, recognized its relevance and fitness. "What better way," they may have said, "to climax an already heroic life than by dying true to His convictions and breathing a prayer of forgiveness for His executioners! The strength of the man is His splendid death."

2. But He was just a man, they have insisted. "The Son of God, never! Why spoil the beauty of this man's life by attaching some fantastic claim of godhead to it? Why all this fairy tale stuff about miracles and rising from death and ascending to heaven? Must we be children about this?"

B. Even we Christians—unless God preserves us in His truth—are subject to this most serious error.

1. Our problem: Every day we are bombarded by the diabolical error described above, especially diabolical because it is sometimes promulgated by churches calling themselves "Christian." In fact, the failure to recognize Christ's deity is one of the main weaknesses of Protestantism today. We are not immune to this propaganda.

2. Jesus' solution: the Transfiguration. Verses 34–35 report: "While he thus spake, there came a cloud and overshadowed them, and they feared as they entered into the cloud. And there came a voice out of the cloud, saying, 'This is My beloved Son; hear Him.'" Nothing could be plainer: God calls the man Jesus His own Son.

As we proceed toward the Lenten season, therefore, may we grasp the twin truths of the Transfiguration: (1) The Son of God must die; it's fitting and proper and a part of God's plan. (2) He who dies is not mere man but the Son of God. None less than Moses and Elijah testified to the first truth. And none less than God Himself testified to the second. Death and deity (Lent and Epiphany)—they go together. They were harmonized on a mountaintop many centuries ago.

FRANCIS C. ROSSOW

Ash Wednesday

EPISTLE   2 Corinthians 5:20b–6:2

Sermon Notes/Introduction

Lent marks the beginning of a journey that leads from the agony associated with the cross to the victory manifested at the tomb. It is not a morbid journey that keeps focusing on the terrible suffering of Christ but a joyous one that keeps the outcome, the resurrection of Christ, in view.

The Epistle points to our sin, which caused Christ's bitter agony. It also points to the favor God showed us in Christ's suffering, death, and resurrection.

Because the Lenten season gets us into the heart of Christianity, it is an appropriate time for renewal of faith. The goal of the sermon is that the hearers will be renewed in their faith that God has acted favorably toward them in Christ.

It is time once more for a Lenten journey that will take us from the events surrounding Golgotha to the victory of the empty tomb. The purpose of this journey is to increase our faith in God's favor toward us in Christ. We need this assurance of God's favor constantly because of our tendency to think that success and happiness and position are to be preferred to what God has actually done for our salvation. As we begin our journey, St. Paul reminds us that "God Has Acted Favorably Toward Us."

Sermon Outline
GOD HAS ACTED FAVORABLY TOWARD US

I. He has made it possible for us to become righteous before Him.
   A. By our own efforts we could never achieve the righteousness or goodness we need to be acceptable to God.
      1. Our deeds are never perfect, and the holy God demands perfection.
      2. God had to take the initiative and become reconciled to us; only then could we be reconciled to God by receiving through faith God's announcement of His reconciliation with us.
   B. God found a way to accept us as righteous people.
      1. He let Christ, who had no sin, become sin for us.
      2. When we believe in Christ, a marvelous exchange

takes place: our sin actually becomes Christ's sin, and Christ's righteousness actually becomes our righteousness. This exchange we received at our baptism.

God has acted favorably toward us. Of this we can be assured on our Lenten journey. After all, God Himself has accepted us as righteous people.

II. He assures that each day is an opportunity for us to be reconciled to God.
    A. Our day of salvation is every day.
        1. Each day we must be on guard that we do not despise God's offer of salvation.
        2. As long as we are on this earth and God is making His salvation known through Word and Sacrament, there is always the opportunity for God's Holy Spirit to remind us of our sin and of our need to be acceptable before God through what Christ has done.
    B. Each day God wishes to draw us to Himself.
        1. God's time of favor is always now, for God's primary concern is always our salvation.
        2. As we make this Lenten journey, we therefore take seriously and rejoice in God's invitation to be reconciled to Him.

To have been strengthened in the conviction that God has acted favorably toward us will make for another beneficial Lenten journey.

GERHARD AHO

Ash Wednesday

GOSPEL   Matthew 6:1–6, 16–21

Sermon Notes/Introduction

We sometimes associate Lent with giving up certain things that may be sinful or that may easily lead to sin. This negative approach to the Lenten season thwarts a proper Gospel emphasis and promotes self-righteous attitudes. The Gospel for Ash Wednesday is a section of the Sermon on the Mount in which Jesus warns us not to practice certain piety only to secure the praise of others. He was speaking to the self-righteousness that can dominate our thinking about repentance. Beginning in verse 1 with a warning not to practice our righteousness for the primary purpose of being seen and honored by others, He moves in verses 3–4 to a specific admonition not to concentrate on all the good we are doing by keeping a detailed account of how we have provided for the needs of others. In verses 5–6 He proceeds to prayer, which was such an important part of the Jewish worship and which is also a profound characteristic of the Christian life today. We are not to make a display of our prayer life but to pray naturally and quietly, though also publicly if necessary. A similar admonition is given in verses 16–17 regarding fasting; it is not to be done for display and ostentation but privately before God as a genuine expression of what we are experiencing in our spiritual life.

Such a performance of Christian duty will mean that we are gathering treasures in heaven, not on earth (vv. 19–20), and that our hearts are already in heaven with God and Christ, in whom alone true treasures are to be found. With Jesus as our heavenly treasure we are able to serve Him with a piety that flows naturally and joyously from faith in Him.

It is easy to become so earth-oriented that we forget that Jesus and heaven are our highest treasures. Lent again reminds us that where our treasure is, there will our heart be also. In the section of the Sermon on the Mount from which the Gospel is taken, Jesus says that by focusing on Him as a treasure, we maintain a balance in our Christian life between the earthly and the heavenly.

Sermon Outline
HOW GOOD IT IS TO HAVE JESUS AS OUR TREASURE!

I. We can be more keenly aware of the distinction between the earthly and the heavenly.
   A. Christ embodies all the spiritual values that are not of the earth.
      1. In Him are found basic truths conveying assurance that God is our gracious Father, who has opened heaven's doors to us because of what Christ accomplished at the cross and at the empty tomb.
      2. In Him we find real peace in all the changes of this life and also joy in death.
   B. What we have in Christ cannot be taken away from us by thieves or by rust or any earthly corruption.
      1. All our earthly treasures—our health, too—are temporal.

2. But what we have in Christ provides a basis for enjoying all these earthly treasures, because Christ has secured for us an anchor that holds in all the changes of life.

We receive Christ and His treasures of forgiveness and peace with God fully and freely at our baptism. Yet we continue to gather for ourselves heavenly treasures as we cling to Jesus as our highest treasure.

II. We can gather for ourselves treasures in heaven.
   A. We gather for ourselves heavenly treasure when we do not need to publicize the good we are doing for others.
      1. We do good to others so naturally that we are hardly aware of doing it.
      2. When our primary concern is not to get the praise of others but simply to meet their needs in response to what Jesus has done in meeting our needs, our Father will reward us. His ways of rewarding go far beyond what we can imagine here on earth or in heaven. Men may praise us, but it is far more significant to gather heavenly treasure by having God's blessing.
   B. We gather heavenly treasure when we don't need to show others how beautiful our prayers are.
      1. God does not look at the form, length, or pithiness of our prayers. Since prayer is an expression of our faith, what matters is that we are praying from the heart and without fear or doubting.
      2. By so praying we gather treasures in heaven. When we pray in response to God's promise that He will answer our prayers, His answers to prayer are a far higher reward than any human recognition for our praying.
   C. We gather treasure in heaven when no pious activity on our part is carried out for ostentatious display.
      1. Fasting, for example, has its place in the Christian life, but we don't fast to call the attention of others to how pious we are.
      2. There is reward in such recognition, of course, but what is that human recognition in comparison to the heavenly recognition God gives us who are fasting as a genuine expression of our relationship to Christ?

How good it is to have Christ as our highest treasure! From Him we gain insight into the distinction between the earthly and the heavenly. From Him we gain power to keep on gathering treasures in heaven.

GERHARD AHO

First Sunday in Lent

EPISTLE   Romans 10:8b–13 (KJV)

Sermon Notes/Introduction

1. The Old Testament Reading for this Sunday (Deut. 26:5–10) demonstrates the same close connection that the text does between faith and confession, between heart and deed.

2. The Gospel for this Sunday (Luke 4:1–13) indicates that the Word, which St. Paul assures us in the text is "nigh" us, was also "nigh" Jesus when He did battle with Satan during the temptation in the wilderness. The Word was at hand, ready for use; indeed, it was in the Savior's heart and mouth. He clearly and boldly confessed it, even as St. Paul urges us to do in the text.

3. The verses immediately before the Epistle show how simple salvation is (simple for us, that is, not for God—it cost Him the death and damnation of His own Son). But from our point of view, nothing extraordinary needs to be done (no ascending into heaven or descending into the deep). God simply gives us salvation through the words about that salvation— and those words are "nigh" us to boot! What those words effect in us in more detail is the concern of our text. The verses immediately after the Epistle express the apostle's concern that the Word be made "nigh" to others as well, that also others experience its blessed effects.

4. Throughout the Epistle there is frequent reference to Old Testament passages. (For instance, compare vv. 6–8 with Deut. 30:11–14; v. 11 with Is. 49:23; v. 13 with Joel 2:32.) Evidently, the Word was "nigh" Paul too, in his heart and mouth. But what is interesting is not so much the frequency of Paul's usage of the Old Testament but the nature of his usage, especially evident in his treatment of the Deuteronomy passage. In Deut. 30:14 the "word" is the Law, God's commandment. But in Rom. 10:8 the "word" is identified as "the word of faith," that is, the Gospel, the Good News. Plainly, that Good News is the theme of the Scriptures, and the Old

Testament takes on its full meaning in the light of New Testament revelation.

5. The words of verse 8, "The word is nigh thee, even in thy mouth, and in thy heart," are more literal than we perhaps realize. For God's Word ushers God Himself into our beings. Our bodies are temples of the Holy Spirit. Jesus and His Father make their abode in us. Not only the Word is in our mouth and in our heart—God is!

6. The words of verse 9, "believe in thine heart," emphasize two aspects of our Christian faith. First, it is something internal, inside, deep down within us, going to the core of our being, permeating every nook and cranny; it is not superficial, not merely external. Second, faith is more than intellectual assent. More than the mind is involved—the heart is also. We don't merely agree to a proposition about God, but we also trust Him with everything we've got.

7. Note that in verse 9 confession with the mouth is mentioned first and believing in the heart second, but in verse 10 the order is reversed. May we not infer from this (what the Bible states explicitly elsewhere) the close connection between belief and confession, between faith and works? They're inseparable. Where belief is, confession is. Where faith is, works are also present. The logical order, of course, is in verse 10. Faith is the cause, confession the result. First, God declares us righteous; then He begins to make us righteous. But in our zeal for systematizing, let us be careful not to put asunder what the text joins together. Belief and confession, heart and mouth, faith and works—they go together—they're inseparable in the Christian life.

8. The words "mouth" and "confession" remind us of the truth that "we cannot but speak the things which we have seen and heard" (Acts 4:20). Praise, prayer, and proclamation are the external evidence of the faith that the Gospel works in our heart. But "mouth" is probably an instance of synecdoche (the part standing for the whole); that is, the mouth represents the whole Christian person whom we see, and confession is a "for instance" of the entire external behavior. Thus Paul not only emphasizes praise, prayer, and proclamation but also embraces all Christian conduct. He talks about "conversation" in both its current narrow sense and in its older wide sense.

9. "The name of the Lord" in Rom. 10:13 is more than a combination of letters that spell a name of Jesus. It is more than a label by which we address Him. The "name" of the Lord is His whole being, His nature. It is He Himself ("I am

that I am"). It is everything He has done for us ("Thou shalt call his name Jesus; for he shall save his people from their sins"). To "call upon" His name, therefore, means to call on *Him,* to want Him, yearn for Him, trust Him, love Him—and all that He has done for us.

The season of Lent with its extra services and its concentration on the message of Christ's death naturally leads us to consider "The Unique Goodness of the Good News."

Sermon Outline
THE UNIQUE GOODNESS OF THE GOOD NEWS

I. Its nearness.
   A. God brings it to us through preachers (v. 8).
   B. It actually enters us and resides in us (v. 8).
II. Its achievements.
   A. It creates the faith in Jesus in our heart through which God declares us righteous and pronounces us saved (vv. 9–10).
   B. It creates the confession of Jesus in our mouth (in our life) by which we evidence the saving faith in our heart (vv. 9–10).
III. Its universality.
   A. It is never biased; it does not discriminate (v. 12).
   B. Whoever accepts it will be saved (v. 13).

In view of the unique goodness of the Gospel, let us cherish the message of Lent by exposing ourselves to it regularly and by receiving it enthusiastically.

FRANCIS C. ROSSOW

First Sunday in Lent

GOSPEL   Luke 4:1–13 (RSV)

Sermon Notes/Introduction

In treating this text, the preacher may wish to emphasize, in place of the introduction suggested in the outline, the timing of the temptation and the application of that timing to the 40 days of Lent. The devil comes shortly after the Savior's baptism, that great event ushering in His ministry and during which He receives the witness of the Father and of the Spirit. Further, special mention is now made that Jesus is *plērēs pneumatos* (see John 3:34) and *ēgeto en tō pneumati.* A combination of this "high" time in the life of the Savior and what Satan believes is a time of physical vulnerability prompts his attack just now. In the same way he tries to catch us off guard during the days of Lent, when we have the special privilege of meditating on our Lord's Passion and when we may practice fasting and/or other spiritual exercises intended to sharpen our focus on the Lord's redeeming work.

The outline suggests that at least a paragraph be devoted to a description of each of the three temptations. Note that in answer to the first temptation Jesus' reference to Deut. 8 (Matthew gives a longer quotation) will remind the devil that God is not bound by ordinary means in maintaining human life. This was graphically portrayed in the life of God's people during their days in the wilderness and indeed throughout their history.

The power of the tempter is seen in the second temptation when he is able *en stigmē chronou* to give the Lord a view of all the kingdoms of the world, later described by Satan as *tēn exousian tautēn hapasan*, "this whole domain." In the third temptation he slyly omits a portion of Scripture when quoting from Ps. 91.

Note also the different treatment in the Synoptics. Mark devotes only two verses to the event (Mark 1:12–13). He uses the verb *ekballei* for the Spirit's action in bringing Jesus to the wilderness, here obviously not in the sense of casting out (as it is often used regarding the exorcisms performed by the Lord) but in the sense of sending (see Matt. 9:38; Luke 10:2). Mark mentions Jesus among the wild beasts and includes reference, as does Matthew, to the ministry of the angels.

Matthew has a different order for the temptations, and his may be the chronological order. Luke simply mentions three temptations and does not undertake to tell us in what order they occurred. Although the first evangelist simply says that the devil left Jesus after the third temptation, omitting the *achri kairou*, the omission does not suggest that Matthew saw this as the last attempt to lead the Savior astray. In Matthew's account we hear the Lord order the devil away: *Hupage, Satana.*

This Gospel gives us a great opportunity to speak of the *active* obedience of our Lord for our salvation, a topic seldom treated from our pulpits. Here is the Gospel power. Our people are to be led to see this victory of the Lord over Satan as His victory also for us.

Sermon Outline
TEMPTED BY THE DEVIL

I. There are three temptations.
   A. The first is to doubt the goodness of God.
      1. Temptation comes to the Savior in His hunger after His 40-day fast.
      2. Temptation comes to us in periods of testing—pain, family problems, bereavement: "Why isn't God doing something about this?"
   B. The second is a temptation to the glitter of the world.
      1. For Jesus, there is a price: "Worship me, [and] it shall all be yours" (v. 7).
      2. There is a price also for us—sacrifice of principle, eyes taken from eternal truth.
   C. The third urges presumptuous behavior, tempting God.
      1. Satan asks Jesus to jump from the temple.
      2. Satan says to us: "There is no danger. Skip the medicine; join the wild party; you don't need church every Sunday. You're God's child."
II. They are sly temptations.
   A. The devil tries to use what God intended as blessing for evil.
      1. In Jesus' case it was the fasting, something that can be a great blessing.
      2. In our case, the birth of a baby, a promotion, or a new home may be all we need to keep us from Christ and His Word.
   B. The devil lives up to his reputation as the father of lies.
      1. He acts as though it is in his power to give power.
      2. He lies to us about the gravity of sin—before: "it is nothing"; after: "it is unforgivable."
   C. Satan quotes Scripture.
      1. See how he twists Ps. 91 when speaking to the Savior.
      2. To us he says: "There is no hell. Doesn't the Bible say, 'God is love'?"
III. All these temptations failed.
   A. Our comfort.
      1. We have often lost battles with the devil; we have succumbed.
      2. Jesus overcomes him *for us* (Rom. 5:18–19).
   B. Our instruction.

1. Jesus used Scripture to overcome Satan.
2. We can in His power do the same. Prayer, yes. Meditation, yes. Above all, the Word.

May the Lord bless our observance of Lent as we find both comfort and power in this account.

KARL BARTH

Second Sunday in Lent

EPISTLE   Philippians 3:17–4:1 (NIV)

Sermon Notes/Introduction

It is characteristic of sinful human beings that we do what we please for ourselves and for the here and now. Illustrations of this truth abound in the world around us. Madison Avenue takes advantage of it in its selling techniques. Both of the other readings for this day illustrate how this same characteristic dominates in many who call themselves God's people but who reject His Word and go their own worldly way. The result is that they put more confidence in the flesh than in the Lord, to use Paul's words in the first part of Phil. 3. In their pitiful effort to become something before God on their own, they lose sight of the beauty and power of what believers already are through union with Christ by faith. The apostle's appeal just before today's Epistle is a fitting and necessary reminder for us: "Let us live up to what we have already attained" (v. 16).

The high value of the dollar in the last few years has impelled record numbers of Americans to visit foreign countries. Wherever they go, they carry with them their American citizenship. They have both the rights of citizens and the responsibility of representing their homeland. Hopefully, they will be recognized as good citizens. The same truth applies to our membership in God's kingdom, of which we are citizens through Christ (Eph. 2:19). How essential it is that each of us "Live on Earth as a Citizen of Heaven."

Sermon Outline
LIVE ON EARTH AS A CITIZEN OF HEAVEN

I. It is to be expected that all believers walk to the same drumbeat in expressing their oneness in Christ (Phil. 3:16–17).

    A. By his appeal to follow his example Paul urges Christians to grow in sanctification, to become more and more Christlike (Matt. 16:24; John 13:15; Rom. 15:5; Phil. 2:5; Heb. 12:2).

    B. A significant factor in Christian living besides the working of the Spirit in the Word is having and following positive examples of faith found in Scripture and in other saints both past and present (1 Cor. 11:1; Heb. 11).

II. It is a sad reality that many who profess allegiance to Christ show just the opposite in their lives.

    A. Paul defines the characteristics of such false citizens of Christ's kingdom.

        1. They are given to shameless gratification of the desires of the flesh. (Illustrations from our culture abound.)

        2. Their hearts are set on the things of this world, not on the things of God.

        3. Such "Christians" love and serve the things from which Christ, by His cross, came to free us.

    B. We need to recognize and shun such "enemies of the cross of Christ" lest they become an influence on us, at the same time grieving over what has happened to them (Luke 13:34).

III. Paul leaves no doubt about what genuine citizens of the kingdom are like.

    A. Their lives are all wrapped up in Christ alone.

        1. Instead of all the things that promise to satisfy, their one treasure is Christ (Phil. 3:7–9).

        2. Their aim in life is to serve Him, not sin (Rom. 6:1–7; 2 Cor. 5:14–15).

    B. Their hope for the future is also centered in Christ (John 14:1–6; 1 Cor 15:42–58, esp. v. 58; Col. 3:1–4).

During this Lenten season, as we reevaluate the citizenship that our lives reflect, we do well to heed Paul's final admonition in the Epistle: "Stand firm in the Lord, dear friends!"

ED DUBBERKE

Second Sunday in Lent

GOSPEL   Luke 13:31–35 (KJV)

Sermon Notes/Introduction

1. Note the symmetry in this text, the progress from specific hostility toward Jesus (from Herod) to general hostility toward Jesus (from Jerusalem). The direction is from small to large, from an individual to a group. In addition, it moves from the jurisdiction in which Jesus' death would not occur (Herod's) to the jurisdiction in which it would occur (Jerusalem's).

2. The time references in verses 32–33 are probably proverbial and indefinite rather than literal and specific. Cryptic and general as they are, however, they are richly suggestive, indicating (1) Jesus' calm determination to carry on His work no matter what dangers exist (He will be "the same yesterday, and today, and forever"); (2) His awareness that His work is programmed, "scheduled," that there is a pattern behind it climaxing ("the third day") in the accomplishment of His goal ("I shall be perfected" [KJV], "I shall finish my work" [TEV]); and (3) His sense of urgency over the brevity of the time remaining to Him ("work while it is day," etc. [John 9:4]).

3. Exegetically, "the third day" of verse 32 does not refer to the bodily resurrection of our Lord on "the third day" (no more than it refers to any other specific act in our Lord's ministry). Yet, used as a Gospel handle, the phrase can remind us of that event. That "third day" on which our Lord was raised from the dead was indeed the climax of our Lord's work, its perfection, the ultimate goal accomplishment!

4. Verse 33 is devastatingly ironic and satirical. Jesus says, in effect, "Actually, I am in no danger of death in Herod's jurisdiction because My death is bound to occur at Jerusalem, the jurisdiction that has a monopoly on prophet killing. That's the place—as Biblical history shows—where prophets go to die. So what else is new?" Yet the verse constitutes much more than divine sarcasm. Like the immediately preceding words, it demonstrates a plan of God behind the seemingly relentless and fated chain of events in which Jesus is involved. He is not the helpless victim of circumstances; He is a voluntary agent in an eternal plan of God for the salvation of the world, willingly proceeding toward a sacrificial death that will consummate that plan. He does what He does, not because it can't be helped, but "that the Scriptures might be fulfilled."

5. "Jerusalem, Jerusalem" (v. 34) is an apostrophe, a

digression in which the speaker turns aside to address an absent or imaginary addressee. The repetition calls attention to the intensity of the feeling that prompts the remark and to the importance of the substance of the remark. (Think of "Absalom, Absalom"; "Martha, Martha"; "Saul, Saul.")

6. "Jerusalem" is also metonymy; that is, the city stands for the people of the city—in fact, for the people of the entire nation.

7. Since "Jerusalem" means "city of peace," the name, in view of the people's evil deeds and their dire consequences, is ironic in this context.

8. The present participles "killing" and "stoning" (v. 34) are significant in that they imply that the dastardly deeds described are still being committed. They are not merely past misdeeds; they persist to the present.

9. The metaphor of the hen gathering her chickens under her wings, besides being a concrete and specific description of the God described in more general and abstract terms in Ezek. 33:11 as taking no pleasure in the death of the wicked and in 1 Tim. 2:4 as wishing to save all people, echoes the frequent Old Testament metaphor of God as an eagle whose wings bear us up (Ex. 19:4) or cover us with feathers (Ps. 91:4), under which we take refuge (Ps. 57:1). When we bear in mind that the Greek word for hen may also refer to any bird, the parallelism in imagery between the Old and New Testaments is all the more remarkable. Aware of this parallelism, the preacher and his audience, when confronting the Epistle, may have a delightful "Aha!" experience, suddenly recognizing in the coupling of the eagle-hen image a powerful tribute to the unity of the two Testaments as well as a reassurance that Jesus is indeed "the same yesterday and today and forever" (Heb. 13:8), a concept perhaps echoed in the similar language of Luke 13:32–33.

10. If only our Lord's addressees would respond to His plea to be gathered together under His protection as chickens are gathered together under the wings of a hen, they could avoid both the "Roman eagle" that later destroyed their city in A.D. 70 as well as the divine eagles of judgment described in Luke 17:37 and Matt. 24:28 as hovering over the carcass.

11. Note in verse 34 the sharp contrast between the "would" of Jesus and the "would not" of His addressees ("how often *would* I have gathered thy children together" versus "and ye *would not*").

12. "House" (v. 35) is regarded by many commentators

as the temple at Jerusalem. Note how subtly God's absence is communicated by calling the temple *"your* house" (not *"God's* house"). Since the temple was the heart and center of Jewish worship and life, God's absence from it signifies His absence from His addressees if they persist in their godless conduct.

13. "Desolate" (v. 35)—bereft of God; thus a symbol of that final and permanent absence of God more commonly called hell.

14. Note the contrast within verse 35. If the first half of the verse threatens the absence of God, the last half promises His presence (a superb Law-Gospel combination). Not all is hopeless; at some future time (after Jesus' resurrection? at Pentecost? at the Second Coming? perhaps better left unspecified?) some of Jesus' addressees will welcome Him in words similar to those used by the Palm Sunday multitude (see also Ps. 118:26). In so blessing the Lord, they, of course, will themselves be blessed.

Sermon Outline
GOD'S "WOULD" VERSUS OUR "WOULD NOT!"

I. Our "would not" (sin).
   A. The evidence.
      1. Then.
         a. Specific (Herod, Jeremiah's enemies in the Old Testament Reading).
         b. General (Jerusalem, "the enemies of the cross of Christ" in the Epistle).
      2. Now.
   B. The outcome: "Your house is left unto you desolate."
II. God's "would" (grace).
   A. The evidence.
      1. Stated generally and abstractly in Ezek. 33:13 and 1 Tim. 2:4.
      2. Stated specifically and concretely in Luke 13:34.
      3. Demonstrated dramatically on the cross.
   B. The outcome.
      1. We repent and welcome the Lord; we say (in effect), "Blessed is he who comes in the name of the Lord."
      2. Jesus says to us, "Come, you blessed of my Father, inherit the kingdom prepared for you from the foundation of the world."

FRANCIS C. ROSSOW

Third Sunday in Lent

EPISTLE   1 Corinthians 10:1–13 (RSV)

Sermon Notes/Introduction

"Fifty million Frenchmen" can be wrong! Truth and the issues of life are not determined by majority vote. Lent is a reminder of this fact, and today's Epistle expressly states that God was not pleased by the attitudes and action of most Israelites who had been set free from Egypt. The greater part of that special people was wrong and perished. The apostle introduces these "fathers" (v. 1) as examples to warn us (v. 6) of the false security and even indifference that have their source in the failure to realize that "The Majority Can Be Wrong."

Sermon Outline
THE MAJORITY CAN BE WRONG

I. Serving the truth takes more than belonging.
   A. The apostle stresses that those Israelites of the majority which perished in the desert, *all* (five times the word *pantes* occurs in vv. 1–4) shared in the sacramental life of God's people.
      1. They all crossed the Red Sea and so experienced a baptism "into Moses" (v. 2).
      2. They all ate of the manna, and they all drank of the miracle water that flowed from the Rock (vv. 3–4).
      3. The cloud (v. 1) of God's presence covered them all, just as the shining cloud overshadowed the three disciples on the Mount of Transfiguration (cf. Mark 9:7).
      4. Yet the majority went down to destruction for (a) their lusting, (b) their idolatry, (c) their grumbling, and (d) their insolence in daring to put God to the test to meet their own expectations.
   B. This case study is offered as a paradigm (*tupos*, v. 6) for all who share in the life of the church.
      1. We have been baptized into Christ.
      2. We participate in the Lord's Supper.
      3. God's gracious presence attends us constantly in Word and sacraments.
      4. Yet our belonging to the church does not, of itself,

offer an automatic guarantee that we shall reach our Promised Land.

5. Lent, as a penitential season, reminds us that we must struggle to avoid the same sins that led the majority in ancient Israel to their destruction.

II. The qualities of Christian living are not determined by a Gallup Poll.

A. Discipleship consists of a life of proper and even rugged response:

1. To God's redemptive acts as exhibited in the crucifixion and resurrection, whereby we have become the new Israel, God's people of the end-time (1 Cor. 10:11);

2. To God's saving power as offered to us in Word and Sacrament;

3. In differentiation from and even opposition to the life-style of the majority (cf. 1 John 2:16).

B. Discipleship incurs the risk of being strongly tempted:

1. To join the majority (1 Cor. 10:9);

2. To reject God on His terms;

3. Thus to create our own criteria and system of values (e.g., situation ethics; cf. the *tupikōs* of v. 11).

C. Discipleship calls for dependence on divine resources:

1. God's constant (the *pistos* of v. 13) attendance on us;

2. His will to keep us from enduring temptations beyond our strength (v. 13);

3. His sustaining power that creates a way out so that we may endure in times of temptation (v. 13).

We observe Lent, for one thing, as a way of recalling the need for Christian discipline, for example, to refrain from doing what "comes naturally." Our Lord Himself practiced that discipline (cf. Heb. 5:7–8) and resisted temptation (cf. 4:15), thereby becoming the "pioneer and perfecter of our faith" (12:2). The majority of His countrymen rejected Him and finally had Him crucified. The majority can be and often is wrong about God. Our life in the church, therefore, is a call to minority service, created and sustained as we are by Word and Sacrament.

MARTIN H. SCHARLEMANN

Third Sunday in Lent

GOSPEL   Luke 13:1–9 (RSV)

Sermon Notes/Introduction

Pilate's massacre of the Galileans was brought to Jesus' attention presumably in the hope that He would be incensed at this outrage and take sides with the nationalists against the hated Romans. Refusing to choose sides, Jesus talks instead about the need for repentance. His reference to another calamity in Jerusalem emphasizes that, although certain punishments may result from particular sins, every untoward incident should not occasion a why on our part. We do not always know God's purposes. All misery is the result of sin, but the circumstance that one individual has a heavier load than another is a part of God's unfathomable ways. The question we ought to be asking is, What does a particular tragic occurrence impel us to do? The need for repentance is firmly established by the parable. "Vineyard": God's order of salvation. "Fig tree": Israel. "Owner": God. "Vinedresser": Jesus. "Three years": era of grace granted Israel then and us now.

The central thought of the Gospel is the urgency of repentance. The goal of the sermon is that the hearers would make their lives a daily repentance. The problem is that Christians become careless about producing the fruits of repentance—confessing their sins, relying on mercy, and doing good deeds. Yet the Lord in His grace gives us time to repent.

God gives us time for living. How we use it is of crucial importance for the present and the future. That is why we need to take to heart Christ's words: "Let it alone this year also."

Sermon Outline
LET IT ALONE THIS YEAR ALSO

I. These words tell us that God's patience will end.
   A. God's patience ended for Israel.
      1. The vinedresser does not ask that the tree never be cut down.
         a. The request is only for an extension of time.
         b. Despite the extension, Israel repudiated God's love; it resembled the tree by the roadside (Matt. 21:19).
      2. Unrepentant Jerusalem was destroyed and the people dispersed (Luke 13:3, 5, 7, 9; 19:41–44).

   B. God's patience with the unrepentant today also ends.
      1. We cannot sin with impunity, excusing our failures.
      2. Are we playing with Christianity, saying "Lord, Lord" while our hearts are far from Him, substituting ritual for repentance?

"Let it alone this year also" is a warning for us. We are in a probationary period. God's patience has an end. There will come a time when He will say, "Cut it down."

 II. These words also tell us that God deeply desires our repentance.
   A. God gives opportunities to repent.
      1. He gave Israel opportunities not only throughout the Old Testament period (13:6–7), but especially during the ministry of Jesus and the apostles (v. 8).
      2. He gives us opportunities.
         a. He has planted us in His church.
         b. We have unrestricted access to His Word in printed form and through the media, also in the sacraments of Baptism and Holy Communion, and through fellowship with other Christians.
   B. God Himself makes repentance possible (v. 8).
      1. With the Law He digs—laying bare our sin.
      2. With the Gospel He fertilizes—strengthening our grasp on Jesus and producing the fruit of good deeds.
      3. Our life becomes a daily repentance in which we confess our sin, trust in His mercy, and bear the fruit of good works.

"Let it alone this year also." What a comfort! God grants us time, for He deeply desires our repentance.

Now is the accepted time (Heb. 3:7–8). Bring forth fruit (Matt. 3:8). God will make you like a tree (Ps. 1:3).

GERHARD AHO

Fourth Sunday in Lent

EPISTLE   1 Corinthians 1:18, 22–25

Sermon Notes/Introduction

In our pluralistic society we are bombarded with all kinds of claims about whom we should follow, how to run our lives, where to find satisfaction, and how to be sure that we are in

control. The advice is actually spiritual, though it certainly is
not labeled as such, because it deals with the relationships we
have with others (which have much in common with our prior
relationship, or lack of such, with God). It is not always easy
to sort out all the input to discover what is truly in tune with
or helpful for our Christian experience. It is probably easier to
attach ourselves to some person or concept that appeals to us
and to promote it as the best source of power for our lives.
The apostle Paul was aware that the Corinthian Christians were
accepting leadership and advice from all sides and that those
who found what satisfied them were haughty and quarrelsome
with those who did not have what was deemed the best
(1 Cor. 1:10–12). The apostle understood that such behavior
and attitudes threaten the power of the cross of Christ (v. 17),
which is what truly best empowers us. Thus this Epistle still
instructs us as we live in the modern world. What continues
to be the best for us is "The Power of the Cross."

Sermon Outline
THE POWER OF THE CROSS

I. Power is not found in human signs and wisdom.
   A. Signs and wisdom have always been in great demand
      (v. 22).
      1. The Jews demanded signs (John 2:18), and the
         Greeks sought wisdom—systems of philosophy to
         guide one's destiny and keep life under control.
      2. It is still so. The Shroud of Turin or the ruins of the
         ark are considered to be faith-authenticating. Peo-
         ple look to astrology, "how to live" books, and sects
         and their leaders for spiritual direction and power
         for daily living.
   B. But signs and wisdom are found wanting.
      1. Signs do not work faith. The Jewish leaders saw
         Jesus' burial clothes and still did not believe. The
         apostles did not carry them around to convince peo-
         ple of Jesus' resurrection. Ark ruins do not make
         Christians.
      2. All "wisdom" is not true guidance. The "me first"
         concept of our time inhibits good relationships. The
         depreciation of the nuclear family has harmed so-
         ciety. Sects last only as long as their leaders.
   C. Those who seek and find inadequate signs and wisdom

are perishing even as they think they are succeeding
(1 Cor. 1:18).

II. Power is found in the cross of Christ.

    A. The Christ of the cross is God's power and wisdom
(v. 24).

        1. He is the power that saves us when we are weak
and faced with destruction (Rom. 5:8–9).

        2. He is the wisdom that presents God's grace to us
in the midst of our sin and inability to save ourselves
(Eph. 2:8–9).

    B. The world discounts God's power.

        1. It is a stumbling block. The Jews looked to the keeping of the Law rather than the promise of the Messiah. It is still argued that the idea of God's saving us takes away from the dignity achieved in saving ourselves by our own power, in which we can boast (v. 9).

        2. It is foolishness. The Greeks considered the resurrection to be absurd (Acts 17:32), and it is still attacked today. What is regarded as even more foolish is the undeserved forgiveness that God offers. How ridiculous it seems to forgive with open arms, with no vengeance, without even a period of testing repentance (Luke 15:11–32)! It gives up our power over others.

    C. But to us the cross of Christ is the power and wisdom
of God (1 Cor. 1:24–25).

        1. Its foolishness and weakness defeat Satan and destroy the terror of death.

        2. It restores the joy of forgiveness, the power to live
for God and others, the certain hope of heaven.

The power of Christ crucified is for all people (v. 24). Paul
was caught up in preaching it. As it empowers us, we rejoice
as God uses us to engage others in its power and wisdom,
which answer our deepest needs (Luke 15:24).

LUTHER G. STRASEN

Fourth Sunday in Lent

GOSPEL   Luke 15:1–3, 11–32 (RSV)

Sermon Notes/Introduction

The first three verses of the Gospel are not treated directly in the suggested outline but are of course the basis of and rationale for our Lord's trilogy on the Lost Sheep, the Lost Coin, and the Lost Son. Each of these stories emphasizes God's concern for the individual, a theme found throughout the Third Gospel.

The profligate life of the son is graphically described in verse 13 with the verb *dieskorpisen* (literally, "scattered" his property). (See the only similar usage in 16:1.)

The son did this, living *asōtōs*—"dissolutely." This is the only New Testament usage of the adverb, though the noun *asōtia* is used by both Paul and Peter.

The imperfect *epethumei* in verse 16 indicates that there was a continual yearning in the prodigal's heart and that it took him a while to "come to himself." (Note also *edidou*, v. 16.)

The repetition of "Father, I have sinned" (vv. 18, 21) highlights how the son must have thoroughly rehearsed what he would say to his father, no doubt wondering how the father would react. *Esplanchnisthē* is that grand verb for feeling compassion. Significantly, in the New Testament it refers only to the Savior, the forgiving King (Matt. 18:27), and the father in this passage.

The words of verse 24 apply to us as well: we were dead and came to life again, were lost and have now been found.

The father goes out to meet the older brother, just as he ran to meet the prodigal (Luke 15:28). More than that, he pleaded with him. (Again the continued action is indicated by the imperfect *parekalei*.)

So bitter is the older brother that he can refer to his brother only as *ho huios sou*, the one who has "devoured [*kataphagōn*] your living with harlots" (v. 30).

There is a tenderness here in the father that must melt our hearts. What a privilege to proclaim this Gospel to our people!

Sermon Outline
A SON, A FATHER, AND A BROTHER

1. Have you ever asked, "Is God aware of and concerned

about *my* fears, worries, temptations, home . . . ?"

2. If so, read again the Gospel of St. Luke. The stories of common, ordinary *individuals*—widow of Nain, Zacchaeus, the woman who washed Jesus' feet.

3. It is this personal and human touch in the story of the prodigal son that has led many to call it "the pearl of parables."

  I. A prodigal son (vv. 11–20).
    A. He leaves.
      1. "He squandered his property in loose living" (v. 13).
      2. This is *our* story. (How easy it is to apply it to others, "modern youth," etc.)
    B. His sin has tragic results.
      1. "He began to be in want" (v. 14) in the fields feeding swine; his friends were gone.
      2. We see what sin does. Disobedience to the Father leads ultimately to despair and damnation.
    C. "He came to himself" (v. 17).
      1. He can no longer blame others; there are no more excuses. "Father, I have sinned" (v. 18).
      2. How do you plan to come before the Father? Join the publican and this prodigal. Any other approach means you are still in "a far country."
 II. A merciful father (vv. 20–24).
    A. He forgives.
      1. Waiting for his son, "he had compassion" (v. 20), ran to him, and ordered the fatted calf to be killed.
      2. Does our Father forgive us? Think of your worst sins; the Father waits.
    B. Look at "the robe of righteousness" (Is. 61:10). It was purchased for us with the blood of the Savior.
III. A cold brother (Luke 15:25–32).
    A. He reacts poorly.
    B. Of whom does he remind you? Jonah at the repentance of Nineveh? the scribes and Pharisees? What about us with our suspicions about the convert?

The more we realize that salvation is by pure grace, the less we shall be prone to playing the cold brother; we will rejoice at the goodness of God in Christ. "He has not dealt with us according to our sins."

KARL BARTH

Fifth Sunday in Lent

EPISTLE   Philippians 3:8–14

Sermon Notes/Introduction

Cheap grace and self-righteousness—neither of these gives glory to God, but they do bring into focus a paradox of the Christian faith. In Christ, we have perfect righteousness. All the perfection of Jesus Christ is imputed to the believer by faith. Yet this truth is never an occasion for complacency or indifference; instead, it spurs us on to ever greater conformity of life to confession. Although we are perfect in Christ, we strive for perfection more and more each day.

Sermon Outline

THE PARADOX OF THE RIGHTEOUS

I. Righteousness that we possess perfectly.
   A. We receive righteousness apart from the Law.
      1. We are tempted to glory in our own accomplishments, pedigree, endurance (cf. the context of the Epistle).
      2. These can never make or give perfect righteousness (v. 9).
      3. They are counted as loss for the sake of Christ (v. 8).
   B. Righteousness comes from God alone.
      1. It is founded in God's actions, not our own efforts (v. 9).
      2. It comes for the sake of Christ by grace through faith (v. 9).
      3. Although righteous in Christ, we strive for righteousness (v. 13).

II. Righteousness for which we strive.
   A. The righteous are aware of their own imperfection (lack of righteousness).
      1. We are not perfect (vv. 12–13).
      2. We have comfort and assurance but are not complacent or indifferent (v. 12).
   B. We press on, reaching for what lies ahead of Christ.
      1. We use the means by which God sustains us (vv. 10–11).
      2. We fulfill the purpose for which Christ has called

us (v. 14).

NORBERT H. MUELLER

Fifth Sunday in Lent

GOSPEL   Luke 20:9–19 (KJV)

Sermon Notes/Introduction

My sermon today is going to start out by doing something that a sermon should never do (but that even the best-intentioned sermon sometimes does anyhow because of listener perversity); it's going to make you think of the sins of others—the only difference being that this time the attempt is conscious, deliberate, and open.

Sermon Outline
SENDING YOUR SON

I. Most of you, no doubt, have had the experience of trying over and over to cure someone of a pet sin that makes the person and/or those around him or her miserable. The sin may be cheating, overeating, excessive drinking, a bad temper, a nasty tongue, a martyr complex, poor sportsmanship, fickleness, or irresponsibility, and the sinner may be someone close to you—a parent or child, a husband or wife, a brother or sister, a boss or secretary, a friend or fellow worker, a colleague or roommate.

A. At any rate, more times than you can number you have approached the person tactfully and kindly, trying to straighten him or her out for the sake of everyone's happiness, and again and again you have run up against the proverbial stone wall. The person you talk to either gets hurt or angry or accuses you of a holier-than-thou approach or acts surprised and dumbfounded (not having the foggiest notion what you're talking about) or, worse yet, agrees with you too quickly, promising prompt reform but the next day going on as always. In the language of the Gospel, you send the person, so to speak, servant after servant, and each is beaten and wounded in rapid succession. Ultimately, you make some herculean effort, some supreme sacrifice (call it sending your own son), but the result is even worse: the person kills the son, so to speak; your efforts get nowhere. Desperately, you mumble something about leopards never changing their spots, and the thoughtless cliché may cross your mind of letting the person "go to hell"—which, ironically, is precisely what could happen.

B. By now you may be saying, "I know somebody just like that, Pastor, and you've described him/her to a T." Well, if my opening remarks have tempted you to sin by thus focusing your attention on the other person's sin, let me say in my defense that I have so tempted you in order that grace might abound. For here is the point of my dubious approach. Just as this particular person has repeatedly frustrated your attempts to amend his or her ways, so you and I have frustrated God's efforts to eradicate some fatal flaw in ourselves. Either we're damnably unaware of our habitual failing (although it's plain as day to God and perhaps to many people as well—including those who have already identified us as the rascal I described in my opening remarks), or we're aware of our flaw but have successfully (at least in our own thinking) rationalized it away. There it stands, our pet sin, a monkey wrench in God's eternal plan, a cause of misery to both Him and our acquaintances and often a source of unhappiness to ourselves, too. Over and over—and now I am *not* doing violence to the language of our parable—over and over God has literally sent us His servants and prophets, and we have beaten them and wounded them. Finally, He made the supreme sacrifice; He literally spared not His own Son, and even Him we have crucified anew on occasion.

II. Although there is considerable historical significance to this parable, let us today restrict ourselves to its contemporary application. It is also you and I, centuries later, to whom God has entrusted His vineyard (the church, the Christian life, whatever). It is you and I from whom God expects produce (faith, good works). It is you and I to whom God sends His servants (pastors, teachers, parents, anyone who tells the Good News of God's love in Christ). And it is you and I to whom God sends His Son, Jesus (now in the Gospel and in the sacraments).

A. And we need to remind ourselves that this is a serious sending. God means it. There is nothing casual or cavalier about God's action. It is not done with a take-it-

or-leave-it attitude. God is not to be regarded lightly. "Be not deceived; God is not mocked." Although God's sending has only our eternal happiness in mind, and although He has a love and a patience beyond the farthest reaches of our imagination, the Bible still confronts us with the possibility that one can turn God down once too often. It reminds us, together with assurances of God's love, that "our God is a consuming fire" and that "it is a fearful thing to fall into the hands of the living God." Our parable, after referring to Christ as a beneficial cornerstone, says it this way (in verse 18): "Whosoever shall fall upon that stone shall be broken; but on whomsoever it shall fall, it will grind him to powder."

B. But if the Scriptures remind us that "our God is a consuming fire," they flood us, they bombard us, with the assurance that "God is love." Again and again the Scriptures tell us of God's incredible mercy and infinite patience. A while ago we admitted how quick we are to give up when our efforts to help a friend overcome a fault are constantly frustrated. But God in His relationship with us is not disposed to quit. He is not a cynic. He does not wish to consign us to hell. "God is love." He keeps sending His beloved Son to us, over and over, in the Gospel and in the Sacrament, hoping that we will someday embrace the truth He speaks to us in such great love and that then the truth will make us free: free from our pet sin, free from the spiritual death in which it is miring us, free to serve Him here and hereafter, free to enjoy the glorious liberty of the children of God in God's eternal home.

And God does this, and keeps doing this, although He has to live with us even more intimately than we have to live with our erring relatives and friends. For He is not only with us, as we are with them, but He is also *in* us. Our body is His temple. Whatever our pet sin, it rubs Him *directly*. But still God loves—and loves—and keeps loving. This is His goodness that, He hopes, will lead us to repentance.

C. By now, I'm sure, my first objective is plain: that we might gain a new appreciation of our sin and a new appreciation of God's efforts to save us from and cure us of our sin. Just as So-and-So constantly blocks our efforts to help him or her, so we, no doubt—at least

some of the time and more often than we think—block
God's efforts to help us. And the compassion and despair we feel toward So-and-So are but an inkling of
the same combination of feelings God experiences toward us, except that God doesn't tire, doesn't quit. He
does not grow weary or faint in well-doing. He continuously speaks the truth in love. His mercy endures
forever. Let us with His help respond to His love and
mercy.

D. More than that, let us with His help imitate His love
and mercy. That is my other objective. Don't quit
speaking the truth to old So-and-So. And don't quit
loving old So-and-So. Keep sending your servants and
prophets, so to speak, to that crusty old codger
(whoever it may be). Best of all, keep sending God's
Son in Gospel and Sacrament. The person may crucify
Him anew (that's the risk you take), but send Him again
and again and again. The day may come when He will
be accepted. That will be the beginning of a glorious
day. Heaven—for that person—will have dawned. And
the leopard, believe it or not, will start changing its
spots.

FRANCIS C. ROSSOW

Palm Sunday: Sunday of the Passion

EPISTLE   Philippians 2:5–11 (KJV)

Sermon Notes/Introduction

1. Preceding today's Epistle, Paul states his objective: that
we might be "of one accord, of one mind" (v. 2).

2. Such like-mindedness consists principally of two ingre-
dients: humility (v. 3) and unselfishness (v. 4).

3. The Epistle presents Christ as both the *model* for and
the *means* to the goal of like-mindedness that consists chiefly
of humility and unselfishness.

4. Paul's approach is delightfully logical. His goal is that
Christians have the same mind. If Christian A has "the mind
of Christ" and if Christian B has "the mind of Christ," they
do indeed have the same mind, that is, "the mind of Christ."
Thus harmony results, for "things equal to the same thing are
equal to each other."

5. "Let this mind be in you, which was also in Christ Jesus"

(v. 5) is more literal than we're inclined to think. This is more than an appeal to have an attitude of humility and unselfishness similar to Christ's. According to the Bible elsewhere, if we keep God's Word, the Father and the Son make their abode in us, and our body becomes the temple of the Holy Spirit. Christ is in us—literally. Hence His mind is in us—literally ("which is yours in Christ Jesus"—the RSV rendering of v. 5).

6. Verse 6 makes clear that Christ is indeed "of one substance with the Father," "Very God of Very God," but that, in the words of the Modern Language Bible, He "did not consider His equality with God something to cling to." He did not insist on His rights but humbled Himself and dedicated Himself to the service of others as described in the unique language of verses 7–8.

7. To accomplish our salvation, Christ not only became a man, in itself a radical step since He was a spirit to begin with, but He also (1) took on the form of a slave (better than KJV's "servant") and (2) "became obedient unto death, even the death of the cross." The latter expression contains levels of meaning—actually, levels of degradation: (a) crucifixion (like hanging today) not only killed—it also humiliated; (b) to make sure this point was clear, Jesus' enemies crucified our Lord between two thugs, placing Him not only geographically between them but also socially on their level; and (c) Christ was accursed of God, forsaken, damned for those sins of ours that He literally carried on His person while He was on the cross.

8. "He that humbleth himself shall be exalted" was Jesus' generalization after telling the story of the Pharisee and the publican praying in the temple. Christ is a classic "for instance" of the truth of that generalization, as verses 9–11 make clear. After His "state of humiliation," there follows His "state of exaltation."

9. Although we should never humble ourselves *for the sake of* being exalted, exaltation is exactly what happens to us Christians. If we humbly confess our sins and trust in the Lordship of Christ, God exalts us too by making us His sons and daughters and sharing His life and His quarters with us forever. As God exalted the humbled Christ, so He exalts the humble Christian. Christ is the first fruits in this respect too, a truth, though not overtly stated, that is perhaps implied by verses 9–11. (In this connection, note that the verse immediately after the Epistle, verse 12, directs our attention to the Christian's outcome, salvation.)

The traditional Gospel for Palm Sunday shows Christ both

humbled and exalted: on the one hand, meek, entering Jerusalem on a lowly beast of burden; on the other hand, applauded and honored by the crowds. In its own way, this incident is an epitome of the stages of humiliation and exaltation in Christ's saving work, stages in which we Christians are urged to share.

Sermon Outline
SHARERS IN CHRIST'S HUMILITY AND GLORY

I. We Christians are urged to share Christ's humility (v. 5).
   A. Christ is the model for the trait of humility.
      1. He did not insist on His "divine rights."
      2. He changed from a spirit into a man to achieve our salvation.
      3. He became not only a man but also a certain kind of man, a slave.
      4. He "became obedient unto death, even the death of the cross."
         a. The cross humiliated Him in the eyes of people—it was a disgraceful death.
         b. The cross humiliated Him in the eyes of God—He bore our sins, and God damned Him for them.
   B. Christ is the means for the trait of humility.
      1. The barrier of our sin being removed by Christ, the Triune God moves into our bodies.
      2. We literally have Christ in us; hence we literally have "the mind of Christ" in us.
      3. Among all the other good things God freely gives us with Christ is the trait of humility ("which is yours in Christ Jesus"—RSV rendering of v. 5).
II. We Christians are promised that we will share Christ's glory.
   A. God exalts Christ.
      1. He gives Him superior honor (v. 9).
      2. He gives Him universal honor (v. 10).
   B. God will exalt us too:
      1. Not because we have the trait of humility;
      2. But because, when we humbly confess our sins and accept Christ as our Savior, God makes us His sons and daughters and shares His life and His quarters with us (cf. vv. 12–13).

Only the Gospel can give us the trait of humility. Only the

Gospel can give us heaven. Both humility and glory are God's gifts to us through Jesus Christ.

FRANCIS C. ROSSOW

Palm Sunday: Sunday of the Passion

GOSPEL   Luke 23:39–43 (RSV)

Sermon Notes/Introduction

The first two Synoptists tell us that both thieves reviled Jesus. Luke uses an even stronger term that denotes intemperate and insulting language (v. 39). But watching Jesus as He hung patiently on His cross, one of these misguided men changed his opinion (v. 40). He rebuked his compatriot in crime (v. 41), admitting that his own sentence was just while Jesus' punishment was not deserved. According to v. 42, the penitent looked forward to Jesus' coming again in kingly power and glory. Thus he alone had read aright the inscription on Christ's cross, "This is the King of the Jews." The thief asked only that Jesus would not forget him at His coming. Jesus assured him (v. 43) that He would remember him on that day, for before night fell he would be in Paradise where the souls of the righteous find a home after death has separated soul and body.

The central thought of the text is that a saved person relies on divine mercy. The problem in the hearers' lives is that they do not always grasp the magnitude of divine mercy. The goal of the sermon is that the hearers would live with a keener awareness of Christ's mercy to them.

The Gospel offers two radically different reactions to the culminating episode of Christ's Passion. At first both men had reviled Christ, but then one man changed completely. There is no limit to the good a person can come to when God works change. Change is evident especially in the criminal's words, "Jesus, remember me."

Sermon Outline
JESUS, REMEMBER ME

I. Sorrow for sin.
   A. The robber saw himself as guilty (v. 41).
      1. He was now getting what he deserved.
      2. He blamed no one but himself.

        3. His observation of Jesus on the cross induced remorse over his sin.

    B. We need to see ourselves as guilty before God.

        1. We cannot point self-righteously to the robber; so much evil comes from our heart (Matt. 15:19).

        2. Our words and actions reveal other forms of sin—selfishness, indifference, hypocrisy.

    C. Are we sorry for our sins?

        1. This means not just sorry that we got caught but a godly sorrow (2 Cor. 7:1–10).

        2. We see that our sins were the cause of Christ's death (Is. 43:24).

"Jesus, remember me!" Let these words express heartfelt sorrow for our sins.

The robber's prayer was not only humble but hopeful.

  II. Reliance on mercy.

    A. The robber had amazing faith.

        1. He asked only to be remembered, leaving it to Jesus how mercy would be shown (Luke 23:42).

        2. He regarded Jesus as an innocent sufferer (v. 41) who was thus in a position to show him mercy because of his sins.

        3. He knew Jesus to be a King who could do anything He wanted to do.

    B. Faith looks beyond what the eyes see.

        1. You may see only the sin in your life and feel only estrangement from God.

        2. Faith sees forgiveness in Christ's blood and life in Christ's death.

    C. Christ's mercy does not fail.

        1. That day the robber would be in Paradise (v. 43).

          a. In the first Paradise the first Adam sinned and doomed all humanity.

          b. The second Adam, Christ, repaired the damage and brought one of the most miserable of Adam's children to heaven.

          c. What a day for this dying man! What a contrast between its opening and its close!

        2. We now have the assurance of heaven and of being there when we die. "Jesus, remember me!" Let these words express reliance on His mercy.

GERHARD AHO

Maundy Thursday

EPISTLE   Hebrews 10:15–39

Sermon Notes/Introduction

The Epistle, though long, is an apt description of the Lord's Supper. What is the Lord's Supper but an expression of the new covenant that God foretold in Jer. 31:34, to wit, that He would remember our sins no more (Heb. 10:15–17)? The Lord's Supper also expresses our confidence to enter the presence of God. God's presence, symbolized by the Most Holy Place in the Old Testament temple, could not be entered by the people because animal sacrifices could not take away all sin. But we can come boldly to God in the Lord's Supper and thus into His presence because Christ offered His body (symbolical of the curtain between the Holy Place and the Most Holy Place, which was torn when Christ died) as the living way through which all our sins were actually washed away. We all received this cleansing in our baptism (vv. 20–23).

Now comes a series of exhortations that can be applied directly to our use of the Lord's Supper (vv. 24–31). We are to consider how to spur one another to love and good deeds, also by not giving up meeting together to partake of Holy Communion. If we deliberately keep on neglecting the Lord's Supper and the Word, knowing of the forgiveness available to us in these means, we can lose our faith and fall under God's judgment. If someone who rejected the law of Moses could die on the testimony of two or three witnesses, how much more severely a person deserves to be punished who insults the Spirit of grace by despising the means of grace. What a serious offense it is against God to neglect His Word and sacraments!

There was a time when the Hebrew Christians deeply appreciated what they were receiving in public worship, also in the Lord's Supper, and encouraged one another to receive these benefits (vv. 32–34). The Epistle concludes with an exhortation not to lose confidence of salvation in Christ (vv. 34–39). That confidence is ours only through faith. So the argument of the writer of Hebrews has come full circle. The complete forgiveness offered in the Lord's Supper is available only to the person who has faith in Christ's atonement.

Many Christians avoid the Lord's Supper due to fear that they are not good enough to partake or that too frequent participation will make the Supper seem too casual and less important than it really is. The Epistle reminds us that "We Can Frequently and Boldly Come to Holy Communion."

Sermon Outline
WE CAN FREQUENTLY AND BOLDLY COME TO HOLY COMMUNION

I. We are assured that God remembers our sins no more.
   A. The Lord's Supper is Christ's new covenant, in which we have full cleansing from our sins (v. 17).
      1. This cleansing became possible because of what Jesus did in His body on the cross (vv. 19–21).
      2. This cleansing is conveyed to us in a powerful and visible way in both Baptism and Holy Communion (v. 22).
      3. Without forgiveness we would have no hope of God's favor or of heaven (v. 23).
   B. Since our greatest need is the forgiveness of sins, we will want to encourage one another to partake frequently of the Lord's Supper.
      1. Failure to partake can show contempt for a precious means God has provided for us (vv. 26–29).
      2. Failure to partake can ultimately result in our falling into the hand of a judging, condemning God (vv. 30–31).

II. We have the certainty that faith makes us worthy communicants.
   A. Faith that Christ's body and blood are present and are given for us guarantees our benefitting from the forgiveness being offered us.
      1. No matter how unworthy we feel about going to the Lord's Supper, we can go, simply believing Christ's words, "Given and shed for you for the forgiveness of sins" (vv. 35–36).
      2. We may have suffered physical and material losses, but faith, by receiving forgiveness in the Lord's Supper, secures for us better and lasting possessions (vv. 32–34).
   B. When we live by faith, we realize that the Lord's Supper is a gracious and powerful means of preserving that faith.
      1. Our justification by faith is constantly assured to us also by this means of grace, the Lord's Supper.
      2. We can daily live in the assurance that forgiveness

is available for the times when we neglected to partake of the Lord's Supper or when we thought that something we do or have makes us worthy of Holy Communion.

We can frequently and boldly come to Holy Communion in the assurance that God remembers our sins no more and that our faith makes us worthy communicants.

GERHARD AHO

Maundy Thursday

GOSPEL   Luke 22:7–20 (RSV)

Sermon Notes/Introduction

The Passover lamb had to be slain by the head of the family (v. 7—cf. Ex. 12:6). Jesus has Peter and John take the initiative (v. 8). "Passover" in this context refers to the meal, the feast day, or the whole period of celebration (John 18:28). Reclining was the custom when eating (v. 14). Jesus here seems to have in mind the heavenly banquet (v. 16). The cup referred to is one of several passed during the Passover meal itself (v. 17). Which cup is meant is uncertain, but it evidently came just before the formal introduction of the Lord's Supper. There is another reference to the heavenly feast at the consummation of the Kingdom (v. 18).

Some manuscripts omit the last part of verse 19, beginning with the words "which is given for you," and also all of verse 20. According to *The Greek New Testament*, edited by Kurt Aland et al. (Stuttgart, 1966), there is only limited evidence to question the genuineness of verses 19b and 20. The New English Bible omits these verses, but the *Good News Bible* (TEV) and the New American Standard include them. Early editions of the RSV also omitted them, but the most recent edition includes them with a note that they are omitted in some manuscripts. The textual evidence appears to support their genuineness. If verse 20 is omitted, Luke would have no reference to the sacramental cup, unless the cup in verse 17 is regarded as the cup of the Lord's Supper. In that case Luke would have the order reversed from all the other accounts, the cup before the bread.

The central thought of the text is that Jesus instituted a New Testament meal that supersedes the Old Testament Passover. The problem of the hearers is that they may restrict their participation in the Lord's Supper to a few special occasions in their life or once or twice a year. The goal of the sermon is that the hearers would come often to the Lord's Supper.

We are gathering tonight for a meal that has remained the same for almost 2,000 years. It is a simple meal and yet the most important one this side of the heavenly banquet. It is not, like the Old Testament Passover, intended to be celebrated only once a year but is to be observed throughout the year. It is "A Meal for All Seasons."

Sermon Outline
A MEAL FOR ALL SEASONS

I. This meal displaces the Passover.
  A. The Passover was an important meal for God's people in the Old Testament.
     1. It was a Passover to the Lord in which the Jews celebrated annually God's deliverance of their fore-fathers from the bondage of Egypt.
     2. The Passover meal required preparation (vv. 7–20).
     3. Jesus especially desired to eat this Passover with His disciples (v. 15a).
        a. It would be His last meal with them (v. 15b).
        b. He would not eat it again until He shares it as a heavenly banquet (vv. 16b, 19b).
  B. The Passover is superseded by another meal (vv. 19–20).
     1. There is no need to celebrate the Passover meal any longer because the deliverance to which the Passover pointed has been accomplished.
     2. The Lord's Supper commemorates the deliverance not only of God's chosen people but of all people.
     3. The Lord's Supper is the incomparable Christian meal for all seasons.
II. It offers Jesus Christ.
  A. Jesus Christ is central in this meal.
     1. Christ was prefigured in the Passover lamb.
     2. The real Christ is given to all who eat the bread and drink the wine (vv. 19b, 20b).
  B. Christ's body given for us and His blood shed for us on the cross assure us of forgiveness.
     1. The Passover was basically a remembrance, but the

Lord's Supper is both a remembrance of Christ's
death and a seal of His forgiveness.
2. We can be sure of forgiveness even when we feel
unforgiven.
C. Christ's body and blood received in bread and wine
also strengthen our faith.
1. We can resist temptation.
2. We can live as Christians.

Since we need all the assurances of forgiveness we can
get and all the strengthening of the faith that is possible, the
Lord's Supper is indeed a meal for all seasons.

GERHARD AHO

Good Friday

EPISTLE   Hebrews 4:14–16; 5:7–9

Sermon Notes/Introduction

In 4:14 the author begins a discussion of Jesus' entry
through the heavens. Whatever the spheres of created heavens, Christ went beyond them into heaven itself, into the presence of God. In the Old Testament the high priest passed
through the veil, that is, through the earthly symbol of separation between God's holiness and man's sinfulness. He moved
into the earthly symbol of eternal glory, the Most Holy Place,
while Jesus, the great High Priest, has passed through the heavens to the eternal glory itself. In considering that we have such
a High Priest, we are to hold fast to our faith. A besetting danger
for us, as well as for the Hebrew Christians, is shrinking from
a full and open confession of Him.

In verse 15 the author emphasizes that Christ was tempted
in all things as we are, except that He was without sin. The
power of sympathy is adduced to remind us that Jesus was
similar to the other high priests in that He had a sympathy for
those for whom He was mediating with God. Christ can sym-
pathize with us in our trials because He has experienced what
we have experienced (Matt. 8:17). His sympathy for us is great
because His temptation was great, and He overcame all these
temptations. Even though He successfully resisted temptation,
that does not mean that Satan did not fiercely assail Him. When
Christ in His human nature experienced human fear, grief,
indignation, and shrinking from suffering, He showed that His

identification with our humanity was complete. Such human affections are not in themselves sinful, but under temptation any of them can become a motivation for sinning. Even though Christ did not sin, He felt within His human nature the power to seduce, and thus He had a real human and personal experience of how great our temptation can be. Because we have a High Priest who actually felt the power of temptation but gave no internal assent to the seduction, we can (Heb. 4:16) receive grace to help in time of every need.

In 5:7 the author discusses in greater detail Christ's human experience. His offering of prayers and petitions with loud cries and tears is clearly a reference to Gethsemane and the cross. Christ prayed that the "cup" might pass from Him. Yet He knew that obedience to His Father was the first requirement, and if that obedience had to involve the dreadful agony of taking human sin on Himself, He would not waver in carrying out His Father's will. And He was heard—the Father answered His prayer—for the Father raised Him from death. Christ's human will thus conformed to His heavenly Father's will through entire submission to that will. Otherwise His participation in human nature would not have been complete, and He would not have felt our infirmities. Even though He was the eternal Son of God, He had to learn obedience to be truly sympathetic with us. He had now been called on to obey to an extent that He had never before experienced, but He came through the temptation. Thereby He showed Himself to be not only our perfect High Priest but also the source of eternal salvation. In a sense Christ was not heard by right of His Sonship; as a Son He knew that the Father had heard Him always. He learned in a human way the lesson of obedience. The prayers and supplications that He offered in His own behalf flowed from His entire participation in humanity, down to the agony and bloody sweat caused by human sinfulness.

Thinking of the terrible agony that the cross caused Jesus, why do we call this Friday on which Christ died "good"? Among other reasons, "At the Cross We Find Help in Time of Need."

Sermon Outline

AT THE CROSS WE FIND HELP IN TIME OF NEED

I. Jesus, as our great High Priest, mediates help.
    A. He endured all the affliction to which our human nature is subject.

1. He experienced the fierceness of temptation but did not give in.
2. Now He is able to be all the more sympathetic and supportive toward us.

B. No matter what we experience in the way of guilt, loneliness, weakness, or pain, the cross is the supreme expression of it all.

1. Since Jesus experienced so fully our anguish and agony by taking our place on the cross, we can look to that cross and find in Him who hung there the help we need to endure our afflictions.
2. He is able to understand and to help in a way no one else can.

II. Jesus, as the source of eternal salvation, mediates help.

A. He showed Himself to be the source of salvation by submitting completely to His Father's will.

1. It was agonizingly difficult for Him as a man to submit to such pain.
2. It was natural for His human nature to abhor it.

B. Now at the cross we find forgiveness and life eternal.

1. We find God's forgiveness for all our refusals to submit to our Father's will and for all our grumbling in the midst of our submission.
2. At the cross we find the assurance of eternal salvation in heaven. God, who heard the prayer of Jesus and at the grave on the third day made the cross the symbol of eternal salvation, has guaranteed eternal life for us who look to the cross as the place of sin's atonement.
3. When we need to become more certain of our salvation, we can find that certainty at the cross.

The cross is not only a sign of the dreadfulness of our sin. It is above all the place where we find help in our need. We can find sympathy and support and assurance of eternal salvation.

GERHARD AHO

Good Friday

GOSPEL   John 19:30 (RSV)

Sermon Notes/Introduction

The other evangelists record yet another word of divine submission: "Father, into Thy hands I commit my spirit." John ends his account of the death of Christ with the climactic words spoken by Jesus, "It is finished." The inscrutable fact of Christ's death is thus presented in its awful grandeur. The debt of sin was paid. The types of the Messiah in the Old Testament were fulfilled. The great work undertaken by Christ to realize the expectations of the prophets was done. The reality has arrived of which the temple, the Sabbath, the priesthood, and the offerings were all shadows. Death became not Christ's shame but His glory, for God reconciled the world to Himself by the death of His Son.

The central thought of the text is the triumphant completion of Christ's work. The problem of the hearers is that they do not always think and act as if Christ had completed His work of saving people. The goal of the sermon is that the hearers will be confident that salvation is an accomplished fact.

A dying person is often aware that many tasks have been left undone. But Jesus could say just before He died, "It is finished."

Sermon Outline
IT IS FINISHED

I. He finished fulfilling prophecy.
   A. He fulfilled Old Testament prophecies about His Passion.
      1. His betrayal (Zech. 13:7).
      2. His suffering (Is. 53:1–3).
      3. His death (Ps. 22:7, 18).
   B. Thereby He showed Himself to be the promised Messiah.
      1. He revealed God to humanity.
         a. Many want to know God.
         b. They keep looking for new revelations (mysticism, esoteric religions).
      2. No new revelations of God are needed, for Jesus is the final Word from God (Heb. 1:1–2).
II. He finished keeping the Law.

    A. He observed it perfectly.
      1. His enemies (John 8:46), Judas (Matt. 27:4), Pilate (John 18:38), and Satan (Luke 4:34) could find no wrong in Him. And God the Father said so (Matt. 17:5).
      2. Through faith in Him, His perfection is ours; God does not hold against us our infractions of His law.
    B. Christ bore its curse.
      1. Those who break laws face the consequences.
      2. Jesus took our punishment for breaking God's law; we are freed from the curse.
III. He finished everything necessary for our salvation.
    A. His death was a victory.
      1. Jesus died when He chose to die, only when He knew that all had been accomplished (John 10:18).
      2. His words "It is finished" are like the exhausted but triumphant shout of members of a mountain rescue team who, after arduous effort, succeed in rescuing an injured climber.
    B. It makes a travesty of Christ's death for anyone to think that one's own sighs and tears, struggles and prayers, words and deeds are still necessary for salvation.

When your unloveliness oppresses you and you go about dejectedly, let the words "It is finished" give you confidence. When death comes and you realize there is still much to be done, let the words "It is finished" calm and cheer you. Because Jesus has finished His task, Easter was possible, the resurrection is ahead of you, eternal life is yours.

GERHARD AHO

The Resurrection of Our Lord: Easter Day

EPISTLE   1 Corinthians 15:1–11 (NIV)

Sermon Notes/Introduction

Holy Week is hectic for a pastor, but he may take heart. This Epistle has nothing new or tricky in it. In fact, Paul indicates that he is going to tell his readers again—to remind them—of what he has preached to them before. Here is another chance to preach the Gospel—this time to assure the people of their resurrection. And the preacher may bask in this Gospel message himself and be fortified in his own spirit to proclaim:

"Christ is risen!"

"Christ is risen! I guarantee it!" Such a bold statement might evoke this question: "What would become of me if He were not risen?" Well, "if Christ has not been risen, your faith is futile and you are still in your sins," and those who have fallen asleep in Christ are lost. In other words, if Christ did not rise from the dead, you and I are in deep, deep trouble (1 Cor. 15:17–19). But Christ is risen! It is with a great sense of relief and joy that we hear from God's Word the Good News that "Your Resurrection Is Guaranteed."

Sermon Outline
YOUR RESURRECTION IS GUARANTEED

I. We need this guarantee of our resurrection. In a world that is moving fast on an unstable course, we need something solid on which to hang our hopes.
  A. The Corinthians had somehow lost this fundamental teaching of the resurrection.
    1. Paul had proclaimed it to them as a primary teaching of the Gospel, and they had accepted it.
    2. Something happened to raise doubts in their minds—the appearance of a teacher, perhaps, or some rationalization.
  B. We are not above forgetting or doubting it either.
    1. We have plenty of outside influences banging away at our faith.
    2. We tend to forget because of our natural fear of dying. Since we talk little about death, why mention rising from the dead? How many times have we stared at a corpse and wondered how it could ever live again?

We need assurance; we want a guarantee that Christ lives and that we will live also.

II. The Gospel offers this guarantee to us.
  A. The Gospel is a valid source.
    1. Paul declares that he did not make it up. He had witnesses to the resurrection: Peter, the Twelve, 500 brothers, James, and, finally, Paul himself (vv. 5–8).
    2. The Gospel has guaranteeing power. It assured Paul so much that he could taunt, "Where, O death, is your sting?" (vv. 55–57).
    3. The Gospel assures people today. The unbeliever

is resigned to death with an attitude of "whatever will be, will be." Believers assign themselves to God in the firm and real hope of rising again. Was not this the peace of our departed loved ones who died in Christ? It works!

B. The Gospel guarantees because of its content. Christ died and lives for us.

1. Christ died for our sins according to the Scriptures (v. 3). Isaiah had predicted that the Messiah would be led as a lamb to the slaughter.

2. Christ was buried (v. 4). He was really dead. This makes the resurrection more certain than if He had been dead for only an hour or so.

3. Christ was raised on the third day according to the Scriptures. Psalm 16:10 proclaims: "You will not abandon me to the grave, nor will you let Your Holy One see decay."

4. Christ's resurrection is the center of our Christian faith, from which we gather our hope.

III. The Spirit leads us to exercise this guarantee.

A. We receive it in faith, regardless of our feelings. Luther states:

> If you want to judge according to what you see and feel and, when the Word of God is set before you, want to pit your feeling against it and say: You tell me much; but my heart speaks a different language, and if you felt what I feel, you, too, would speak differently—then you do not have the Word of God in the heart but have quenched and extinguished it by your own thoughts, reason, and brooding. In short, if you will not let the Word mean more to you than all your feeling, eyes, senses, and heart, you must be lost, and there is no further help for you. For we are concerned with an article of *faith,* not an article of your reason or wisdom or human power and ability.
>
> Therefore you must judge solely according to the Word in this matter, irrespective of what you feel and see. (*What Luther Says,* p. 1215)

B. We stand firm in faith. "This is what we preach, and this is what you believed" (1 Cor. 15:11).

1. We preach this message over and over because the Gospel is the soil to which the roots of our faith cling.

2. The only way to remain confident of our resurrection is to remain sure of Christ's resurrection.

3. We live confidently. We live expecting a resurrection. We live as though there is a tomorrow.

The Gospel guarantees our resurrection. We say with Job, "I know that my Redeemer lives. . . . In my flesh I will see God" (Job 19:25–26).

LOWELL F. THOMAS

The Resurrection of Our Lord: Easter Day

GOSPEL   Luke 24:1–11

Sermon Notes/Introduction

1. A text-critical note: "of the Lord Jesus" (v. 3) and "He is not here; He was raised" (v. 6), both of which have been relegated by the RSV to the footnotes, have more than enough manuscript evidence to be regarded as authentic.

2. Jesus Himself does not appear in this text. Nevertheless, Luke gives us at least six indications that He is risen: (1) The women do not find the body of Jesus; this is explicitly stated only by Luke (v. 3). (2) Jesus is called "the Lord" (v. 3), a title that is used especially of the *risen* Christ (Acts 1:22–25; 4:33; 8:16; 1 Cor. 9:1). (3) Jesus is called "the Living One" (v. 5); He lives forever (Rev. 1:18) and by living gives life (Rom. 8:29; 1 Cor. 15:20). (4) The angels report, "He is not here; he was raised" (v. 6). (5) Christ's prediction of His resurrection is recalled; this is only in Luke (v. 7). (6) The disciples are called "the apostles" (v. 10), the title that designates them as eyewitnesses of the risen Lord (Acts 1:22–25; 1 Cor. 9:1).

3. Christ's resurrection is the climax of the entire history of human salvation. The Old Testament foreshadowed and predicted it (Luke 24:25–26, 46); Christ predicted it (9:22, 44; 17:24–25; 18:31–33); and the church of all ages proclaims it (24:9, 46–47). It was necessary for Christ to die and rise from the dead (v. 7) that there might be forgiveness for all humanity (24:46–47). Thus, Christ's resurrection gives meaning to all history and to all of life.

4. The text says that Jesus "was raised" (v. 6), denoting the work of the Father, and that He rose (v. 7), denoting the work of Christ Himself. Both of these verbs as well as "be betrayed" and "be crucified" (v. 7) are aorists; they refer to

God's one-time action in our Lord's death and resurrection as the center and climax of history.

5. The disciples' early unbelief gave way to faith when they saw the risen Lord. Christ now overcomes people's unbelief through His Word (vv. 25–27, 32, 45), which centers in His death and resurrection (vv. 25–26, 44, 46).

6. Christ's resurrection gives purpose to our life in this world. In His name we proclaim repentance and forgiveness of sins to all nations (vv. 46–47).

Sermon Outline
LIFE NOW HAS MEANING

Have you ever felt that life has no meaning?

I. The meaninglessness of life is a problem of human nature.
   A. Many have no purpose that reaches beyond this life; hence despair and hopelessness arise.
   B. The fall robbed human beings of their life, hope, and future.
   C. Because of our sin, our only future is death and damnation.

II. Christ gives meaning to our life.
   A. His *work* gives meaning.
      1. He suffered and died (v. 7a).
      2. He rose again (6 indications in the text).
      3. This work was necessary (v. 7) for people to have forgiveness (24:26–47).
   B. This gives meaning to *all* history.
      1. The previous ages looked forward to it.
         a. God's saving acts in the Old Testament prefigured it (e.g., today's Old Testament Reading: Ex. 15:1–11).
         b. The Old Testament predictions foretold it (e.g., Is. 52:13–53:12).
         c. Christ Himself predicted it (Luke 9:22, 44; 17:24–25; 18:31–33).
      2. Due to His work, forgiveness of sin is proclaimed to all (24:46–47; 1 Cor. 15:1–11—today's Epistle).
   C. This gives meaning to *each of us.*
      1. Through the proclamation of Christ God offers the forgiveness of sin.
      2. With sin forgiven, we have life through the Living One (Luke 24:5; Rom. 8:29; 1 Cor. 15:20).
      3. We now have a future and a hope—eternal life.

4. We now have a purpose in life—to proclaim repentance and forgiveness.

Life is no longer meaningless, because "He is not here;
he was raised."

PAUL E. DETERDING

Second Sunday of Easter

EPISTLE   Revelation 1:4–18

Sermon Notes/Introduction

Verses 4–6 are a greeting, and verses 5b–6 are the dox-
ology within the greeting. Verses 7–8 Martin Franzmann calls
"a sort of introit" to the worship service of which the reading
of the letter was to be a part. These verses are the theme song
of the entire book. Verse 7 speaks of the triumphal return of
Christ, while in verse 8 the Lord speaks of Himself as the eternal
and almighty One. Jesus supplies the power to endure patiently
the tribulation that comes to all Christians as members of
Christ's kingdom (v. 9). Verse 13 makes clear that the eternal
Son is in the midst of His church as tribulations come. Although
He now wears a human form, He is the glorified Messiah whose
divine attributes are graphically described in verses 13–16.
Verse 17 describes the reaction of a sinful human being to
divine holiness, but also the great comfort given by Jesus
Christ.

Most people believe in God, but what kind of God? God
is known only through Jesus Christ. The Epistle presents the
first in a series of visions of the Lord God in the person of
Jesus Christ.

Sermon Outline
WHAT A LORD WE HAVE!

I. He is above us.
   A. He is above us in dominion.
      1. He, not Caesar (the emperor Domitian called him-
         self "lord and god"), is the Lord (v. 13b).
      2. He rules our world and the universe.
   B. He is above us in glory (vv. 14–16).
   C. He is above us in holiness. He has eyes from which
      nothing evil is hidden, feet that will pursue evil to pun-
      ish it, and a mouth that judges all evil.

A Lord who is so far above us can frighten us as he did John. But Christ came to John, touched him gently, and said, "Fear not." He is not against us.

II. He is for us.
  A. Christ showed that He is for us by dying for us (v. 17).
    1. The Eternal, the First and the Last, actually died.
    2. He died to atone for our sins.
  B. He showed that He is for us by rising from the dead (v. 18).
    1. He lives forever (Rom. 6:9).
    2. He has authority over death (Rev. 1:18). We need not fear death, for Jesus went through it and conquered it for us.

He will support us with His power by being with us at the time of death. But every day, right now, He is also with us.

III. He is with us.
  A. He is with us in our tribulation.
    1. Christ was with His suffering church when John wrote (v. 13).
    2. He is still with His church, which may not be afflicted in the same way as was the church in John's day, but which nevertheless is plagued with apathy, indifference, and lovelessness.
  B. He is with us to renew and strengthen us.
    1. Through the Word and sacraments He moves us to repentance and firmer faith.
    2. He supplies us with the endurance we need to overcome defeat and discouragement.

In Christ we see what a Lord we have, one who is above us, for us, and with us.

GERHARD AHO

Second Sunday of Easter

GOSPEL   John 20:19–31 (KJV)

Sermon Notes/Introduction

V. 19: The scene is Easter Sunday evening. The fearful disciples were aware of the preceding events: the report of the women, the appearance to Mary, the account of Peter and John, and the report of the Emmaus disciples. Luke implies that more than the Eleven had gathered. "Jesus stood in the midst" in His glorified body, subject to the laws of neither time nor space. "Peace be unto you": This is the peace He won and He alone can give (John 14:27). *V. 20:* "He showed unto them His hands and His side": He is the living One who was dead but is now alive. "Glad": extreme dejection and fear are converted into the joyful conviction of the truth. The disciples heard, saw, and handled the Word of Life (1 John 1:1). *V. 21:* The first "peace" gave a new revelation; the second "peace" was a summons to service. "As My Father hath sent Me," etc.: This is Christ's divine commission to His church. *V. 22:* "Receive ye the Holy Ghost": The Holy Spirit is Christ's parting gift to His church. *V. 23:* "Whose soever sins ye remit," etc.: This is the office of the keys, the power Christ gave to the church to forgive the sins of penitent sinners and to retain the sins of the impenitent. Cf. Matt. 18:15–19; Acts 2:37–39. *V. 24:* Thomas is an example of an anxious skeptic. "Thomas . . . was not with them": That was his first mistake. *V. 25:* Thomas's second mistake was that he discounted the testimony of witnesses. *V. 27:* Note the patience of Jesus. *V. 28:* Thomas is now convinced and boldly declares Christ's divinity. *V. 29:* Believing is seeing; that is faith. *V. 31:* The miracles are a part of Christ's proclamation of Himself as the Son of God; they are His sign language attesting to His Messiahship. The goal of the sermon is to encourage the hearer to live by faith and to bring forth faith's fruits in a life of service.

We worship a living Lord, who is with us always.

Sermon Outline
JESUS IS IN THE MIDST OF HIS CHURCH

I. He commissions His Church.
   A. He gives the command (v. 21; Matt. 28:18–20; Acts 1:8).
   B. He gives the message (John 20:21, 23, 25).
      1. It is a message of the peace that He won (Luke 2:14; Col. 2:14).
      2. It is a message of pardon (John 20:23; 2 Cor. 5:19).
   C. He gives the power (John 20:22).
      1. The Holy Spirit's power came at Pentecost.
      2. The Holy Spirit is Christ's abiding gift to the church (John 16:7–15; Acts 1:8).

What a challenge we have! What power! But, alas, we are sometimes faithless when we ought to believe. But Jesus deals

with our doubts.
II. He strengthens the faith of the doubters.
   A. Thomas lived by the philosophy: "Seeing is believing" (John 20:25).
      1. Thomas was not with the other disciples.
      2. He discounted the testimony of witnesses.
      3. In times of adversity we are tempted to behave just like Thomas.
   B. Jesus encourages the philosophy: "Believing is seeing" (Heb. 11:1).
      1. We have a sure Word to guide us.
         a. The Word is given by inspiration (2 Tim. 3:15; 2 Peter 1:21).
         b. The Word points to Christ and His promises (John 5:39; Matt. 28:20).
      2. Faith clings to the Word.
         a. It holds on in all circumstances (Luke 5:5).
         b. It prevails over our feelings (Ps. 42:5).
         c. Faith is rewarded by sight; cf. Abraham, the children of Israel at the Red Sea and at Jericho, Gideon against the Midianites.

Let's walk in the confidence of faith, bringing forth the fruit of Christian witness, because Jesus is alive and with us.

HENRY J. EGGOLD

Third Sunday of Easter

EPISTLE   Revelation 5:11–14

Sermon Notes/Introduction

The preceding thought unit (vv. 6–10) focuses on the Lamb, Christ, who brings an end to the weeping (hopelessness) of the world. By taking from the Creator the scroll on which the future of the church and of the world is written, He shows that He has taken up His power and reign. This action evokes the new song of praise that continues in the Epistle, praise that Christ has redeemed all people. The Epistle begins with the host of angels joining in the song of all creatures. This song of praise focuses on Jesus Christ and what He has done. Following the Epistle, chapter 6 begins with an account of the troubles to be released on the world before the final consummation. The praise given to the Lamb in the Epistle makes clear that in the midst of the troubles the Lamb is in control and that all creatures must eventually acknowledge Him to be Redeemer and Lord. The song of praise climaxes by ascribing might and glory to the Lamb alone; all who sing His praises fall down in silent adoration.

Worship can be a human-centered experience directed toward our own well-being and improvement, so that we become concerned only with our personal returns in worship, with what we individually are going to get out of it. That is a misplaced emphasis. From this obsession and preoccupation with ourselves the Epistle would free us. The heavenly hosts by their action are calling us to "Give Adoration to Jesus Christ."

Sermon Outline
GIVE ADORATION TO JESUS CHRIST

I. He was slain for our redemption.
  A. His blood alone could redeem us.
    1. We could not ransom ourselves, and yet blood had to be shed (Heb. 9:22).
    2. His precious blood had power to redeem, for He Himself was innocent (Eph. 1:7; 1 Peter 1:18–19; 1 John 1:7).
  B. Through His redeeming blood we have come into His kingdom (Rev. 5:10).
    1. This kingdom is hidden now.
    2. It will ultimately be revealed, and we will reign with Him.

II. He is the supreme Lord.
  A. The symbol of His supremacy is the throne (v. 13). Jesus has been exalted (Phil. 2:9).
  B. His supremacy manifests itself (Rev. 5:12).
    1. He has all power (Matt. 28:20).
    2. He has all wealth (2 Cor. 8:9; Eph. 3:8).
    3. He has all wisdom (1 Cor. 1:24, 30).
    4. He has all might (John 10:18; the resurrection).
  C. He is to be worshiped as the supreme Lord (Rev. 5:13).
    1. Everything on the earth, under it, and above it praises Him (Ps. 148).
    2. There is satisfaction in acknowledging God in Jesus Christ for who and what He is. We do this well in such canticles as the Te Deum Laudamus.

When we focus on God, we will be helped. When we

adore Christ, we will be built up. So let us not only wail our litanies and cry our petitions. Let us also learn the language of praise. There is something mysterious, beautiful, and uplifting taking place when we, with the four living creatures, say, "Amen," and fall down and worship Jesus Christ.

GERHARD AHO

Third Sunday of Easter

GOSPEL   John 21:1–14 (KJV)

Sermon Notes/Introduction

The disciples left Jerusalem for Galilee to await Christ's appearance (Matt. 28:10, 16). Galilee was the place where Jesus gathered all his disciples except Judas, fed the 5,000, and walked on the water. V. 2: The other two disciples may well have been Philip and Andrew. V. 3: Waiting for Christ's appearance, the disciples would not be idle. "They caught nothing": without God's blessings our best efforts are futile. V. 4: Christ comes when people have reason to be most despondent. V. 5: "Meat": literally, anything eaten at a meal with bread. V. 6: When the ingenuity and industry of the disciples failed, Christ stepped in to help. So great was the catch that they could not get it into the boat. V. 7: John is the first to recognize Jesus. V. 8: Two hundred cubits is about 100 yards. V. 9: God will provide our daily bread. Ours is but to work faithfully at our calling without giving in to sloth or anxiety. The provision of bread and fish is the second miracle in this narrative. The goal of the sermon is to encourage people to live with a consciousness of the Lord's presence, power, and grace.

Many people look at life simply as a dog-eat-dog existence. Life to them is simply a matter of the survival of the fittest. Christians count God in the equation of living. That makes all the difference in the world (Rom. 8:31; Phil. 4:13). In the midst of fruitless toil John cries out: "It is the Lord."

Sermon Outline
IT IS THE LORD

I. The Lord is with us.
   A. The disciples toiled fruitlessly.

      1. Waiting for Christ's appearance in Galilee, the disciples returned to their vocation as fishermen.
      2. A night of fishing proved fruitless.
      3. So often life is like that.
         a. We do not seem to get ahead.
         b. Reverses like sickness or unemployment cause us to go backwards.
         c. We become anxious and ask, "Where is God?" (Mark 4:38).
   B. Jesus appears.
      1. He knows about the disciples and appears to them.
      2. Our loving Lord knows about us, too (Ps. 27:5; 139:7; Jer. 23:24; Matt. 28:20; John 10:14; 1 Peter 5:5).

If God knows, we can take comfort, for He also has power to help.

II. The Lord is with us with His power.
   A. Jesus performs a double miracle.
      1. He gives the disciples 153 large fish.
      2. He prepares a table before them (Ps. 23:5).
      3. Jesus often proved his power: lepers were cleansed; the blind received sight; the lame walked; the dead were raised.
   B. Christ's power is available to us, too.
      1. He supplies our daily bread (Ps. 145:15).
      2. He helps us in every need.
         a. At times He removes our trial.
         b. At other times, He gives us strength to bear our trials (1 Cor. 10:13; Phil. 4:15).

What power we have available! Hence we pray (Phil. 4:6). As we pray, we trust (Matt. 21:22).

III. The Lord is with us with His grace.
   A. It was love that brought Jesus to the seashore.
      1. He came to provide for the immediate needs of the disciples.
      2. He came to strengthen them for their future work as fishers of men.
   B. Jesus is with us with His grace, too.
      1. He showed His love for the world by His sin-atoning death (John 10:11).
      2. His resurrection guarantees His victory for us over sin, death, and hell (1 Cor. 15:55–57).

3. This love attends us, too (Is. 49:15).
   a. It guides us in life (Ps. 73:23–24; Matt. 6:31).
   b. It brings us to our heavenly home (2 Tim. 4:8).

"It is the Lord." He is with us. Therefore, we can live in humble dependence, grateful for the blessings He daily gives, and trusting His love to provide also for the future.

HENRY J. EGGOLD

Fourth Sunday of Easter

EPISTLE   Revelation 7:9–17

Sermon Notes/Introduction

The most widely known Scandinavian hymn in English-speaking countries is *Lutheran Worship* 192 (*TLH* 656). It is based on today's Epistle and begins:

Behold a host, arrayed in white
Like thousand snow-clad mountains bright.
They stand with palms And sing their psalms
Before the throne of light.

The question put to John by an elder was "Who are these, clothed in white?"

Sermon Outline
WHO ARE THESE, CLOTHED IN WHITE?

I. Amazingly, they have survived the great tribulation (Dan. 12:1; Matt. 24:21).
  A. The exchange in Rev. 7:13–14 echoes that in Ezek. 37:3, where only the Lord could give the answer. ("Can these bones live?" "O Lord God, thou knowest.")
    1. Dead bones beginning to live—that's amazing! Compare today's First Reading, Acts 13:15–16a, 26–33, where Paul preaches the miracle of Christ's resurrection.
    2. For weak and mortal people to survive the great tribulation is just as amazing (Matt. 24:22)!
  B. The evils and suffering caused by people's sins against others (Rev. 6:1–8) must be included in the great tribulation along with the wrath of God against sin.
    1. This means that each of us is a cause of the tribulation.

    2. According to God's law, each of us therefore ought to be a victim also; for who is able to stand on the great day of God's wrath (vv. 15–17)?

II. Their salvation (victory) is the work of God and the Lamb (7:10).

    A. Christ's precious blood, shed during His trial and execution under Pilate, washes away sin (1 John 1:7) and provides the garments of white (Rev. 7:14—echoes of Is. 1:18).

    B. The Good Shepherd not only promises life (compare today's Gospel, John 10:22–30) but also dwells with His sheep to shepherd them forever (Rev. 7:17—echoes of Ps. 23).

III. "Their" salvation is "our" salvation.

    A. God's grace (His kind disposition toward us because of Christ) is universal, not limited to a certain number of people (echoes of the promise regarding the number of Abraham's children, Gen. 15:5).

    B. Christ sacrificed Himself for *all* (2 Cor. 5:15), so that people of every nation, tribe, people, and tongue (Rev. 7:9) could serve and worship God forever (echoes of Is. 49:6).

Who are these, clothed in white? They are the saved of all ages and climes; they are the church triumphant. By God's grace, because of the blood of the Lamb, you and I can see ourselves among their number.

JERROLD A. EICKMANN

Fourth Sunday of Easter

GOSPEL   John 10:22–30 (RSV)

Sermon Notes/Introduction

1. *Series C Pericopes:* The appointed lessons for the fourth and fifth Sundays of Easter present what at first may appear to be a muddle of ideas without reasonable connection. But there is a consistency (at least in the two Sundays noted above) in the Biblical books used. Each Sunday has a reading from Revelation, Acts, and John. On closer examination, one is struck with the unifying approach of "Future, Past, and Present." The Revelation readings point the hearer to the consummation of God's plan of salvation ("Salvation belongs to our

God" and "Behold, I make all things new"). The readings from Acts deal with the continued growth of the church, giving specific instances of how the Gospel was preached and spread in the early Christian church. Finally, the Gospels direct the hearer to this present life, calling for a comfortable feeling of assurance ("My sheep hear my voice, and I know them") and a glorious way of life ("A new commandment I give to you, that you love one another"). To build a unified whole for the worship service, one might choose hymns that emphasize these aspects.

2. *The Gospel of John:* If the texts for the sermons on these Sundays are drawn from the Gospel of John, one might ask whether there is an overriding approach of the gospel writer that would carry through to the sermons. If we consider that John's gospel has a more theological (religious) than biographical focus, it would at least be logical that we approach the texts asking "Why?" rather than "What?" or "How?" Given this lead, the Gospel motivation of the sermon would focus on the rationale behind the truths that Jesus speaks and how this rationale works itself out in daily Christian living.

3. *Miscellaneous items of interest:* The "feast of the Dedication" mentioned in the Gospel is the Hanukkah celebration of the reconsecration of the temple for Jewish use under the Maccabees. The idea of renewal is parallel to the Psalm verse: "Create in me a clean heart, and renew a right spirit." One might note that although the temple had been renewed, the hearts of some temple users had not.

It is curious to note that the "porch" where Christ walked reminds a person of the *stoa* in Greece where great men taught and from which we get the word "stoic." The contrast is that Christ not only changes minds but does something about the concerns of heart and soul.

John's use of the term "eternal life" is further explained in 6:68. One soon learns that "words" for John have power and are living and effective. Their effectiveness consists in ability to bring people into real relationships with God through "the Word." This special life is enjoyed by believers *now*.

Probably all people have experienced the embarrassment of asking for something in a supermarket while standing right in front of it. The item is overlooked because of the confusion of items all around or because the searcher's image of the item sought is inaccurate. Something similar develops in the Gospel as the Jews ask for information about something that is right before their eyes.

Sermon Outline
ASKING QUESTIONS ALREADY ANSWERED

I. Why ask the question?
  A. The Jews who asked Jesus about His mission were motivated by a hostile and argumentative spirit. Their question is preceded by argument (v. 19) and followed by hostility (v. 31).
  B. People today often ask for the same reason: the Gospel message of Christ as Messiah seems to them absurd in a world so beset with problems. They are angry and hostile toward the God who would let all these awful things happen.
  C. Influences of this type and the old Adam of the Christian tempt him/her also to ask in a doubting and troubled way, "Jesus, are you *really* the Christ?"
  D. The question needs to be asked by each person, but as a genuine seeking for peace and comfort, a sincere reaching out for help in the midst of helplessness. God's Spirit leads, guides, and encourages us toward such an asking.
II. Why Christ's answer is so wonderful.
  A. Jesus phrases His answer with love, caring, and compassion. He uses the image of the sheep and the shepherd. He reaches out without argument or hostility to a reality of relationship in which one cares completely for another.
  B. Jesus' answer is filled with the power of God, who rules all things. Christ affirms that it is the Father's will that the sheep be His and that the Father's power shields the sheep. ("I and the Father are *one.*")
  C. The Shepherd, Christ, calls each to partake of His genuine peace and comfort. Not only are the mundane cares of this life coming under His protection but the relationship described as "eternal life" is given to them.

The final joy and comfort of the answer comes in the works that the Christ has done and still does in the Father's name. His work of suffering and death has made possible the new relationship of sheep and Shepherd. Today, tomorrow, and every day there is no need to question or doubt but only to believe and be comforted.

DANIEL H. POKORNY

Fifth Sunday of Easter

EPISTLE   Revelation 21:1–5 (RSV)

Sermon Notes/Introduction

There is a universal dissatisfaction with the world we have and with the state of human nature. Utopian literature reflects the longing for a "new start." Most people have heard of *The New Atlantis* or Thoreau's *Walden Pond*. Edward Bellamy's *Looking Backward* enjoyed great popularity, and even B. F. Skinner's *Walden II* is well known. Despite the desire for a fresh human start, most people are pessimistic about it. The Epistle reminds us that a new start for humanity is exactly what God has in mind and will bring to pass. He promises "A New People in a New World."

Sermon Outline
A NEW KIND OF PEOPLE
IN A NEW KIND OF WORLD

I. The old kind of people and the old kind of world are to go.

   A. The old kind of people will disappear. We infer the passing away of present human nature with the elimination of "the first earth" (v. 1).

      1. Human beings were created "very good" (Gen. 1:31). What would humanity have been like had it remained that way?

      2. Human nature was corrupted by the first parents. Eph. 2:1 summarizes the condition as "dead through trespasses and sins." Romans 1 is the most devastating indictment of humanity.

      3. Humanity, therefore, has been beleaguered by the results of a corrupted nature (cf. Rev. 21:4). Tears, death, mourning, crying, and pain are the human lot.

      4. God's created people have become "not His people." Compare the Old Testament concept of *lo-ammi* ("not my people"). Sin separates people from God, and they are related to Him only by judgment (Law).

      5. The old human nature must be destroyed. Luther: "The old Adam must by daily contrition and repentance be drowned and die." Those who come

to Judgment Day without the new birth will be eliminated from God's happy plan.

B. The old kind of world will pass away.
1. It, too, was originally perfect.
2. Nature has been corrupted (Rom. 8:22).
3. Concerns of ecologists provide many examples.
4. Though we are uncertain of the precise nature of
the restoration of the physical world, we do know
that the present "polluted" order will pass away
(Rev. 21:1).

II. There will be a new kind of people in a new kind of world.
A. God will make and is in the process of making new
people.
1. The Old Adam dies in contrition as it faces God's
law.
2. Through the work of the Holy Spirit a new person
comes forth. The process of rebirth and becoming
a new creation applies (cf. 2 Cor. 5:17; Gal. 6:15;
Eph. 2:10; 4:24). God is at work in the church with
the Gospel to establish His new kind of people by
justifying and sanctifying them.
3. The results astound us. We are so limited in ap-
prehending what the eventual form of "salvation"
will be that we must hear it in negative terms—tears,
death, mourning, crying, and pain will be gone.
4. How? Here we remember what happens as the
Gospel is proclaimed. God is at work. He works
through Word and Sacrament, creating His own
people, enlightening them, sanctifying them, and
incorporating them into the New Israel, the body
of Christ. In the Epistle He gives them a glimpse of
the glorious future awaiting them.

B. God will provide a new kind of world for the new kind
of people.
1. The exact nature of the new world is beyond our
conceptual ability now. We will await the unveiling,
though we are not now able to describe "the fur-
niture of heaven."
2. But its characteristics are clear. It will be pleasing
according to God's perfect standards. It will be
marked by His own presence. It will exclude all the
problems that afflict us today. We note especially
in the Epistle that God promises three times to be
with His people.

This is all a fine vision. But is it only another utopian dream? We are directed to God's written words: "These words are trustworthy and true" (Rev. 21:5). We are directed for our confidence not to human longings and hopes but to the objective, inspired words of God. We are sure, and we dwell in this hope as we accept the direct promise of our God that He has communicated to us in the written and transmitted words of this and other parts of Scripture.

RICHARD J. SCHULTZ

Fifth Sunday of Easter

GOSPEL   John 13:31–35 (RSV)

Sermon Notes/Introduction

Jesus announces His going away in terms that the disciples are slow to understand. He is to be "glorified." By this He means that He is to be revealed as the Savior and the divine Son of God through His suffering and death (v. 31) and also through His resurrection and ascension (v. 32). In all this the Father is active. The disciples would not be able to walk the same path of suffering that He would walk, nor could they immediately follow Him into heaven (v. 33). Nevertheless, they not only would share in His glory but would also glorify Him themselves through their love for one another while on earth. Jesus' commandment to love is new in the sense that He has provided a new standard and motive: "even as I have loved you" (v. 34). The love He was to show in His death for others was a self-sacrificing love. Such love shown by His followers would be the witness to the world of true discipleship (v. 35).

The central thought of the text is that Jesus is glorified or honored by submitting to death, by God's exalting Him, and by the love of Christians for one another. The goal of the sermon is that the hearers will let the glory of Jesus that they see by faith be reflected in their lives. The problem is that Christians sometimes let other kinds of glory overshadow the glory that is theirs in Christ.

"The paths of glory lead but to the grave." Acclamation by people is ephemeral. One enjoys it no more in death. Jesus walked on paths of glory much different from the world's paths. His paths give all other glory a new dimension.

Sermon Outline
PATHS OF GLORY FOR JESUS CHRIST

I. He followed a path of humiliation.
   A. He was about to suffer and die.
      1. Judas had left the room to carry out the betrayal
         (v. 31).
      2. Jesus was now seemingly helpless against the worst
         that sin, Satan, and death would do.
   B. Yet He was glorified in suffering and death (v. 31).
      1. Here is the brightest manifestation of God's righ-
         teous love (Rom. 3:21–22).
      2. Here is the clearest demonstration of vicarious sin-
         bearing (2 Cor. 5:21).
      3. Here is the complete redemption of the human race
         (Col. 1:14).
      4. None of us could go with Him on this path of hu-
         miliation (John 13:33). He went for us. It was a
         path of glory indeed.
II. He followed a path of exaltation (v. 32).
   A. He descended into hell (1 Peter 3:19–20).
      1. He went to proclaim victory over Satan.
      2. He announced to the condemned their irrevocable
         judgment because of their unbelief.
   B. He rose from the dead (Matt. 28:6; 1 Cor. 6:14).
      1. He conquered death for us (John 11:25–26).
      2. His resurrection gives us new power (Phil. 3:10).
   C. He ascended into heaven (Eph. 1:20–22).
      1. He reigns as head of the church.
      2. He is the ruler of all.

We share in His glory, for we have been delivered from
eternal death and assured of new life here and hereafter (Eph.
2:6). It was a path of glory indeed.

III. He followed a path of love.
   A. We Christians are to love one another "as I have loved
      you" (John 13:34).
      1. It is a new commandment because of the principle
         of self-sacrifice (agapē).
      2. It is a new commandment because of the motiva-
         tion. His love enables us to love.
   B. When we live in love, the glory of Jesus shines through
      us.
      1. Such love is the most evident demonstration to the
         world that we are Christ's disciples (v. 35).

2. It is a marvelous power for healing and service.

Because Jesus' paths of glory have intersected with ours, we need not glorify ourselves. It is glory enough to share in His glory and to reflect it.

GERHARD AHO

Sixth Sunday of Easter

EPISTLE   Revelation 21:10–14, 22–23 (RSV)

Sermon Notes/Introduction

This is the second time John receives a vision of the Holy City "coming down out of heaven from God." The emphasis in verse 2 is on the presence of God with His people in eternal life. Here the vision emphasizes the glory of the new heaven and new earth. The Epistle responds to our natural curiosity about what it will be like to live in eternal life. We cannot envision the reality of it, but God graciously gives us a symbolic picture to help us appreciate and long for it. We do not press the symbolism, but we do learn from the general impression. Thus we stand beside John on a high mountain and get "A Glimpse of Our Future Holy City."

Sermon Outline
A GLIMPSE OF OUR FUTURE HOLY CITY

I. To live forever means to live in the presence of God.
   A. God will be the light of the city of eternal life. (Note: the *phōstēr* is not merely light or radiance but actually the lightbearer.)
      1. We learn that "the lightbearer" is God from verse 23 (cf. also 4:3).
      2. God's presence is like a shimmering, crystal-clear jewel. We can hardly conceive of this symbol, let alone the reality behind it. Yet we do get the impression of majesty, purity, and absolute revelation of the true state of affairs. Note that the benefits provided to us by the sun and the moon in this life are provided by God's presence in the next life.
   B. Our new city will have God's glory.
      1. We are reminded of the *shekinah,* the pillar of cloud and fire that led God's people in the Exodus. It symbolized God's presence to the Israelites. God

visibly demonstrated that He was available to them with all His attributes.

2. Thus in eternal life God's glory or *doxa* is the sum of all His attributes. God's power, creative ability, flawless wisdom, knowledge, etc., are all directly and immediately available. As we struggle with limited resources in this life, we are awed by the possibility of having divine resources directly applicable to any situation.

II. Our new life will be in an exclusive company.

A. The new city is walled.

1. Walls divide; they leave some inside and some outside.

2. Thus some will not enjoy eternal bliss. They will be "thrown into outer darkness" (Matt. 8:12). To be brought to faith in Christ in this life is to be brought from "darkness into His marvelous light" (1 Peter 2:9).

B. Angels guard the gates.

1. They "check the credentials" of the applicants. Contrary to the *opinio legis,* they do not look for blameless lives. In that case none would enter (Ps. 143:2).

2. The only acceptable credentials are faith in the salvation wrought by Christ (cf. Rev. 7:14). Those before the throne of the Lamb "have washed their robes and made them white in the blood of the Lamb."

III. Yet the opportunity for eternal life is open to all.

A. There are gates on all sides with names inscribed.

1. One may approach from any direction. All nations are welcome (cf. 7:9). None is excluded because of race, age, social level, or any other human criterion.

2. The names of God's chosen people are inscribed on the gates. God knows we are coming before we get there. In Christ, our names are in the Book of Life. Furthermore, believers will have the "white stone" to present as evidence of privilege to enter.

B. The revelation through the apostles is the foundation.

1. The Old and New Testaments are represented. The way to the Holy City of eternal life is not hard to find. God has given us His Word by inspiration, and therein we find the true Gospel, which is the power

of God to salvation. The apostolic word is the "Word of life" (Phil. 2:16).

2.. Through the Word we have access to repentance, to faith, to forgiveness, and ultimately to inclusion in the splendors of eternal life.

The sermon may well end with an enthusiastic admonition for Christians to avail themselves of the apostolic words as the avenue of faith in Christ and eternal joys.

RICHARD J. SCHULTZ

Sixth Sunday of Easter

GOSPEL   John 14:23–29 (KJV)

Sermon Notes/Introduction

1. The entire 14th chapter of John is concerned with queries from individual disciples about the Lord's forthcoming departure and the destination to which He is journeying. Thomas, for example, questions whether it is possible for anyone who has no definite knowledge of the final goal of a journey to know the way that leads to it (v. 5). Jesus replies that the way to God lies in the knowledge of the truth about Him and that He, Jesus, is "the way, the truth, and the life" (vv. 6–7). Then Philip raises a question about the indirect knowledge of God even though the intermediary be Christ (v. 8). But the Lord reminds him that since He lives in perpetual union of purpose and will with His Father, His words and actions are God's words and actions (vv. 9–12). But Jesus also says that before He returns to the Father and another Advocate is sent (v. 16), He will come to His disciples in the glory of His resurrection body (v. 19).

2. The Gospel is an exchange between Judas (the other Judas, not Iscariot) and Jesus that grows out of the Lord's promise to appear to the disciples. A confinement of the appearances of the risen Christ to *believers* seems to Judas a limitation of Christ's power (v. 22). "How is it that thou wilt manifest thyself" is more accurately rendered in the New American Standard translation: "what then has happened. . . ." Judas thinks something must have happened for Christ to limit His sphere of influence to a small group instead of going to the whole world.

3. In response to Judas, Christ speaks words similar to

those of verse 21: "If a man love Me, he will keep My words" (v. 23). The spirit of obedience is made prominent, but there is a promise attached to such obedience: "We will come unto him and make our abode with him." This is a spiritual coming and abiding in the heart of the obedient believer. The realization of this promise is conditioned on obedience to His Word. Note that when the Lord said, "We will come," He testified again to His unity with the Father. In verse 24 the same truth is presented negatively: "He that loveth Me not keepeth not My sayings."

4. In verse 26 Christ speaks of the function of the Spirit as teacher and reminder in the period after His departure. But these two functions are closely connected. He will teach the new by recalling the old and will recall the old by teaching the new. In His role as teacher, the Holy Spirit will interpret the person and mission of Christ, and in calling the Words of Christ to the disciples' remembrance, He will open the disciples' minds to the right understanding of His teachings. The Gospel of John is itself an illustration of the fulfillment of this promise. That this Spirit will be sent "in My name" means "on My account" to instruct the disciples in all the things that Jesus had begun to teach them.

5. But Jesus recognizes a more immediate requirement: He must face the needs of His disciples for consolation because the separation is near. In verse 27 He takes up a familiar word of salutation and infuses it with a new meaning (cf. 20:19, 26). He gives them a legacy: "My peace I give unto you." "My peace" is perhaps best translated as the "peace that is Mine" or the peace that He made. He made peace in the blood of the cross: "Therefore being justified by faith, we have peace with God through our Lord Jesus Christ" (Rom. 5:1). Peace with God is the legacy of Christ's death. It is the peace that He made and that we cannot make by virtue of our own efforts or actions. The disciples had witnessed something of what Jesus calls "My peace" when they had seen Him restoring calm to human lives racked by sin. His return to the Father would mean not the lessening but the heightening of the experience of this peace, so they hear His reassuring words, "Let not your heart be troubled."

6. The words "greater than I" in verse 28 were frequently cited by the Arians to support their doctrine of the creaturely subordination of the Son to the Father. But the words mean that He who is one with the Father had taken the place of a servant; He became man. As such He was sent forth by the

Father and did the Father's will. The words do not mean that the Father was greater in power or deity.

All people, even the revolutionary and the warmonger, as St. Augustine noted, desire peace; they are always striving for what they imagine would be a more settled condition of life. To be sure, temporary freedom from distraction, anxiety, and strife is often possible. But it is from our Lord's last bequest to His disciples that we know the meaning of true peace. This last bequest—His peace—is personal, genuine, and seasonable.

Sermon Outline
THE LAST BEQUEST

I. Christ's peace is personal.
   A. It is a peace distinctive of His person and work.
   B. It becomes personal to us; it is independent of and unaffected by outward circumstances.
II. Christ's peace is genuine.
   A. This characteristic is brought to the fore when Jesus contrasts His giving with that of the world.
   B. The difference is twofold when compared with what the world gives.
      1. What does the world offer when it yields the best it can give? Wealth, fame, status, comfort, praise. The world cannot give love, forgiveness, or spiritual consolation.
      2. Further, the way in which the world gives shows how much less genuine is its giving. The Greek saying "Call no man happy until the day of his death" expresses the general feeling of the weak and unsteady grasp any person has over the things of the world.
   C. The gift of God in Jesus Christ is genuine; it is a peace that can never be undone (Rom. 5:1).
III. Christ's peace is seasonable.
   A. At the time of the Lord's last bequest, the disciples were troubled and fearful. He had spoken to them of His imminent death.
   B. We too live troubled lives. Sin abounds; sorrow surges around us; the shadow of death lies on us. But in this bequest is a divine provision for every human necessity. The outward circumstances may remain unchanged, but "we are more than conquerors through

Him who loved us" (Rom. 8:37).

JOHN F. JOHNSON

The Ascension of Our Lord

EPISTLE   Ephesians 1:16–23 (NIV)

Sermon Notes/Introduction

Crucial to the Trinitarian approach to the sermon outline is the distinct possibility that "the spirit of wisdom" in verse 17 of the Epistle is the Holy Spirit. Both the *Good News Bible* and the New International Version capitalize the word "spirit." Moreover, this conclusion better fits the immediate context in verses 13–14, which speak clearly of the Holy Spirit. Even if "the spirit of wisdom" of verse 17 were a mere human trait— as suggested by the lower case *s* in many versions—such a spirit could be ours only through the gift of the Holy Spirit.

The ascension of Jesus commemorates Jesus' visible departure from earth and return to heaven. But despite His physical absence He has not left us. It is true, as He Himself observed, that He had finished the saving work He came to earth to do ("It is finished"). But this does not at all mean that God is finished with us. Jesus Himself once informed His disciples that His leave-taking for heaven would be a signal for the Holy Spirit to come to them (John 16:7), a coming we have witnessed continually ever since the first Pentecost. Today's Epistle is one more assurance that Jesus' ascension is the signal not only for the Holy Spirit to come to us but also for God the Father and even Jesus Himself to come to us in unexpected ways.

Sermon Outline

THE MEANING OF THE ASCENSION
JESUS LEAVES—AND THE TRIUNE GOD COMES!

I. The Holy Spirit comes to us (see first paragraph of Sermon Notes).
   A. God the Father sends Him ("that the God of our Lord Jesus Christ . . . may *give* to you the Spirit of wisdom," v. 17).
   B. The Holy Spirit comes to us through the Gospel (*"revelation,* so that you may know him better," v. 17).

    C. He enlightens our understanding through that Gospel (v. 18).

    D. As a result, we are strengthened in our hope and longing for heaven (v. 18).

II. God the Father comes to us.

    A. We have already experienced His power in the faith He has given us (v. 19; 2:8).

    B. We are promised even more of His power ("his *incomparably great* power"), the same power of God that exalted Christ in His resurrection and ascension (1:19–21).

    C. As a matter of fact, we receive more than His power—we receive Him (John 14:23).

III. Jesus comes to us.

    A. He is over all things (Eph. 1:21–22), yet, paradoxically, He is so for the sake of, the benefit of, the church (*"for the church,"* v. 22).

    B. He fills all things (v. 23), yet, paradoxically, the church completes His fullness just as a body completes the head to a body (vv. 22–23; Phillips paraphrase: "In that body lives fully the One who fills the whole wide universe").

FRANCIS C. ROSSOW

The Ascension of Our Lord

GOSPEL   Luke 24:44–53 (RSV)

Sermon Notes/Introduction

Although vv. 44–49 may well have been spoken by Jesus on Easter Sunday, it is possible that the evangelist here condenses various reports into one, relating in one paragraph what happened on several occasions. In any event, we have recorded the commission to carry on Christ's work and not to begin a new one. As the Father sent Christ (in the past, for His mission was completed), so now Jesus sends His disciples (in the constant present, till His coming again).

Christ's mission was now complete. Jesus indicates that the unalterable agreement introduced by "it stands written" has now been fulfilled. The "must" of fulfillment of the whole Old Testament touching on the work of the Messiah was now completed. In the word translated "must be fulfilled" we have what one can call the key to the work of Christ. Why was this suffering, dying, and rising again necessary? Arndt insists:

1. "It had been prophesied and the divine Scriptures have to be fulfilled."

2. "The fact that the prophecies were in the Scriptures shows that God had decreed the Passion and resurrection of Christ."

3. "It was necessary for the salvation of the human race that these things come to pass."

To these things the disciples had been eyewitnesses. The proclamation of this message "in His Name" was to be their principal task and that of the church until Christ's return.

Thus the continuity not only of the work but also of the message was established. For even as the burden of the Messiah's proclamation was the summoning to repent and receive the Kingdom, so now "repentance and forgiveness of sins should be preached." To the changed heart that in faith laid hold on Christ and His atoning work there was the free offer of forgiveness of sins.

In this work the disciples had the promise of the Christ for the outpouring of the Holy Spirit and also for His abiding presence and help. For even though His visible presence was removed by His ascension, invisibly Jesus continued with them.

Paradoxically, rather than experiencing sorrow at their parting from Jesus Christ, the disciples found joy. This joy is pegged on three specifics that come out of the text: joy in the fulfillment of God's promises prophesied in the Old Testament, joy in the call to purpose and significant service, joy in being blessed and responding in joyful worship in the temple.

Relate the events, resurrection to ascension, as indicated in the text.

Sermon Outline

AN ASCENSION MESSAGE OF JOY

I. There is joy in the fulfillment of God's prophesies in the Old Testament.

    A. The Messianic prophesies of the Old Testament are fulfilled.

        1. "It stands written" is the formula introducing God's unalterable agreement.

        2. The whole Old Testament bears witness to Christ.

    B. "It was necessary."

        1. The Scriptures must be fulfilled.

      2. "It pleased God to bruise Him" was God's decree about Christ's suffering, death, and resurrection.

      3. He came for the salvation of the human race.

   C. Jesus opens the minds of the disciples to understand—here merely an intellectual comprehension.

II. There is joy in the call to purpose and significant service.

   A. "You will be witnesses of these things."

      1. They witnessed the "what" and "why" of the suffering, dying, and rising again of Christ.

      2. They were to carry on the work of Christ (this command is in the "constant present") until Christ's coming again.

      3. They were to begin in Jerusalem and go out into all the world.

   B. They proclaimed repentance and forgiveness in His name.

      1. True repentance involves two things.

         a. First come sorrow and contrition.

         b. Then follows faith, which trusts the promise of God's forgiveness.

      2. It is proclaimed "in His name."

   C. The Holy Spirit would empower them.

III. There is joy in the blessing that found response in joyful worship.

   A. They receive the blessing of Christ, not the least of which was the promise of His abiding presence (cf. Matt. 28:20).

   B. Their worship in the temple anticipates their joy of worship in heaven (cf. John 14:1–6).

The Ascension joy is also available to us in the same way and on the same terms. God has promised, called, and blessed us. We in that blessing respond in joyful service and worship, until in Christ's coming again we are taken "so that where He is we may be also"—in heaven, where we shall serve and worship our God in the fullness of joy that knows no end.

NORBERT H. MUELLER

Seventh Sunday of Easter

EPISTLE   Revelation 22:12–17, 20 (NIV)

Sermon Notes/Introduction

John in exile on the island of Patmos concludes his letter to the seven churches with a promise that Jesus is coming again soon. The believers, torn by false teachers and temptations from within and increasing persecution from without, welcome the coming of Jesus with courage for the present and hope for an eternal dwelling in the city of God.

Thursday we celebrated the Ascension of Our Lord. As the disciples gazed into the heavens, the two men in white explained, "This same Jesus, who has been taken from you into heaven, will come back in the same way you have seen him go into heaven." We still live in the time between Ascension Day and the Second Coming of Christ. As we prepare to celebrate Pentecost next week and face the daily pressures of living in a secular world, St. John in Revelation directs us to "The Coming Again of Our Ascended Lord."

Sermon Outline

THE COMING AGAIN OF OUR ASCENDED LORD

I. His announcement (vv. 12–16, 20).
   A. Death to unbelievers (v. 15).
      1. Jesus strongly asserts His coming again as bringing recompense. To the "dogs" and sorcerers and fornicators and murderers and idolaters His coming means life forever outside the gates of the city of God. They continue in sin and reject the announcement.
      2. Jesus likewise speaks judgment to our sinful, secular world. To the extent that we succumb to false teachers and immorality, we stand in danger of rejecting His announcement. We confess our blindness.
   B. Life to believers (vv. 14, 16–17).
      1. Jesus graciously offers robes washed in His blood and water without price (Is. 55). The persecuted believers are preserved for eternal life in the city of God by Christ, the bright Morning Star, the Root and Offspring of David.
      2. Jesus graciously offers us His cleansing forgiveness as the Son of David, crucified and risen. We can

be preserved from this sinful, secular world as we look to Him.
II. Our invitation (vv. 17, 20).
   A. The Spirit, the bride, and the believer invite Jesus to come and supply courage now.
     1. The persecuted invite Jesus to come and in the process receive living water to strengthen them for faithful ministry.
     2. We likewise stand strong as we invite His early return; we are refreshed.
   B. The church invites Jesus to come and supply hope for the future.

What a joyful announcement from Jesus! What an eager invitation from our lips—power for living from the coming again of our ascended Lord!

STEPHEN J. CARTER

Seventh Sunday of Easter

GOSPEL   John 17:20–26 (KJV)

Sermon Notes/Introduction

In John 16 our Lord has unfolded to His disciples the meaning of His approaching departure; with this He concludes His ministry of teaching. But His priestly ministry is not yet ended, and in chapter 17 He moves toward its culmination in the atmosphere of prayer. He turns His gaze from earth to heaven, from His disciples to His Father, and utters the prayer that can perhaps be described as the prayer of the great High Priest (17:1–26).

The prayer in John is the only long, continuous prayer of Jesus recorded in the gospels. In it He prays for Himself (vv. 1–5), for the welfare of the disciples after His departure (vv. 6–19), and for all believers (vv. 20–26). The Gospel for the Seventh Sunday of Easter contains "Christ's Prayer for His Church."

Sermon Outline
CHRIST'S PRAYER FOR HIS CHURCH

I. Christ prayed for the unity of His church (vv. 20–23).
   A. Although believers are many in number, they are to be one (vv. 20–21). This is Christ's most specific state-

ment on unity. It is far different from some contemporary pleas for ecclesiastical unity in disregard of apostolic beliefs. He prays that the church be one as He and the Father are one; it is a spiritual oneness. Believers are brought to faith by the living Word. That living, powerful Word makes them members of the body of Christ. By His grace we are members of His body. Being one in Him, we are to be one with one another in His church.

B. Christ prays for unity because unity strengthens our witness (v. 21). True unity, based on His Word, will be a powerful witness to the world of the truth of the Gospel. Christ knows that the witness of His followers will be much more effective if the Christians speak with a united voice and if this voice is the true expression of the conviction of their hearts.

C. Christ prays for unity because unity in the church declares His love (v. 23). The world will be attracted by the love of Christians and will be moved to look into it. The Christian can then answer: "We love Him, because He first loved us" (1 John 4:19).

D. It is important for the preacher to underscore that the unity for which Christ prays is not an organic union of religious bodies but the inner unity that consists in the bond of faith in Jesus as the Son of God and our Savior. In other words, there is a difference between unity and uniformity. Church union and church unity can be two entirely different things. (The preacher would do well to reacquaint himself with the meaning of AC VII and its implications.)

II. Christ prayed for the glorification of the church (John 17:24–26).

A. Christ introduces this petition with the words "Father, I will." This signifies His firm intention and deliberate determination. Our eternal salvation is our Savior's concern, not merely something with which we should concern ourselves. When Jesus says, "I will," He is not demanding something contrary to the Father's will; His "I will" has none of the selfishness of our "I will's." His will is always in perfect accord with His Father's will.

B. The Father has given us to Christ. This He did when He brought us to faith through the working of the Holy Spirit. In the Explanation of the Second Article we confess with Luther that the purpose of Christ's whole redemptive activity was "that I may be His own and live under Him in His kingdom." This coheres with Christ's prayer (v. 24). He prays that we may be with Him where He is, that we may behold the glory that the Father has given Him.

In summary, we may say that John 17 reflects the evangelist's strong ecclesiastical interest. But this ecclesiastical concern prompts him to say nothing about church organization; on the contrary, the record of our Lord's high-priestly prayer emphasizes the life in the Spirit, which unites the believer with Christ and sets the true agenda for Christian unity and our eternal destiny.

JOHN F. JOHNSON

Pentecost: The Day of Pentecost

EPISTLE   Acts 2:37–47 (RSV)

Sermon Notes/Introduction

After the Lord's final instructions to the disciples to be witnesses, His promise of power from the Holy Spirit, and His ascension into heaven, the disciples wait prayerfully in Jerusalem. On Pentecost the Spirit fills the house where they have gathered. Jews from many nations hear the Gospel message. Peter preaches a powerful Law and Gospel sermon that culminates in the words of the Epistle. The Jerusalem fellowship of believers in Jesus Christ is initiated with the baptism of three thousand. The fellowship grows in both quantity and quality.

Pentecost is an annual feast in the Christian church year and provides important emphasis on the Holy Spirit, described by one author as the "half-known God." But more significant, Pentecost is an opportunity for you to move back in time and stand in that notable assembly of Jews from around the world where, spellbound by Peter, the big fisherman, you experience "The Powerful Effects of a Pentecost Message."

Sermon Outline
THE POWERFUL EFFECTS
OF A PENTECOST MESSAGE

I. The Pentecost message cuts to the heart (v. 37).
   A. The hearers recognized their guilt in Peter's account of

the rejection of Jesus Christ. They cried out, "What shall we do?"

B. We recognize our guilt as our hearts are sometimes hardened to the weekly message of Jesus Christ.

II. The Pentecost message brings forgiveness of sins through baptism (vv. 38–41).

A. Peter's description of the crucified and risen Christ transformed his hearers, and they were baptized.

B. We hear again the message of the crucified and risen Christ and apply the power of our baptism to daily living (the gift of the Holy Spirit promised to us who are far off, vv. 38–39).

III. The Pentecost message creates a dynamic fellowship of believers (vv. 42–47).

A. The early believers joined in regular worship and study of the Word (vv. 42, 46–47). Despite our times of indifference to the Word, the Pentecost message creates in us a desire for regular reception of Word and Sacrament through worship and Bible study.

B. The early believers joined in meeting physical and spiritual needs (vv. 43–45). They formed a common treasury and shared bread in their homes. Despite our selfishness and individualism, the Pentecost message creates in us a desire to reach out to others to meet their physical and spiritual needs.

C. The early believers joined in word-and-deed witness through which the Lord added to their number (v. 47). Despite our self-absorption and timidity, the Pentecost message creates in us the desire and the ability to witness in word and deed so that the Lord may add to our fellowship those who are being saved.

Because we have been present at Pentecost to hear Peter, the Holy Spirit cuts us to our hearts, brings assurance of Christ's forgiveness through Baptism, and gives us the privilege to participate in a dynamic fellowship of believers—worshiping, meeting needs, and witnessing to others. These are the powerful effects of the Pentecost message.

STEPHEN J. CARTER

Pentecost: The Day of Pentecost

GOSPEL   John 15:26–27; 16:4b–11

Sermon Notes/Introduction

A part of the last discourses of Jesus is His treatment of
the doctrine of the Holy Spirit. John contains frequent references to the person and work of the Holy Spirit and the necessity of His coming to the disciples. We have long since come
to the awareness that the Holy Spirit enables people to embrace Christ and what He said and did in faith and trust, for
He above all bears witness to Christ. In the words immediately
before this pericope Jesus had explained that the hostility of
the Jews toward Him was sinful, for they ought to have recognized His divine mission in His works and words. They hated
Him, not knowing Him, although they ought to have known
Him, but when the "Paraclete" came, He would bear true
testimony to Jesus, being indeed the Spirit of truth. Thus Jesus
in the Gospel calls the Holy Spirit the "Paraclete," the divine
advocate, defending "the Righteous One" against false accusers, pleading the cause of Christ with the world. The Holy
Spirit comes from the Father and bears true witness to the
world of the Truth, the Christ of God.

Because, as Jesus says, He was going to the Father (a
reference to His death, resurrection, and ascension), the persecution that focused on Him would, with His leaving, be directed at His disciples, His witnesses. The Paraclete, whose
office has already been described as one of witness, would also
vindicate the apostles in the testimony that they were to deliver.
Exposed to persecution, they would have a powerful advocate
at their side. "He will be their Paraclete, no less than the Paraclete of Jesus, or rather He will be theirs because He is His."

It is interesting to note that emerging from the Gospel is
the conviction that the Paraclete will convict the disciples' accusers and the accusers of Jesus of being in the wrong.

Jesus renders not only an indictment but also a conviction
on three counts (the word used for "convict" is straight out of
the courtroom): (1) The Paraclete will expose the sin of failure
to discern God in Christ and thus "to believe in Him." The
world is to be convicted of the sin inherent in the rejection of
Jesus. (2) The righteousness of which the world will be convinced to its shame is the righteousness of Christ, that absolute
righteousness that could only be revealed in the risen Christ.
"He goes to the Father" is the statement that authenticates His

mission. For with the Passion, His revelation of the Father is completed, and henceforth the Paraclete will convince the world of the perfect righteousness that is revealed in Christ and made accessible to people. (3) The Paraclete will convince the world of both the justice of God and the inevitability of God's judgment. The world will be judged, and the outcome of that judgment is already determined, because the prince of this world has been judged. In the redemptive act Jesus is victorious. He has conquered Satan. (Luther's words are appropriate: "He's judged, the deed is done; one little word can fell him.")

The message is plain. The Paraclete is both the advocate of the disciples and Jesus Christ and the accuser or prosecutor of the world. As we witness to our Lord, the Spirit performs the same functions today for and through us.

Sermon Outline
THE HOLY SPIRIT—
ADVOCATE AND PROSECUTOR

I. The Paraclete is an advocate—a divine helper.
   A. He is an advocate for the disciples.
      1. He helps in persecution and need.
         a. Jesus had warned them.
         b. With His leaving, the hatred that focused on Christ would be turned on them.
         c. They would need the advocacy of the Holy Spirit.
      2. He supports their witness to Jesus Christ.
         a. They along with the Holy Spirit would bear witness to Jesus.
         b. They were witnesses because they had been with Christ from the beginning.
         c. The coming of the Holy Spirit was to complete Jesus' presence.
   B. He is an advocate of and for Jesus Christ, bearing witness to Jesus and His works.
      1. He defends the Righteous One, pleading the cause of Christ with the world.
      2. He pleads the cause of Christ before false accusers.
      3. He bears true testimony to Jesus as a Spirit of truth.
II. The Paraclete is also the prosecutor. He will not only provide defense, but He will also take the role of the accuser.

He will accuse the accusers of Jesus and His disciples of being wrong. He will convict the world to its shame.

A. He convicts the world of sin.
1. Sin is inherent in the rejection of Jesus.
2. The world fails to discern God in Christ and to believe in Him.
3. The world fails to recognize Jesus' divine mission through His words and works.
B. He convinces the world of Christ's righteousness.
1. His righteousness is absolute and is authenticated by the Passion and resurrection.
2. Righteouness is revealed in Christ and made accessible to people.
C. He convinces the world of judgment (its justice and inevitability).
1. The outcome is already determined and assured.
2. Satan will be expelled from the domain over which he claims rule.

NORBERT H. MUELLER

The Holy Trinity:
First Sunday After Pentecost

EPISTLE   Romans 5:1–5 (RSV)

Sermon Notes/Introduction

The "therefore" of verse 1 logically roots the justification of Paul's readers in the work of Christ that Abraham (chapter 4) appropriated through the same faith understood here (vv. 1–2). The pivotal emphasis on the peace that we now (present tense) enjoy with God (v. 1) provides for Paul's development of the thought that even sufferings serve the Christian's larger pilgrimage (vv. 2–5). The rich and multifaceted *shalom* of the Old Testament is undoubtedly in view with its broad implications of a right relationship with God and with the cosmos. An excellent article that surveys the scope of Biblical "peace" is by H. Beck and C. Brown in *The New International Dictionary of New Testament Theology* (Grand Rapids, Mich.: Zondervan, 1976), 2:776–83. This context converts Pauline hope (v. 2) into a confident longing for the public display of God's glory that has already been manifest in the person and work of Christ. The future aeon had already sounded the end of the present futile age by the invasion of the kingdom of God. Whatever this epoch can serve up in suffering (v. 3), the one who has been justified perceives the partial and passing nature of its power. The new state of affairs that Christ has inaugurated will irrevocably and ineluctably exert its power for those whose hope has been sustained by the gift of the Holy Spirit (v. 5). The coming of the eschatological reality will not disappoint but will confirm the enduring benefits of the grace in which Paul and his readers now stand (v. 2).

Sermon Outline
GOD'S WORK IN CHRIST HAS BROUGHT ABOUT A NEW STATE OF AFFAIRS

I. Juvenal, the Roman satirist, stated: "The wise man, in peace, prepares for war."
   A. The history of humanity—ancient, medieval, and modern—demonstrates Juvenal's point.
      1. Cain's slaying of Abel has provided the paradigm for humankind.
      2. Our technological advances, far from aiding our quest for peace, have augmented our killing abilities and aggravated the threat of even wider destruction and death (e.g., laser and nuclear technology).
   B. The hope of humanity—ancient, medieval, and modern—has been disappointed.
      1. No political system has successfully engineered a permanent peace (socialism, communism, capitalism).
      2. No psychological program has diverted the destructive disposition of its subjects (Fromm, Freud, Rogers).
      3. No person has presented a pattern of enduring peace, be he statesman, diplomat, or guru.
II. Paul, the apostle to the Romans, announced an already achieved peace.
   A. This peace was accomplished in the person and work of Jesus Christ.
      1. The change in the cosmos is the direct consequence of its movement from an unjust state to a state of justification before God.
      2. This justified status bestows peace.
      3. This peace is freely given to the faith that is focused on Christ.

B. This peace permits us to live as those liberated from the futility of false hopes.
   1. Christ's peace endures through the rise and fall of earthly kingdoms.
   2. Christ's peace abides through the ups and downs of our psychological states.
   3. Christ's peace dispels the destructive force of our own rebellion against God.
III. Christ's peace is the new alternative that St. Paul announced.
   A. Every other option is worn out and has been found wanting.
   B. As we live this new alternative of God's peace, the warring and dying world is declared "defeated" and called to a new hope.

DEAN WENTHE

The Holy Trinity:
First Sunday After Pentecost

GOSPEL   John 16:12–15 (RSV)

Sermon Notes/Introduction

1. Which emphasis is best for this Sunday, the First Sunday After Pentecost or the Feast of the Holy Trinity? The Three-Year Lectionary restores this Sunday to its ancient position as the octave of Pentecost. But the Gospel permits us to do justice to both festivals. The work of the Holy Spirit is to communicate the truths about the Trinity and to complete in the hearts and lives of believers the entire work of the Trinity on their behalf. The Spirit's work is to connect us to the operations of Father and Son in the plan of salvation.

2. The Gospel is part of the lengthy instruction and consolation to the apostles given by the Lord as He approaches His week of trial, crucifixion, and death and as He anticipates His resurrection and ascension. We are allowed to listen to the farewell lectures in pastoral theology (or should we say apostolic theology) of Christ Himself. The entire address of John 13–16 is directed to the apostles. The word "you" appears five times in today's Gospel. In each case it refers to the apostles—except Judas, who had left. This distinction is crucial in preaching on this text. If we refer the "you" to contemporary

hearers, we may damage the doctrine of the means of grace. Applied in this way, the words "when the Spirit of truth comes, He will guide you into all the truth" may lead one to believe that the Holy Spirit needs no vehicle. We may fall into a sub-jectivistic enthusiasm. If we leave the impression that the Spirit will guide us without the apostolic Word (moved by the Holy Spirit), we open the way for an undisciplined faith.

3. Questions abound. What are the "many things" that the Lord has to say to the apostles? Why can't they bear them now? By what process will the Spirit guide the apostles? How will He hear things from the Father and the Son? How will He speak? What things of Jesus will He take and declare?

4. Some answers. Since Jesus expressed His intention to tell the apostles "many things," we look for these things in the writings of the apostles. Such doctrines as justification by grace through faith, sanctification, the election of grace, and many others are expounded in the gospels and epistles. The apostles could not bear them because the full drama of the vicarious atonement, resurrection, ascension, and sending of the Spirit at Pentecost as the promise of the Father had not yet been played out before their eyes.

"He will guide you into all the truth" (John 16:13). This is a remarkable promise. The marketplace of ideas, especially "religious" ideas, is confused and confusing. A recent issue of *Good Housekeeping* listed 1,200 "denominations" or religious groups in the United States.

Moreover, truth in religion is not a matter of taste. It is a matter of temporal and eternal destiny. Has God left us on our own to struggle for such important truth? If so, we are left to the vagaries of human opinion. The good news today is that God has provided a means whereby the truth—all the truth we need—is communicated to us.

Sermon Outline
HE WILL GUIDE YOU INTO ALL THE TRUTH

I. We need a sure word of truth from God.
   A. We hear many human words of truth, but they are conflicting and confusing.
   B. The truth we seek is necessary because it involves the basic issues of life. Who are we? Where did we come from? What happens to us after our bodies cease to function?
   C. This human need for truth drives many to despair of

ever knowing the truth or to attach themselves to any who claim an access to truth.

II. We have God's promise that He will guide us into all the truth.

   A. God the Father has known the truth from eternity.

      1. He knows that human beings are lost in their estrangement from Him in time and in eternity.

      2. He sent His Son to be the Savior to release humanity from its lost condition.

   B. God the Son came to share God's truth and to fulfill it.

      1. The prophetic ministry of Jesus, recorded in the Scriptures, brought God's truth to humanity.

      2. In His life and death the Son lived the perfect life and paid the full penalty of our estrangement from God.

   C. God the Spirit gives us this truth.

      1. As a person in the Trinity He knows all truth.

      2. By a miraculous inspiration He communicated it to the apostles.

      3. The apostles wrote it clearly under the guidance of the Spirit.

      4. Their writings have been preserved for us in the Holy Scriptures.

      5. Truth—God's truth—is clearly preserved for us in the writings of Scripture.

Do we need to be uncertain? We can be certain if we read and study the clear words of Scripture and find there the "many things" that our Lord has done for us. The Scriptures, written under the guidance of the Holy Spirit, are our only way to truth and our sure way to truth. Let us bless the Father, Son, and Spirit for what they have done for us, and let us pay heed to the only source of certain truth in matters of the Spirit of God.

RICHARD J. SCHULTZ

Second Sunday After Pentecost

EPISTLE   Galatians 1:1–10 (NIV)

Sermon Notes/Introduction

Paul opens this famous letter with an extraordinary effort

to define his own apostolic identity and mission. He has been "sent not from men nor by man, but by Jesus Christ and God the Father, who raised him from the dead" (v. 1). Several current commentaries (e.g., Hans D. Betz, *Galatians,* Hermeneia [Philadelphia: Fortress Press, 1979]) have rightly focused on the clear conflict that is evident between Paul's claim and those at Galatia who were contesting his credentials and credibility. These studies also show that Paul viewed such challenges not on the personal level of trying to stake out his own turf—he was only too happy to suffer humiliation if that would further the work (2 Cor. 10–13)—but on the theological level of the Gospel itself. The effrontery that Paul faced was not a slap in his own face but a direct assault on the Gospel of Christ, which had been entrusted to him. Therefore, whether it be Paul or even an angel who expounded another "gospel," that alien proclamation is to fall under God's condemnation (Gal. 1:8). As the contours of this contest in the primitive church emerge, a segment of the community clearly was championing a return to such laws as circumcision in a way that rendered Christ "of no value to you at all" (5:2).

The rhetoric of Paul's opening admonition (1:6–10) is more than literary flourish. It is the appropriate language for a community on the verge of abandoning its birthright. The juxtaposition of Paul's gospel with the counterclaim (vv. 6–7), the immediate appeal to eschatological condemnation of those who propound it (vv. 8–9), and the plea of Paul for a hearing (v. 10), all point to the watershed nature of the question for the apostle. Only by articulating the Gospel, regardless of any human tribunal, can Paul remain a "servant of Christ" (v. 10). An illuminating monograph on this point is John H. Schutz, *Paul and the Anatomy of Apostolic Authority* (London: Cambridge University Press, 1975).

Sermon Outline
THE DISTINCTIVE NATURE
OF THE GOSPEL OF CHRIST

I. Humanity by nature makes religious decisions.
  A. The choice to be a "good person" entails a larger set of assumptions about the meaning of our life.
  B. The decision to be a "hedonist," "humanist," "agnostic," or even "atheist," whether consciously or unconsciously made, brings with it a certain understanding and perception of the world around us.

      1. We are here today and gone tomorrow. (Eat, drink, and be merry, for tomorrow you die.)

      2. Man is the measure of all things.

      3. None of us can know life's meaning.

      4. There is such evil that God cannot exist.

II. Human religiosity is worn out.

    A. All the alternatives have been tried and found wanting (cf. Eccl. 1–11).

    B. The purportedly "new" options turn out to be the same old choices in new attire.

III. The Gospel of Jesus Christ is qualitatively different from human religiosity.

    A. The Gospel is a gift.

      1. God bestows it freely when it is proclaimed in Word and Sacrament.

      2. It remains a gift and aloof from any claim that we merit it.

    B. The Gospel communicates the person and work of Christ.

      1. It frees us from the self-deception that we can add to the work of Christ.

      2. It bestows the benefits of forgiveness and faith apart from any quality inherent in us.

    C. The mission of Paul and his own identity were indissolubly intertwined with the character of the Gospel.

    D. As "servants of Christ" with Paul we have become new creatures and forsaken the false gospels of our worn-out religiosity.

DEAN WENTHE

Second Sunday After Pentecost

GOSPEL   Luke 7:1–10 (KJV)

Sermon Notes/Introduction

1. The appointment for this Sunday of a Gospel reading depicting a Roman centurion (a Gentile) and his servant as objects of Jesus' saving and healing ministry is in keeping with the church-outreach emphasis of the Pentecost season, an accent, incidentally, also captured in the Old Testament Reading for this Sunday (1 Kings 8:41–43), in which Solomon, at the dedication of the temple, asks God to look with favor on the prayer of "a stranger . . . not of thy people Israel . . . when he

shall come and pray toward this house."

2. Although the Christian church should be "broad" and "tolerant" about the recipients of its message (no one is to be excluded), it must at the same time be "narrow" and "intolerant" about the content of that message (presenting Christ—and Christ only—as the way to salvation). The Epistle for this Sunday (Gal. 1:1–10) captures this important accent when Paul asserts, "Though we, or an angel from heaven, preach any other Gospel unto you than that which we have preached unto you, let him be accursed" (v. 8). The church should preach to any*body* ("Parthians and Medes . . . strangers of Rome, Jews and proselytes" [Acts 2:9–10]), but the church dare not preach any*thing* (except "Jesus Christ and Him crucified" [1 Cor. 2:2]).

3. As the opening verse reminds us, the incident described in this pericope occurred after Jesus had completed the sayings recorded by Luke in the previous chapter. One can hardly avoid recognizing a connection between the last of those sayings (Luke 6:47–49) and the Gospel. Might not St. Luke be suggesting that this centurion is a stellar example of the man described in 6:47–48, one who hears Jesus' sayings and does them—one, therefore, who built his house on a rock, a house that will not fall when storms and floods assault it?

4. John 4:46—54 records another instance in which Jesus healed *in absentia*. There, to be sure, this peculiar method was Jesus' idea, not the petitioner's (as in the Luke pericope). But in both cases it is remarkable that each—the centurion from the start and the nobleman eventually—believed so unreservedly in the power of Jesus' saving, healing Word. Neither required any power display, any "hocus-pocus" or "razzle-dazzle." (Jesus, for that matter, didn't even have to be present at the healing!) They simply believed the Word that Jesus spoke. Both petitioners walked by faith, not by sight (2 Cor. 5:7). Such a faith—a faith whose strength seems to be in inverse proportion to the amount of tangible evidence supplied—can be only the manufacture of God's Holy Spirit through the Gospel, the Good News, that is "the power of God unto salvation." Truly, both the nobleman and the centurion are among those "blessed" people who "have not seen, and yet have believed" (John 20:29).

Sermon Outline
TRUE WORTH

I. In a way we can be proud of the elders of the Jews in the Gospel who went to bat for a Roman centurion. In doing so, they overcame the prejudices so horribly common among their kind in Jesus' day. They put in a good word to Jesus for a man of another nationality and for a military enemy besides. All of this was in the best Christian tradition. Had we lived then, it undoubtedly would have been a pleasure to know these men personally.

II. And yet, to borrow St. Paul's words, they had "not already attained" nor "were already perfect." In respect to sanctification they had not yet arrived; they still had a little way to go because the reasons for their intercession were somewhat dubious. To begin with, they assured Jesus that the man was worthy. Really, it would have been better if they had left that bit out. Jesus was in the habit of responding to human need, not to human worth. The worth or unworth of a person in need had always been irrelevant. God's actions do not depend on human worth. Christ died for us while we were yet sinners. Furthermore, the elders of the Jews came up with a poor definition of worthiness. The centurion is worthy, they said, "for he loveth our nation, and he hath built us a synagogue." "He scratched our back; now we'll scratch his. One good turn deserves another. What's more, he's respectable. He's got class. He's a church worker and all that. There'll be no talk or scandal attached to helping him. It's O.K., Jesus. You can go ahead." One could be committing the sin of putting the worst construction on what these elders of the Jews said and did, but it does seem remotely possible that they were still in the flesh and still in this world and that even their righteousnesses (like so many of yours and mine) were as filthy rags.

III. Anyhow, the whole thing was straightened out, refreshingly straightened out, by the plea of the centurion himself a few minutes later. To begin with, the centurion denied the worth attributed to him. He was not worthy enough for Jesus to come to his house. For that matter, he was not even worthy enough to approach Jesus in person. "Please don't go to any fuss, Jesus, on my account. Just say 'a word, and my servant shall be healed.' " And it wasn't false modesty either. The centurion wasn't resorting to the timeworn trick of bragging by being humble. He wasn't being gushy or phoney or patronizing. Come to think of it, he claimed to be a man of rank, having people under him, who came and went as he ordered. As the world saw it, he had a certain amount of worth, yes. But as God saw it, no. Because what God saw was his sins. And they made him unworthy.

IV. And in so doing, the centurion came up with an adequate definition of worth. Worth is unworth, the knowledge of one's unworth, a genuine knowledge of one's unworth, an accurate knowledge of one's unworth. In God's scheme of things, he is worthy who is unworthy, who knows he is unworthy, who sincerely knows he is unworthy, and who knows as precisely as it is humanly possible where he is unworthy and where he isn't, who can simultaneously recognize his talents and his sins. Jesus put His stamp of approval on the definition of worth personified by this centurion. "I say unto you, I have not found so great faith, no, not in Israel." Such men are ripe for the Lord Jesus and His saving acts, His life, His death, and His resurrection. To such "worthy unworthies" (to coin a paradox), the Gospel gets through, gets through for all its worth, not because awareness of one's unworth merits salvation, but because God-manufactured repentance is a prerequisite for that God-worked faith through which we appropriate God-prepared salvation.

FRANCIS C. ROSSOW

Third Sunday After Pentecost

EPISTLE   Galatians 1:11–24 (KJV)

Sermon Notes/Introduction

In recent years people have shown much interest in being "open and genuine" in relationships with others. To this end we have been encouraged to become aware of the "real me." The introspective search for the "real me" has been stimulated in the interest of better mental health by behavioral scientists like Carl Jung and Fritz Perls, by Eric Berne with his popular books *Games People Play* and *What Do You Say After You Say Hello?* and by Thomas Harris in *I'm OK—You're OK*. In the "journey into self," as styled by Dr. Carl Rogers in sensitivity groups, the goal is usually self-acceptance and a wholesome self-awareness based on the acceptance, support, and encouragement of a group. But when we take a "journey into self" on the basis of God's holy, saving Word, the Bible, we discover our "real me" in the mirror of God's righteous law. This law tells us, from God's perfect creation, that our heavenly Father has a right to demand perfection or death, and we are driven to our knees weeping in repentance until a loving heavenly Father bids us look to Golgotha and Joseph's empty tomb. There we find forgiveness and hope in Jesus, our Savior; there we come alive in faith by the power of the Holy Spirit working through Word and Sacrament. In the spiritual realm, on the basis of God's saving Word and guided by His Holy Spirit, we consider how the Gospel of God's grace confronts and challenges the "real me."

Sermon Outline
THE GOSPEL OF GOD'S GRACE CONFRONTS AND CHALLENGES THE "REAL ME"

I. The confrontation.
  A. Paul's confrontation—this Gospel of God's grace "is not after man" (v. 11).
    1. It did not come from the "real me"—not from within me.
      a. Before his conversion, following his own instincts, he was zealous for human tradition (v. 14).
      b. He "persecuted the church of God and wasted it" (v. 13).
    2. Nor did Paul learn this saving truth from other human sources.
      a. He did not receive it "of man" (direct transmission—v. 12).
      b. He did not learn it (by learning interaction—v. 12).
      c. He "conferred not with flesh and blood" (v. 16).
      d. He did not go up to Jerusalem, the center of faith (v. 17).
      e. He spent only 15 days with Peter (v. 18).
      f. He briefly saw James, the Lord's brother. (There is hesitation in mentioning him, since he might not be considered an authority, certainly not an apostle—v. 19.)

g. He was "unknown by face" among the churches of Judea (v. 22).

3. He was the picture of a man zealously seeking by way of the traditions of the fathers (the Law) to work out his own salvation.
   a. He achieved nobility and status among equals in his own nation (v. 14).
   b. He recognized the futility of this only after he was called by God's grace (v. 15).

B. Our confrontation follows a similar pattern.
   1. Our "real me" is characterized by compromising and accommodating God's just law and results in an "All-American" concept of goodness: Be a good neighbor, a "nice guy," and God will not be able to do anything but love you and accept you.
   2. Our "real me," uninformed and untouched by the Gospel of God's grace in Christ Jesus, is tempted to rewrite God's holy law to meet limited capabilities (Golden Rule morality).
   3. The "real me," desperate and oftentimes despairing, still meets with frustration (continuing poverty, squandered resources, greed, crime, war).
   4. A righteous God sternly informs us that we are "dead in trespasses and sins," that "no good thing dwells in us."

II. The challenge.
A. For Paul—a Spirit-inspired response to God's power and will.
   1. God called (*kaleō* [v. 15]: the call to faith in Christ as Savior and the call to apostolic responsibility— it is used in both senses) Paul to an apostleship to which he was divinely destined.
   2. Divinely empowered and a wise builder, Paul based the foundation of his faith on the Gospel, the preaching of Christ crucified and raised from the dead.
   3. Paul relied not on the human "real me" but on the revelation of Jesus Christ (v. 12).
   4. Led by God's Holy Spirit, he reflected on God's grace in the Gospel in "Arabia" (v. 17).
   5. Because of all this God was indeed glorified in Paul and in his ministry to the Gentiles (v. 24).

B. For us—we gratefully acknowledge our sure salvation in Christ Jesus and resolve, empowered by God's Holy

Spirit, to live lives that will glorify God and serve humanity in His name according to His will.

1. All uncertainty and doubt are banished by God's gracious plan to save humanity from sin through the vicarious suffering, death, and resurrection of our Lord.
2. God's glory shines through this world-saving mission of our Lord to enlighten the whole world groaning beneath the crushing burden of sin.
3. God's glory shines through His faithful servants, like St. Paul, who appeared in the course of human history with providential justice and mercy.
4. The Christ who is full of grace and truth touches each one of us, transforms the "real me," strengthens the "new man" to combat the "Old Adam," and sanctifies our lives by the influence of His Holy Spirit working through Word and Sacrament.
5. Thus the "new me," given life by the Spirit of God, takes over the "real me" and lives out a productive, significant life of service to Christ and to neighbor, thereby glorifying God (*simul justus et peccator*—Martin Luther).

MARTIN A. HAENDSCHKE

Third Sunday After Pentecost

GOSPEL   Luke 7:11–17

Sermon Notes/Introduction

1. Tenses of verbs contrasted: (a) *eporeuthē* (aor.) versus *suneporeuonto* (imperf.) (v. 11)—Jesus "went" is a simple completed action in past tense versus the continued following of the disciples and the crowd. (b) *ēggisen* (aor.) versus *exekomizeto* (imperf.) (v. 12)—Jesus "came near" the gates is a simple completed act in past time, but the son "was being carried out" in a prolonged retinue of mourners. (c) *elaben* (aor.) versus *edoxazon* (imperf.) (v. 16)—Fear *seized* all as a completed fact, but the glorifying of God continued for some time. (d) *mē klaie* (pres. impv.) (v. 13) versus *egerthēti* (aor. impv.) (v. 14)—To the widow who was weeping, Jesus said, "Stop weeping" ("Cease what you are doing"); to the corpse, who was lying still, Jesus' command involved the beginning of a new action: "Arise." Note that the first three pairs of verbs

are in the indicative and denote punctiliar or continuous action in past time; the fourth pair, in the imperative mood, denotes types of action rather than time, since all imperatives refer to the future.

2. Contrast of two processions (vv. 11–12): The one entering the city no doubt is happy and filled with hope because Jesus is in its midst; the one leaving the city is sad and without hope since it is a funeral procession. The focal point of the one group is Jesus, the source of life; the focal point of the other is death as represented by the corpse.

3. (a) *ochlos polus* (v. 11) implies a retinue of spectators wondering what to expect next from the man from Nazareth. (b) *tethnēkōs* (v. 12), the perfect participle, stresses the continued effect of the son's death, with no human hope of revival. (c) *monogenēs* (v. 12) here means simply "only" son, the same word as in John 1:14, where it also can be translated merely as "only." (d) *tē mētri autou* (v. 12) is a dative case, which suggests more than the son "of his mother" (which would be in the genitive case); he was the sole support "for/to his mother." Her husband had died previously, as she was a widow; now her last hope for financial support also was gone. (e) *esplagchnisthē* (v. 13) in Greek suggests stronger emotion than "had compassion"; the root meaning is "poured out his bowels." The ancients at times made no distinction between the organs below and above the diaphragm; cf. Philemon 7, 12, and 20 in the King James Version. Today we would prefer "poured out his heart" to her. (f) *phobos* (v. 16) could be rendered "awe" or "amazement" rather than "fear" or "fright." Jesus has done nothing to cause fear, but His action should arouse respect. However, some of the spectators could also have experienced "fear" of a person who could overcome death. (g) *Prophētēs* (v. 16) indicates that the people saw Jesus primarily as parallel to an Old Testament prophet who at times performed supernatural deeds involving the conquering of sickness, death, and other bodily ills, not as the Savior from sin and the Redeemer of condemned sinners. (h) *epeskepsato* (v. 16): God, in their opinion, "visited His people" in Jesus, as He had done through Moses and the prophets, but the crowd failed to recognize Jesus for His full benefit to people as the promised Messiah. The root meaning of the verb is "look at," "examine with the eye"; that is, God continually has all people in His purview. (i) *laos* (v. 16) is the usual word for the Jewish people. That is, the crowd considered themselves to be a special race because God had chosen them as descendants

of Abraham. They apparently had forgotten the event of the previous day, when Jesus also helped a Gentile.

Jesus had shown His power over illness by healing the servant of a Roman centurion (a Gentile). He now exhibits His ability to overcome physical death. He shows Himself as "Healer of All Our Ills."

Sermon Outline
HEALER OF ALL OUR ILLS

I. The scene (vv. 11–12).
   A. The happy procession of disciples and spectators eagerly follows Jesus, a worker of miracles, hoping and expecting to witness more wonders.
   B. The sad procession of relatives and friends mournfully accompanies a widow who has lost her last means of support; they are without hope or expectation of any reversal of fortune.
II. The solution (vv. 13–15).
   A. Jesus pours out His heart and He acts. While the two groups follow either Him or the corpse, He is the source of the solution to the tragedy of the widow. He alone as God's Son has the power to heal the predicament of human beings.
   B. Jesus' action reverses things for all concerned in the sad procession. The widow is to stop weeping. Those carrying the corpse stop walking. The corpse sits up, speaks, and is restored to the mother.
III. The sequel (vv. 16–17).
   A. Both crowds experience awe, respect, reverence, and (no doubt, in some cases) fear as a result of Jesus' amazing conquest over death.
   B. They give God credit for Jesus' power over human ills and assume that He is equal to the prophets of old, through whom God frequently spoke and acted. The people consider themselves God's chosen people as a result of their birth.
   C. They spread the report of that day's miraculous event throughout all Judea and the surrounding area. They report that God once more has sent a prophet to His chosen race.

Although feeling the presence of God in Jesus of Nazareth, the crowds did not acknowledge and confess Him as the Messiah. Their understanding perhaps fell short of the centurion's from Capernaum in the previous pericope. We, through God's grace, have the advantage of hindsight afforded by Good Friday and Easter. Through the gift of faith engendered by the Holy Spirit, we acknowledge and confess Jesus as the Son of God, our Savior and Redeemer from sin.

Yet we remain and live in an imperfect world, full of sickness, death, and other misfortunes. Our pericope emphasizes that Jesus, our Savior for eternity, is also the healer of our mortal ills. We should use human knowledge supplied through medical science, for God works through human agents. He also performs miraculous healings today—both when He is approached in prayer/request (cf. the preceding pericope) and at times before He is asked (present pericope).

In brief, faith in Christ as our Redeemer and trust in Him as our healer of all types of ills will give us the peace that transcends human understanding and that we need in a world of outward and inward turmoil. Death, our final enemy, pertains to the realm of darkness. Jesus, who came to proclaim and exhibit the kingdom of God, performed this miracle as an indication of the final destiny God intends for all Christians.

ROBERT G. HOERBER

Fourth Sunday After Pentecost

EPISTLE   Galatians 2:11–21 (RSV)

Sermon Notes/Introduction

The central thought of the Epistle is that Christians should abandon every suggestion of salvation by works. The goal of the sermon is that the hearers will so rejoice in God's grace in Christ that they want nothing to supplement it. The problem is that we, in our weakness, do not live as people saved by God's grace. The means to the goal is the full impact of God's "not guilty" verdict on us because of Jesus' work.

"The question of justification is an elusive thing," Luther said, "not in itself . . . but so far as we are concerned" (*Lectures on Galatians 1535: Chapters 1–4,* ed. and trans. Jaroslav Pelikan; *Luther's Works,* American Edition [St. Louis: Concordia Publishing House, 1963], 26:63). Indeed, we marvel that the great apostle Peter could send such deceptive signals about this all-important matter. In utter humility we examine "The Most Elusive Reality."

Sermon Outline
THE MOST ELUSIVE REALITY

I. As far as we are concerned, justification is most elusive.
  A. Though we know better, we often make Christianity a matter of good conduct.
    1. This seems to make our religion practical.
    2. It seems to maintain our responsibility to respond to God.
  B. If Christianity is good conduct, we can look to others for approval. But we fear not getting it (v. 12).
  C. When desire for approval motivates us, we fall into hypocrisy and compromise the Gospel (see v. 13 and compare FC SD vi 16).
  D. If we compromise the Gospel, we cannot have its power (see v. 14a).
II. In itself firm and sure, the reality of justification takes hold of us.
  A. The sinner is righteous because of Christ.
    1. We are righteous not by works (good conduct) but through faith in Christ (v. 16).
    2. Our goodness fails as much as anyone's. Yet in God's view our sins are covered, else Christ would be a servant of sin (v. 17). In Him our justification (God's approval of us) is
      a. complete (2 Sam. 12:13b; Ps. 85:2–3; 1 John 1:7; see Ap XV 12); and
      b. constant (Ps. 32:1–2; Is. 43:25; Rom. 8:1; see Ap IV 317).
    3. Effectively speaking, only unbelief can harm us. It rejects Christ and returns instead to the condemning Law (Gal. 2:18).
  B. The dead live in Christ.
    1. There is no reason to go back. In Christ we have died to the Law (*dia nomou*, v. 19—Jesus' active and passive obedience) and live, with Him, to God.
    2. He lives in us. We receive our life from Him by faith (v. 20a).
      a. He "removes and absorbs all the evils that torment and afflict me" (Luther).
      b. He empowers spiritual life: " 'Paul is dead.' 'Who then is living?' 'The Christian' " (Luther).
    3. The basis of His exaltation—also in our hearts and

lives—remains His sacrifice for us (v. 20b; see
1 John 4:10).
C. The "Defeated One" is glorified: Christ Himself.
1. There is every reason to stay with Christ's grace.
Its glory consists in His death, which cannot fail to
provide us righteousness (Gal. 2:21; see John
12:23).
2. The highest way to worship Christ is to avoid nul-
lifying His grace or belittling His death (see Ap IV
154, which comments on Luke 7:36–50). This is
practical in the best sense.

Sheep rescued from a burning barn often run back into
the flames. We are the sheep of God's pasture (Ps 100:3).
Why run to the Law? Instead, we "enter His gates with thanksgiving," for "His steadfast love endures forever" (vv. 4–5).

KEN SCHURB

Fourth Sunday After Pentecost

GOSPEL   Luke 7:36–50 (KJV)

Sermon Notes/Introduction

I'd like to do two things with the Gospel just read to you:
first, deal with an old problem it poses, a problem so familiar
that it hardly bothers us anymore; and second, extract from
this Gospel a new thought that may prove exciting.

Sermon Outline

THE RELATIONSHIP OF FORGIVENESS AND LOVE

I. As you perhaps are aware, *for* can be a pesky word. Sometimes it describes a causal relationship. Take this sentence,
for instance: The window is wet, for it is raining. Here we
would agree that the rain is the cause of the wet window.
But sometimes the word *for* describes a different relationship. Take this sentence, for example: It is raining, for the
window is wet. Certainly, you will agree that the wet window did not cause the rain. Rather, the wet window is the
proof or the evidence of the rain. Now take a look at the
Gospel. "Her sins, which are many, are forgiven, *for* she
loved much" (v. 47). Lifted out of context, the passage
might sound as if it were expressing a causal relationship,
as if it were saying that the reason the woman was forgiven

was because of her lavish display of love. She washed Jesus' feet, wiped them with her hair, kissed them, and anointed them with oil. The result? Jesus forgave her. But such an interpretation would contradict not only the Bible elsewhere but even the particular parable that Jesus told Simon right before He forgave the woman her sins. Neither debtor, you recall, did anything to merit the cancellation of his debt. Actually, the correct interpretation is the opposite. The reason the woman displayed so much love was because of her having been forgiven. The lavish display of love toward Jesus was the proof or the evidence of a prior forgiveness. Forgiveness the cause, love the result—that is the correct formula, and not the other way around.

II. So much for the polemics. Now for a fascinating new thought, new to me at least. This Gospel suggests an intriguing correlation between sin and love. Which debtor in the parable loved his creditor more? The one who had the bigger debt erased from the books. What does Jesus say? "Her sins, which are *many,* are forgiven, for she loved much." The more forgiven, the more you love; the less forgiven, the less you love. How's that for a new way of confessing yours sins? Not just in sackcloth and ashes. Not just in crying, "Mea culpa! Mea culpa!" Not just in singing dirges. Not just in the confessional booth or in the public service. And not just in recognizing broken resolutions and renewing them. But in loving. Every deed of love we do somehow says, "There's a sin in my past." There seems to be a strange connection between the amount of love and the amount of our sin.

A. Now the obvious error we are flirting with is that a premium, it seems, is being put on sin. Like some of St. Paul's addressees, we are tempted to conclude, "Let us, therefore, sin that love may abound." Or another error is possible: a lid, it seems, is being placed on love. If love is a confession of sins, if the amount of our love is somehow indicative of the amount of our sin, we may in a discreet, respectable moment conclude, "For goodness' sake, let's stop loving before *all* of our skeletons are hauled out!"

B. Now I'm not too eager to tackle these errors because, for one thing, I'm sure they're more hypothetical than actual—who in the world would think this way anyhow, and it sounds as if I am just setting up some straw men to knock down—and, another thing, I don't want any explanation to emasculate the intriguing correlation between sin and love that we have already suggested. One can sometimes play so safe with a text that he completely negates it. Some texts, I believe, are meant to puzzle us—it's good that they do—and maybe this is one of those. The paradox should be retained, not explained.

1. But perhaps in dealing with this text it would be helpful to keep two things in mind. One is that it isn't the sin that triggers the love but the forgiveness of the sin. It wasn't the five hundred pence that caused the debtor to love his creditor more, but the remission of the five hundred pence. "Her sins, which are many, are *forgiven,* for she loved much." The correlation is not merely between sin and love but between forgiven sin and love. The cross, you see, is needed to complete our formula. Hence every act of love we do says, "There's a sin in my past, yes, a lot of them, in fact, but, thank Jesus, they've been forgiven."

2. The other thing to keep in mind is that it isn't the amount of sin that counts but the awareness of that amount. Actually, the disreputable woman of the Gospel was no more an evildoer than Simon, that pillar of respectability. She was a sinner. So was Simon. The woman was just a bit more obvious about it, that's all. Simon simply played it cooler. After all, sin isn't a thing you measure by the number. It's a state of being, a condition you carry around with you whether you are a member of a red-light district or a country club. The only difference between sinner woman and sinner Simon is that the woman knew her condition. She was conscious of the number of her sins. She was aware of the amount.

If, then, your sins are many—and who of us doesn't this hit right smack between the eyes?—there is hope for you. Since you have much to be forgiven, you have the potential for loving much. But only if you are aware of that "much." And only if, through Jesus, you are forgiven that "much." Those are the conditions that in God's goodness can bring good out of your evil.

FRANCIS C. ROSSOW

Fifth Sunday After Pentecost

EPISTLE   Galatians 3:23–29

Sermon Notes/Introduction

A large recreational van roared by me on the toll road flaunting a prominent rear bumper sticker that said, "We're spending our kids' inheritance." Boasting of our temporal earthly pleasures illustrates what St. Paul meant by the law of the flesh. Since our materialistic appetites can never be satisfied and continually war against our private and social best interests, God gave the laws of Mt. Sinai as a disciplinarian to restrain us from self-destruction. But neither the greedy passions of our flesh nor the Law given to restrain us can ever provide the breakthrough to eternal salvation. Only the God-given inheritance of Christ's saving grace can make us "People with a Promise."

Sermon Outline
PEOPLE WITH A PROMISE

I. We are reborn as "sons of God" (v. 26).
   A. People with a promise see their origin as children created by their heavenly Father.
   B. People with a promise see their relationship to God enhancing life.
II. We are clothed with Christ (v. 27).
   A. People with a promise find identity in their saving relationship with God through Christ.
   B. People with a promise find motivation and assurance through the role of Christ's grace.
      1. They know that by grace through faith they are properly clothed for the wedding banquet of God's Son.
      2. They are motivated to share their clothes with those who are needy, thus expressing their faith and love.
III. We are baptized in the Spirit (v. 27).
   A. People with a promise are washed clean of unrighteousness.
      1. The water of Baptism washes away sin and assures us of forgiveness.
      2. The word of Baptism miraculously creates and sustains faith, whereby we trust in the saving promise of the Spirit.

B. People with a promise are born again into the kingdom
of God.

IV. We are justified by faith (v. 24).

A. People with a promise are given the justifying righteousness of Christ as a gift.

1. They no longer endure the shadow of the custo-
dian, the Law, to worry them about their salvation.

2. They have the glorious liberty of the children of
God with an inheritance that is incorruptible.

B. People with a promise are given the gift of faith and
are assured of the heavenly home.

V. We are unified in freedom (v. 28).

A. People with a promise are freed from divisive and par-
ticularistic prejudices to move toward inclusive unity in
Christ's kingdom.

B. People with a promise are freed from oppressive bond-
ages for servanthood among the friends of Jesus.

C. People with a promise are freed from the separating
interpretations of sexist selfishness for oneness as
brothers and sisters in the family of Christ.

1. Sexists create discouraging separations of men and
women.

2. Christians edify, love, and help one another in the
family of Christ.

Without the saving grace of Christ proclaimed to Abraham, we have no promise. The promised inheritance of salvation is not something we earn, nor is it something that can
be taken away from us by a selfish generation of pleasure-
seeking people who do not concern themselves with the future
(the attitude expressed by the travel trailer's bumper sticker).
The most precious inheritance that can be communicated to
us is that we are secure as divinely destined people with a
promise of salvation.

HAROLD H. ZIETLOW

Fifth Sunday After Pentecost

GOSPEL   Luke 9:18–24 (RSV)

Sermon Notes/Introduction

1. A comparison of this text with its Synoptic parallels
yields some helpful insights (cf. Mark 8:27–35; Matt. 16:13–

25).

The account in Matthew makes it especially clear that Peter (who represents the apostles) is right on target when he confesses Jesus as "the Son of the living God" (16:16). Peter keenly recognizes and boldly confesses that Jesus is the expected Messiah and that He is God. Jesus confirms that Peter has made the proper confession by asserting that the Father has revealed this truth to him (v. 17), and that the whole church will be built on faith in this confession (v. 18).

But both Mark and Matthew help us to understand that the apostles' expectations about Jesus, expressed by Peter, did not include suffering, death, and resurrection. Deceived by Satan, their expectations were colored by the common Messianic misconception of Jesus as the king of an earthly realm (cf. Mark 8:32–33; Matt. 16:22–23). Because of this misconception, closely tied to the misunderstood term "Messiah," Jesus commands His apostles not to advertise that He is "the Christ" (the Greek equivalent for the Hebrew "Messiah"; see Luke 9:21).

2. St. Luke's account reveals three responses to the question, Who is Jesus? (1) the crowds (*ochloi*) view Jesus as a great prophet of God (v. 19); (2) Peter (representing the view of the apostles) properly confesses Jesus as the divine Messiah (v. 20), but misunderstood as a utopian king, not the Suffering Servant; and (3) Jesus proclaims He is the "Son of Man" who must suffer, die, and rise on the third day (v. 22). The term "Son of Man" (cf. Dan. 7:13–14) packs a lot of Gospel and is the corrective for the misunderstood term "Messiah"; for the Son of Man is the God-Man who, though highly exalted, humbles Himself, suffers death, is glorified again, and comes to judge the world.

As the preacher unravels this material, he will want to help his hearers identify aspects of their lives that display the false views of Jesus (Law) and proclaim the correct views of Him (Gospel).

3. The proper identity or nature of Jesus' disciples follows directly from His identity as the Son of Man. The disciple is one who does not seek to preserve (*sōzein*) his own sinful, selfish nature with its false goals and ideals but gives himself over to Christ and the way of His kingdom, which is the cross (vv. 23–24). As he does so by the power of Christ, the Son of Man saves and preserves (*sōzein*) him.

Here again the preacher will want to make pertinent Law/ Gospel applications for his hearers.

4. The goal of the sermon is to motivate hearers to probe their present expectations of Jesus and discipleship to see where they are false and to rediscover the true identity of Jesus as the Son of Man who suffered, died, and rose for us, and who now empowers us daily to take up our cross and follow Him.

The church in every age, and every Christian in his/her life, is confronted with the same radical questions: Who is Jesus? What is my role as His disciple? History shows that basic responses to those questions rise again and again. Today's Gospel outlines the inadequate as well as the faithful responses. Which are ours?

Sermon Outline
THE JESUS QUESTIONS

I. Who is Jesus?
  A. Many believe that Jesus is nothing more than a prophet of God.
    1. The crowds in Jesus' day held that He was John the Baptizer, Elijah, or some other great prophet risen from the dead (v. 19).
    2. Many in our day hold that Jesus was just another prophet—e.g., Mormons, Jehovah's Witnesses, etc.
    3. We sometimes treat Jesus as just a great prophet—e.g., when we are more interested in Him as a model for morality than as Savior from sin.
  B. Some correctly profess faith in Jesus as the Christ but disregard the cross and expect Him to establish a utopia on earth.
    1. As expressed by Peter, the apostles harbored Messianic delusions and expected a kingdom without the cross (v. 20; see Sermon Note 1).
    2. Are the present fascinations with spectacular experiences, the "electronic church," and the "theology of glory" of television's Christian "clubs" symptoms of the same false expectation?
  C. Jesus claims to be the Son of Man, who came to suffer, die, and rise again for sin.
    1. Jesus proclaimed this to His apostles (v. 22; see Sermon Note 2).
    2. Jesus proclaims the same to us in Word and sacraments.
II. What is the role of Jesus' disciple?

   A. Some claim to be Jesus' disciples while preserving their own selfish, sinful views and ideals of Jesus (see Sermon Note 3).

     1. The crowd of Jesus' day and to a degree His apostles followed their own dreams (v. 24).

     2. How often do we disregard what we know to be God's will and follow a Jesus of our own making?

   B. The true disciple follows Jesus in the way of the cross (v. 23; see Sermon Note 3).

     1. Jesus' apostles were led through Good Friday to Easter, to suffering and martyrdom.

     2. In Baptism our old sinful self is crucified with Christ and a new self rises, whom Christ empowers to follow Him (Gal. 3:26–29).

May God the Holy Spirit grant us always the true vision of Jesus as our Savior from sin and the faithfulness to follow as His disciples in the way of the cross.

TERENCE R. GROTH

Sixth Sunday After Pentecost

EPISTLE   Galatians 5:1, 13–25 (KJV)

Sermon Notes/Introduction

1. This particular pericope is clearly related to the Pentecost season to which it has been assigned in that it speaks of the miracle that the Holy Spirit still works in us today, centuries after the first Pentecost. That the Holy Spirit enters us at all is part of the miracle. And what He achieves there is an even greater miracle, for He gives us spiritual life, a life whose marks (vv. 22–24) are every bit as astounding as the tongues of fire, the mighty wind, and the gifts of language that characterized the first Pentecost.

2. The Epistle, of course, contains a familiar Scripture paradox: that we can be free only by being slaves to Christ and to one another. Verse 13 best states this paradox, reminding us in one breath that we are "called unto liberty" and yet urging us in the next breath that we should "serve one another" (*douleuete* being the Greek word used). Technically, no one is ever free. One can be either a slave of sin (John 8:34) or a slave of God (Rom. 6:22). But in the latter slavery the Christian discovers, to his pleasant surprise, that he is ac-

tually free (John 8:32; Rom. 8:1).

3. The Epistle is another familiar reminder that Christian liberty does not mean license, that Christian freedom does not mean licentiousness. Obviously, we are free from all human commandments intended to serve as substitutes for doctrine. To be sure, we are free from the ceremonial laws of the Old Testament. Thanks to Jesus, we are free from the all too easily self-imposed burden of keeping the moral Law for the sake of earning heaven. Above all, we are free from the condemnation of the Law, damnation. But we are still expected to "delight" and to "walk" in the law of the Lord (Psalm 1), a requirement so easily fulfilled by one activity: "love" (Gal. 5:14), an activity, incidentally, that God Himself will perform in us (v. 22). Indeed, His "yoke is easy" and His "burden is light"! That such adherence to God's law is, paradoxically, freedom is confirmed by Paul's mildly humorous observation in verse 23 (after listing a host of virtues): "against such there is no law" (i.e., in performing such virtues we are really not in the realm of Law at all).

4. Verse 15 uses imagery ("bite," "devour," "consume") especially appropriate to the "dog-eat-dog" world we often describe ourselves as living in today.

5. "Flesh" (v. 16), of course, is not "the body" but "the sin-power in the body" (human rebellion against God). It is not "avoirdupois" but "corrupted human nature." This is especially evident from the ear-filling catalog of sins mentioned in verses 19–21, some of which are clearly sins of the mind rather than sins of the body ("emulations" and "envyings," for example).

6. "Faith" (v. 22) is better translated "fidelity" or "faithfulness." "Temperance" (v. 23) had a broader meaning then than the word has now. Modern usage so often restricts the word to the proper use of alcohol. But it is the Holy Spirit's intention that we apply the word to all areas of life: food, pleasure, work, emotion, etc.

7. Mention of Christ in verse 24 calls to Paul's mind His crucifixion, leading Paul to state one of his favorite concepts (cf. Rom. 6:1–11; Gal. 2:20), namely, that we Christians share in Christ's crucifixion. Incidentally, there is a possible tie-in between this concept and the circumcision (vv. 2–12) advocated by some of Paul's readers. *Circumcision* of literal flesh is not needed, no. But *crucifixion* of the flesh (i.e., the body of sin) is needed, yes! Paul's proposal, in a sense, is more revolutionary than that of his readers. Paul goes them one

better.

Paul begins chapter 5 with an urgent appeal to "stand fast" in the freedom Christ has given us (v. 1). Why does he consider it so important? What is such freedom like? And how do we get it? We can best answer these questions by considering the theme: "Freedom in Christ."

Sermon Outline
FREEDOM IN CHRIST

I. The necessity for freedom.
   A. The Law enslaves us and eventually kills us eternally.
      1. Bible characters in the Old Testament Reading and in the Gospel for this day testify to this.
      2. Both the Epistle (vv. 1b and 17b) and parallel passages (e.g., John 8:34; Rom. 6:19, 23) testify to this.
   B. Only Christ can free us and make us alive forever.
      1. He promised us such freedom and life (John 8:32, 36).
      2. He kept His promise: He made freedom and life available to us through His life, damnation, death, and resurrection (Rom. 6:23; 8:1; Gal. 5:1, 18).
II. The character of freedom.
   A. Freedom in Christ does not mean license (Gal. 5:13).
      1. Consider the characteristics of such license (vv. 19–21).
      2. Consider the results of such license.
         a. It is destructive of others and self (v. 15).
         b. It prevents us from inheriting the kingdom of God (v. 21).
   B. Freedom in Christ means loving one another.
      1. Consider the characteristics of such love (vv. 22–23).
      2. Consider the results of such love.
         a. It obviously helps our neighbor (v. 13).
         b. It fulfills the Law (v. 14).
III. The means to freedom.
   A. By God's power our old self, our flesh, is killed.
      1. The Holy Spirit wars against our flesh (v. 17a).
      2. He crucifies it through Christ's crucifixion (v. 24).
   B. By God's power a new self is created.
      1. The Holy Spirit leads us out from "under the Law" (v. 18).

2. The Holy Spirit makes us alive through Christ's resurrection (v. 25a; Rom. 6:4).

Since we're alive, let's look alive. "If we live in the Spirit, let us also walk in the Spirit."

FRANCIS C. ROSSOW

Sixth Sunday After Pentecost

GOSPEL   Luke 9:51–62 (RSV)

Sermon Notes/Introduction

1. This pericope seems to begin a major section of the Gospel according to Luke. As the opening verse stresses, the emphasis is on the growing hostility to the Lord and His eventual and impending Passion.

2. The Old Testament Reading in Series C for this Sunday is 1 Kings 19:14–21. Elijah laments that the people of Israel had broken the covenant and slain the prophets. "And I, even I only, am left; and they seek my life, to take it away" (1 Kings 19:14). The Lord assures Elijah that, despite the gloomy prospects, the hand of the Lord is still powerful and the debacle will not be total. As we apply this to the position of Jesus, we appreciate the reminder that God is in control, no matter how evil the days may become.

3. The Epistle is Gal. 5:1, 13–25. The problem for the Galatians is knowing how to live in evil days. In spite of religious errorists and in spite of the seeming fragility of the true Gospel, we are to remember that its power does not fail but gives believers great spiritual and moral power to live nobly in its freedom.

4. There is a note of hope in the description of Jesus' Passion as the time for His being received up. There will be suffering and death, but the culmination lies even beyond the resurrection. The Suffering Servant will be the ascended Lord!

5. Why did the Samaritans not receive Him? They did not like the direction He was taking. He was going to Jerusalem. He was not coming to them. He was ignoring the religion of Mt. Gerizim, and this did not please them.

6. Verses 54–56 are accorded a "C" rating in the United Bible Society's apparatus. The preacher will have to determine whether he wishes to use these verses. It is reasonable to suppose that they might have been omitted because they are un-

complimentary to the apostles and might even be seen as casting aspersions on Elijah. The event is homiletically useful in pointing out that Jesus will not use or allow His disciples to use physical force in the battle that lies ahead.

7. The reports of three encounters with potential disciples stress the same theme, that is, the cost of discipleship. The cost must be counted, and nothing in the worldly life must interfere. We are not told what any of these men decided. Therefore, we should not use them as "whipping boys" in the sermon.

8. One needs to guard against undue harshness in preaching on this text. None of the men concerned with discipleship is manifestly evil. The point is not that they were bidden to turn from evil ways before they could be disciples. Attending to the funeral of a father and bidding farewell to one's family are natural and not evil in themselves. The question is of primary loyalty, even in the choice of acceptable and normally laudable practices.

9. Likewise, to interpret Jesus' words about letting the dead bury their dead to mean that only the spiritually dead should be concerned about burying the physically dead will get one into a difficult position pastorally. Do we not "officiate" at funerals? Do we not encourage Christian burial practices? A person who has died is beyond the reach of our prayers and preaching. If it comes to a choice between disposing of the body of a dead person and proclaiming the Gospel to one whose eternal welfare is still in the balance, the choice is obvious.

The preacher will find some interesting comments on these verses and some excellent quotations in *The Cost of Discipleship* by Dietrich Bonhoeffer (Macmillan: New York, 1959). We speak glibly at times of being "Jesus' disciples." Do we understand and appreciate what it means? Do we truly want to be disciples? The Gospel confronts us with the challenge of being a Christian disciple. It asks us to examine our relationship to Christ not only in what we believe about Him but in how faith becomes active in Christian living.

Sermon Outline

THE CHALLENGE OF CHRISTIAN DISCIPLESHIP

I. Discipleship is our response to the invitation to follow a remarkable Lord.

   A. His path to saviorhood led to suffering and death.

      1. He set His face toward Jerusalem to suffer and die as the atoning Lamb of God.

      2. His love for humanity moved Him to assume the burden of saviorhood.

   B. His path to saviorhood led to glory.

      1. The ultimate end of suffering, crucifixion, death, and resurrection was His ascension and His sitting at the right hand of the Father.

      2. To follow Him is to follow the Lord of lords and King of kings.

      3. He lays claim to those for whom He died by sending His disciples to proclaim the Good News of His rulership.

II. Discipleship is a challenge to serve our remarkable Lord.

   A. It is a challenge that He issues and that we do not assume for ourselves on our own terms.

   B. It is a challenge to trust the power of His Gospel and to reject all human religions and processes.

   C. It is a challenge to make the kingdom of God the first priority in our lives and to resist the temptation to be drawn into the toils of a secular view of life.

Who is able to be a disciple? Left to ourselves this is impossible. The Holy Spirit calls us by the Gospel, enlightens us with His gifts, and strengthens us in discipleship. He who issues the challenge supplies the spiritual power to respond and to grow in discipleship (see Phil. 3:12–14).

RICHARD J. SCHULTZ

Seventh Sunday After Pentecost

EPISTLE   Galatians 6:1–10, 14–16 (RSV)

Sermon Notes/Introduction

This pericope speaks especially about our good works: to bear one another's burden, to "forgive those who trespass against us," to share all good things with him who teaches us, and to do good. But the apostle Paul does not forget to make it clear that these good works come only from a "new creation," from those who are able to "sow to the Spirit."

1. The natural human impulse is to act, to judge one's act, and to approve or correct oneself (conscience).

2. For this reason it is so difficult for us to understand and

impossible for us to believe that God forgives without our being able to correct our mistakes and to justify ourselves before God. (This is due to our natural *opinio legis.*)

3. God has to change our minds (*metanoia*) and make us accept forgiveness by faith in Christ (1 Cor. 2:6–16).

4. The question is why Paul can insist with the Galatians and tell them and us all: "Let Us Do Good."

Sermon Outline
LET US DO GOOD

I. We are God's new creation.
   A. Paul told the Galatians that the old creation, the natural self, has to be crucified.
      1. Our natural drive to do good leads only to restricted results.
         a. It is good as far as God's orders of creation after the fall are concerned.
         b. It is good for civil righteousness, family care, government, and care for the poor.
      2. Our natural drive ends with death.
         a. Before the justice of God it is sin, because we are sinners.
         b. It leads to corruption (Gal. 6:8) and death eternal.
      3. This world (and we are part of it) has to be crucified (v. 14) before it leads us to final death and condemnation.
   B. In Christ the world was crucified and a new creation came into being.
      1. Christ entered our world and saved it.
         a. He took our nature on Himself and fulfilled God's will perfectly: His works are holy, pure, and perfect.
         b. He suffered and died for our sins (our imperfect works) and so crucified the world in our stead (v. 14).
      2. Through faith Christ crucified us to the world.
         a. Through faith we are forgiven and saved.
         b. We were made a new creation (v. 15) by the Spirit given to us.
         c. According to the new spirit in us, we no longer want to offer our works as righteousness before God.

      3. We are now the Israel of God (v. 16), able to do good (v. 10) and sow (vv. 7–8) in this world according to the new rule (v. 16) and law of Christ (v. 2).

II. We can sow to the Spirit.

  A. We were crucified to the world and were made a new creation by faith.

    1. As the Israel of God we are still in the world.

      a. Our flesh and all its implications are still with us.

      b. But we received God's Spirit, who created a new spirit in us that fights our flesh (Luther's *simul justus et peccator*).

    2. As a new creation we were called to decide for the Spirit in all our actions.

      a. We are able to fight sin.

      b. We are able to do good, although in weakness— to sow to the Spirit (v. 8).

    3. As a new creation we have to examine again and again our own works (v. 4), repent, and receive forgiveness.

      a. In Christ crucified our sins are forgiven.

      b. In Christ our sowing to the Spirit reaps eternal life (v. 8).

  B. We are in the world; here "let us do good."

    1. We will see others sin as we do.

      a. But we have the forgiveness, and we are being asked to forgive and to restore them (v. 1) as Christ restores us.

      b. We are being asked to bear the burden with one another (v. 2).

    2. We received the freedom to give and share.

      a. The good thing we received we are being asked to share. Let us be grateful to those who taught us the good things (v. 6).

      b. We most certainly will spread the good things throughout the world ("sow to the Spirit," v. 8).

    3. As a new creation we will do good to all people.

      a. To be sure, we will start with those close to us— our family, our friends, our church.

      b. But we will want to share our love, our gifts, and our help in action with all people (v. 10).

As the Israel of God, we have peace and mercy (v. 16) through Jesus Christ. We can and will do good. Christians are active in love at that place and in that opportunity that God gives them in their daily callings. Our doing good does not have to be anything special or exceptional; our daily faithfulness in our family work, in our business, in our neighborhood, in our country, and in our church is what is meant. Let us do good while and where God gives us the opportunity.

MARTIM C. WARTH

Seventh Sunday After Pentecost

GOSPEL   Luke 10:1–9, 16 (RSV)

Sermon Notes/Introduction

"After this" (v. 1) refers to the incidents in the preceding chapter. "The Lord appointed seventy others" in addition to the twelve disciples who had already been sent on a similar mission (9:1–2). "I send you out as lambs in the midst of wolves" (v. 3) is a picture of the risks Christian preachers take, for they are seemingly weak and defenseless. Yet they are not to worry about their livelihood but are to work with a joyous abandon (v. 4a), nor are they to dally in aimless conversation with individuals they meet (v. 4b). "Peace be to this house!" is more than a common salutation (v. 5). It is an offer of divine peace, as is evident from verse 6, which describes the peace spoken of as resting on a son of peace. "And remain in the same house" (v. 7) indicates that one house and family were to be selected as the center of the work. The missionaries were also to eat whatever was set before them without fussing about clean or unclean foods (vv. 7–8). To attest that they had been sent by the Lord with an offer of divine peace, they also healed the sick (v. 9). God saw that this miraculous power was needed in the early days of the church. Those appointed hardly believed that they had such power, even after Christ had announced the gift to them (v. 17). The reception accorded their message reflects the attitude of the hearers toward Christ Himself (v. 16).

Our problem is that we sometimes wish and perhaps even expect God's kingdom to come near us through something more spectacular than human beings and the words they speak. The goal of the sermon is that the hearers would see pastors and their message as an altogether adequate way of bringing God's kingdom to people. Introductory thought: Since we associate God's kingdom (God's grace, presence, and rule in our hearts) with something superhuman—God Himself and divine goodness and strength—we tend to think that it ought to come near us in ways that transcend the ordinary. But Jesus reaffirms the down-to-earthness of God's kingdom by pointing to "God's Way of Bringing His Kingdom Near."

Sermon Outline
GOD'S WAY OF BRINGING HIS KINGDOM NEAR

I. He brings the Kingdom through men whom He sends in answer to prayer.
  A. The Lord who sends Laborers into the harvest (vv. 1, 2b; John 3:15; Eph. 4:11).
    1. He wants us to pray for pastors, and He promises to answer such prayers.
    2. He works through individual Christians to recruit men for the pastoral office, and He works through Christian congregations to call men into that office.
  B. The Lord is able to send the right laborers.
    1. He sends men who know that God will provide for their daily needs (Luke 10:4a).
    2. He sends men who are not unappreciative of what Christians give to support them (v. 7; 1 Cor. 10:27).
    3. He sends men who have a sense of urgency because the time is short (Luke 10:4b).

Is there a shortage of pastors? Pray the Lord of the harvest that He will send them. That is God's way of bringing His kingdom near. The primary task of the men God sends is to speak the Word He has given them.

II. He brings the Kingdom through words He gives these men to speak.
  A. Their words point to a remarkable peace (v. 5b).
    1. It is peace with God through His Messiah (2:14; John 14:27).
    2. It flows from the forgiveness of sins (John 20:21).
  B. These words offer peace.
    1. All who receive the Word of God in faith have peace with God ("sons of peace," Luke 10:6a), for to hear with a believing heart the Word of God spoken by the pastor is to hear Christ Himself (v. 16a).
    2. All who reject God's words in unbelief lack peace with God, for they thereby reject Christ (v. 16b).
      a. The rejection of God's offer of peace brings dire consequences (context, vv. 12, 14–15).

b. People can spurn the kingdom, and many do.

The words spoken by men seem so ordinary, so common. But if that word has its basis in God's written Word, Holy Scripture, it is God's effective way of bringing His kingdom near. God continues to bring His kingdom near through men and the words they speak—which shows how near God wants to be to us and how real He wants His kingdom to be.

GERHARD AHO

Eighth Sunday After Pentecost

EPISTLE   Colossians 1:1–14

Sermon Notes/Introduction

Paul gives thanks for the Colossians' faith and love (vv. 3–4) grounded in their heavenly hope (v. 5). The Gospel, not a local perversion of it, had produced this hope in them, and this same Gospel was manifesting its power wherever it was being preached in the world (v. 6). Having reminded them (v. 7) that they had heard the Gospel of the grace of God from Paul's helper Epaphras, from whom Paul had in turn heard of the Colossians' love (v. 8), Paul informs the Colossians (v. 9) of his continuing prayer for them that they would grow in the knowledge of this Gospel so that they would not be ensnared by false wisdom but would have the ability to discriminate between the false and the true and to grasp the relations in which things stand to each other. Such spiritual wisdom and understanding, centering in the Christ whom the Gospel reveals, issue in right practice (v. 10). God Himself supplies the power to lead a life pleasing to Him and to persist in so doing with patient joy. With God strengthening them, the Colossians would be able to lead lives of continual thanksgiving to the Father for the great things He has done through His Son— redemption, forgiveness, deliverance from darkness, and qualification of a heavenly inheritance (vv. 12–14).

In trials we appreciate knowing that fellow Christians are praying for us. Intercessory prayer supports and sustains us. It is important to pray for each other—and not only in times of trial. The greater the number of Christians praying at other times, too, the greater the opportunity for the power of prayer to be shown. Implicit in Paul's prayer for the Colossians is an exhortation to us: "Let Us Always Pray for Our Fellow Christians."

Sermon Outline
LET US ALWAYS PRAY
FOR OUR FELLOW CHRISTIANS

I. We pray that they would grow in their knowledge of the Gospel.
   A. It is the message that announces our deliverance from the dominion of darkness into the kingdom of God's Son (v. 13).
      1. Christ secured our redemption (v. 14).
      2. He assures us of forgiveness (v. 14).
      3. Through Him God has qualified us for a heavenly inheritance (v. 12).
   B. Growing in the knowledge of the Gospel means to be filled with the knowledge of God's gracious will (v. 9).
      1. This knowledge is not merely intellectual.
      2. Spiritual wisdom and understanding are needed— the knowing of faith (v. 9).
II. We pray that they would experience the power of the Gospel.
   A. It is the message that enables us to walk in a way worthy of the Lord (v. 10).
      1. The more we live in the Gospel, the more we are able to love one another (vv. 4, 8).
      2. The more we live in the Gospel, the more we are able to bear fruit in every good work (v. 10).
   B. It is the message that strengthens us with divine power.
      1. We can endure steadfastly whatever life brings with patience and joy (v. 11).
      2. We can give thanks always to the Father and for each other (v. 3).

   Let us always pray for our fellow Christians. We have great things for which to ask.

GERHARD AHO

194

Eighth Sunday After Pentecost

GOSPEL   Luke 10:25–37 (RSV)

Sermon Notes/Introduction

"Lawyer" (v. 25) refers to a scribe or expert in the Law of Moses. He "stood up," probably to attract Christ's attention. His reason for testing Jesus was possibly to convict Him of some unorthodox statement that would injure His reputation as a teacher. Jesus cleverly turned the tables on His cross-examiner (v. 26) by showing that the lawyer already knew the answer to his question. The answer was drawn from Deut. 6:5 and Lev. 19:18, correct as far as the words went (v. 28). But no one can do what the Law requires toward God and neighbor. Yet inability to keep the Law for eternal life does not mean there is to be no effort to keep it. Implicit in Jesus' words (v. 28) is the idea that we are not merely to theorize about love but to practice it. Now the lawyer, probably embarrassed and perplexed, tried to show that he had acted in good faith by putting another question, "And who is my neighbor?" (v. 29). Where am I to draw the line? What followed was not to answer the man's question but to show him that it was the wrong question. The right question is not "Whom am I to regard as neighbor?" but "To whom can I be a neighbor?" The right answer to that question is "to anyone in need of my help."

The distance from Jerusalem to Jericho (v. 30) was 17 miles of dangerous, rocky road. Two pillars of the Jewish church, a priest and a Levite (a minor clergy), come along but do not help. They might have thought the man was dead, and their duties in the temple prevented them from defiling themselves by touching a corpse (Num. 19:11). Or they might have been afraid that the robbers were still hiding nearby and would attack them (vv. 31–32). The hero of the tale is the Samaritan, a half-breed heretic who took one look at the man and was moved to pity (v. 33), extravagant in his solicitude and love (vv. 34–35). When Jesus asks the final question (v. 36), the lawyer gives the only possible answer but even then cannot bring himself to name the hated Samaritan. The lawyer had asked, "How can I love my neighbor if I don't know who he is?" The point of the parable is that one's neighbor may well be the person we least expect. Love knows no bounds of race, space, or character.

The goal of the sermon is that the hearers will actually

love their neighbor in deed as well as in word. The problem is that the hearers do not always make love a practical matter. The means to the goal is the love Jesus showed in a practical way to redeem and renew us. Introductory thought: The Samaritan loved in a practical way, but how practical is it for us? Can we "go and do" what he did? Is it not beyond us? Not if we remember the love Jesus showed us by keeping the Law and dying for us. He has put His love (*agapē*) in us so that we can "go and do likewise." For us who are in Christ, "Love Is a Practical Matter."

Sermon Outline
LOVE IS A PRACTICAL MATTER

I. Love is extended to all who need help.
  A. There are no restrictions based on race.
    1. The lawyer excluded hated Samaritans from those to be helped.
    2. Many today exclude other races from the neighbor concept—Jews and Arabs in the Middle East, minorities in the U.S. How much racial prejudice is there among us?
    3. Love does not ask, "Are they like us?" but goes out to all, regardless of ethnic background.
  B. There are no restrictions based on acquaintance.
    1. People in Christ's day tended to limit their love to friends and acquaintances.
    2. It is hard even today to think of people in other countries as neighbors.
    3. Yet people we do not know may have just as great a claim on our love as friends and acquaintances. (The Samaritan did not know the injured man personally.)
  C. There are no restrictions based on character.
    1. The lawyer and others like him are ready to love good people but not publicans and sinners.
    2. Likewise today we are ready to love people who are upright, will be thankful for what we do for them, and will love us in return.
    3. But we must extend love also to the reprobates and outcasts of society.

Love is a practical matter. We cannot narrowly restrict it. We can see how practical love is in Jesus, who loved you and me and every sinner enough to redeem and renew us. Now we can extend love to all.

   II. That choice is truly rewarding.

       A. Love comes without excuses.

          1. We do not know why the priest and the Levite were so callous, but they no doubt could have offered excuses.

             a. They might have been late for the temple service.

             b. They might have feared defilement.

             c. They might have feared being attacked by the robbers.

          2. We can usually rationalize our way out of helping someone.

             a. We have no time.

             b. We have no money.

             c. "It won't do any good anyway."

       B. Love comes with specific aid.

          1. The Samaritan gave the help that was needed.

          2. We can give concrete help.

             a. We can help someone find a job.

             b. We can give food and clothing.

             c. We can give money to bring medicine and the Gospel Word.

             d. We can speak words of comfort and encouragement.

       C. Love comes with generosity.

          1. The Samaritan did not skimp in the help he gave.

          2. Love is extravagant in the giving of time, the sharing of self, the bestowing of gifts (cf. the widow's mite, Mark 12:41–44).

Jesus offered no excuses to escape the cross but generously came through with the specific help we needed to be His own. That is why we can now stand ready to do whatever needs to be done to help our neighbor. That is why love can be for us such a practical matter.

GERHARD AHO

Ninth Sunday After Pentecost

EPISTLE   Colossians 1:21–28 (RSV)

Sermon Notes/Introduction

1. The Epistle begins with a confrontation between the *pote* and the *nuni*. In former years the Colossians had been far away from God ("in a foreign country") and enemies of Him according to their minds as expressed by their evil deeds, but now they have been brought near because of Christ's work of reconciliation, through which He presents them "holy and blameless" to Himself (vv. 21–23; cf. Eph. 2:1–10; Col. 2:13). The Colossians will remain steadfast in faith when they are sure in the hope of the Gospel, which is proclaimed throughout the whole world; of this Gospel Paul himself became a servant (Col. 1:23). He worked hard at the call that he had received (v. 24); he fulfilled his office by following Christ's suffering, by sacrificing himself through his ministry to the churches. He was totally devoted to God's Word now revealed to the Lord's saints (vv. 25–26). Christ is the mystery proclaimed as "the hope of glory" to all nations, through whom everyone is presented as perfect in His sight (vv. 27–28).

2. Thus the apostle's ministry stands in the center of this pericope. It is not his person or performance but his service under God's Word that is and must be proclaimed to churches and individuals through preaching, admonishing, and teaching (v. 28). This message of Christ's redeeming work leads people back from their lostness to sin and Satan into saving communion with God.

3. There is always the danger that a congregation considers its pastor as a leader in many areas and fields of a parish, a synod, or even a community, while the proclamation of the Gospel and pastoral work in the strict sense of the word are not judged to be of major importance anymore. This more or less reflects a misunderstanding of what the Gospel really means in the daily life of every Christian. The less God's message is the foundation of our existence, the less pastoral service is expected.

4. The question might also be asked whether the pastor always understands his office correctly. Is his work centered in the proclamation of God's Word in every respect? Does he care for "every man"? Does he fulfill his calling in the same sacrificial way as Paul describes? A sermon on this text will not only address the congregation but also the preacher himself.

5. The majority of the parish might not have experienced the contrast between "once" and "now" (vv. 21–22) as did the members of the congregation at Colossae. But there is a parallel condition to be observed: once many of them were only "Christians" by tradition. When the Lord called them back into a living trust in Him, they became aware that they were nearly lost in sin and hopelessness. They experienced the danger connected with a lazy and merely traditional devotion. They will therefore be ready to help the minister in calling others into the saving *koinōnia* with Christ, the revealed mystery for the saints of all nations.

6. This passage of Paul's letter to the Colossians can remind the congregation of the importance of the Lord's saving message as offered by the holy ministry.

The countries outside the Roman Empire, the barbarian or "foreign" countries, were without civil law and were always acting in the name of injustice, and people living in these countries were constantly in danger of torture and death. In contrast, the Roman Empire was considered a refuge of law and order. Those who could live in it were relatively safe and free. This is how it is for people who have been alienated but are now promoted into God's kingdom through Christ's saving work. Like Paul, we are called to proclaim the message of redemption.

Sermon Outline
THE TASKS OF THE HOLY MINISTRY

I. Offering Christ's message to all nations.
  A. The character of the message.
    1. Of Christ the Savior.
    2. Of Christ the revealed mystery.
    3. Of Christ the hope of glory.
  B. The character of the ministry.
    1. As ordered in God's household.
    2. As "fulfilling" God's Word.
    3. As sacrificing itself for the churches.
II. Preparing everyone for eternity.
  A. By admonition.
  B. By teaching.

Thus through Christ Jesus we can be perfect in God's eyes. This motivates our confession of gratitude with words and deeds.

HANS-LUTZ POETSCH

Ninth Sunday After Pentecost

GOSPEL   Luke 10:38–42 (KJV)

Sermon Notes/Introduction

1. There is a marked contrast between the accent on Christian activity in the account of the Good Samaritan, immediately before today's Gospel, and the emphasis on Christian passivity in this pericope. Each account, as it were, supplements the other, acting as a "corrective" to any reader who might mistakenly promote one aspect of the Christian life at the expense of the other. Together, the two accounts present a complete, "balanced" picture of the Christian life. Further, the Mary-Martha episode indicates the source (the Gospel) that alone can provide the power for the life of active charity mandated in the story of the Good Samaritan.

2. The discussion on prayer immediately after the Gospel seems to be a logical continuation of the portrait of "that good part" that Mary had chosen. Once a person has initiated an intimate relationship with Jesus by sitting at His feet and listening to His Word, prayer is the next glorious step in that daring, delightful intimacy.

3. Verse 39 informs us that Mary "sat at Jesus' feet and heard His Word." More accurately translated, it should read that she "*kept hearing* His Word" (imperfect tense in Greek). The reception of God's Word is never a momentary or once-for-all event; it is a process—regular, continual, persistent.

4. The Lord Jesus praises inactive Mary and scolds active Martha, who, after all, was only being active in His interest and for His welfare! This is a classic instance of the topsy-turvy world so often portrayed in Jesus' ministry on earth, a world in which publicans and harlots enter the kingdom of God before scribes and Pharisees; a world in which a notoriously sinful woman who washes Jesus' feet with her tears and anoints them with oil is extolled above Simon, the respectable Pharisee, into whose house she intrudes; a world in which the pure Son of God dines with publicans and sinners; a world in which laborers who have worked only one hour are paid as much as those who have endured the burden and heat of the day; a world in which the last are first and the first are last.

Sermon Outline
THE BETTER PART

I. The story of Mary and Martha is familiar—we've heard it scores of times—and for that reason the jolt it's meant to give us has become somewhat reduced. But the jolt is still there, no getting around it. The Lord Jesus praises the adoring, dreamy-eyed, meditative Mary, sitting at His feet, and scolds the hustling, bustling Martha, who, after all, was only hustling and bustling in His interest and for His welfare. When not on our guard, we're inclined to disagree with Jesus' evaluation. Had I written this story, I would probably have turned it around. I'd have had Jesus praise active Martha and scold inactive Mary. And chances are, that's the way you'd have written it, too. But you didn't write the story. And I didn't either. God did. And He must have had a good reason for writing it the way that He did. We want to find out that reason today.

A. Let us be sure to get the full force of the shock the Gospel intends to give us. The Martha that Jesus scolded was not a bad woman. She wasn't a slacker or delinquent. She was a close friend of Jesus. She loved Him. She was an energetic worker for the kingdom. She was active. In fact, that's what was wrong with her; she was too active. But if she were present in the congregation today, we wouldn't hesitate a minute about calling her a good church member.

B. Nor was Martha's action a bad action—at least not in itself. To contemporize the story, Martha wasn't sleeping in on a Sunday morning, nor was she out on the golf links. She was, if anywhere, in the parish kitchen preparing the church dinner. She was working for a good cause. She simply meant to serve the Lord. After all, isn't that what He wanted? Hadn't He said time and again that His followers should serve Him? The Lord wanted activity—and she was giving it. To all appearances she was doing the right thing. So sure was she that she was doing the right thing that she asked Jesus to send Mary into the kitchen, too. And what did Jesus do? He scolded her for her activity and praised the inactive Mary. What an unexpected turn of events!

II. Sometimes a person is said to have a choice between two evils. But Martha, we might say, had a choice between two goods. There was the good of serving the Lord. And there was the good of sitting at His feet and listening to His Word. Mind you, both were good. But now get this, and let it be indelibly written in your memory: the good of hearing God's Word is better than the good of serving God. Project and meditation—both are good—but meditation is better. Committee work and worship—both are good—but worship is better. Actively to work for the Lord and passively to receive His Word—both are good—but given a choice, it is better that the Christian be in the passive voice, so to speak.

A. Normally, to be sure, the Christian does both: he or she works and worships, labors and listens, serves and is served. That's the ideal; that's the way it should be. But while doing both, the Christian, remembering the story of Mary and Martha, is ever aware that the worship is more important than the work, the listening more essential than the laboring, and the being served more blessed than the serving. And should there ever arise a conflict between these two good things, serving the Lord and hearing His Word, the Christian, like Mary, chooses the good part and sits at Jesus' feet.

B. Why was Mary's the good part? Well, Jesus said so, and I suppose that settles the matter. But this wasn't really an arbitrary choice by Jesus. If we search the Scriptures elsewhere, we soon discover that He had a good reason for endorsing Mary's action. And that reason is this: You can't really serve the Lord unless He first serves you. You can't actually do good things unless the good Lord first comes into you through His Word and manufactures those good things. You can't be a man or woman of God unless you've first got God, and you can get Him only through His Word. You can't be a fruit-producing branch unless you're first connected with the Vine. You can't really be a Martha—at least a proper Martha—serving in the kitchen unless you're first a Mary sitting at Jesus' feet. In the Christian life there can be no output without input. Oh, to be sure, a person can do what *seems* like good things without God's help. Our world is filled with hustlers and bustlers engaged in good causes. But without Christ's help their motives are all wrong and their methods are all wrong. We need to remember that God doesn't simply want us to do good things; He is even

more concerned that we let Him do them—in us.
FRANCIS C. ROSSOW

Tenth Sunday After Pentecost

EPISTLE   Colossians 2:6–15

Sermon Notes/Introduction

The baptismal theology expressed by St. Paul throughout his writings provides for the Christian a great source of strength and encouragement. Luther said, "There is on earth no greater comfort than Baptism." This pericope offers the preacher an excellent opportunity to share the meaning of Baptism as it empowers the contemporary Christian's daily walk.

Aimless wanderers—that is what many individuals appear to be today in our society. They have no direction, no purpose, no solid basis for living. At times we all may even ask, "Where is life leading me?" In the midst of the questioning comes Good News; in Jesus Christ we are "More Than Wanderers."

Sermon Outline
MORE THAN WANDERERS

I. Many wander in life due to the confusion and contradictory directions offered in our world.
   A. Some seek direction through a philosophy that is based on financial power.
      1. Money appears to offer security and control.
      2. Money does not answer the real questions of life.
      3. Money usually fails, as recessions and stock market fluctuations of recent years prove.
   B. Some have no real direction in their lives because they live by a philosophy that says "satisfy the self."
      1. The media's many voices constantly tempt us to satisfy our own desires first.
      2. Such a philosophy alienates others and leaves one alone without approval or support.
      3. On account of the fickle nature of humankind, "satisfaction" always needs to look for new highs. How much is enough?
II. Life that is rooted and united in Jesus Christ has meaning and direction, today and for eternity.

    A. People will be nothing more than wanderers until they find purpose and direction in their God.

       1. God has revealed Himself and His care for the individual in the person and ministry of Jesus Christ.

       2. To know Jesus Christ is to know life in its fullest meaning. Jesus has demonstrated Himself to be the source of life in His resurrection.

    B. Christians partake of Jesus' life and all its merits as they are united with Him through the water of Baptism.

       1. In Baptism they are united with Christ in His death and resurrection. They partake of His victory, of His life, and are coheirs of His Father. Life has meaning because heaven is their destination.

       2. The meaningless existence of the individual is put aside. A new beginning is made by God's creative grace. There is true satisfaction as God empowers us to give and to serve, replacing the emptiness of self-service.

       3. A new life is created through Baptism. This life has meaning and direction because of its attachment to Jesus Christ. His mission becomes our mission.

    C. The baptized believer is more than a wanderer because in Jesus the way is laid and the life is secured.

"Where is life leading me?" The life that is found in union with our Savior is leading us through the current struggles to the eternal arms of a loving and waiting heavenly Father.

WM. G. THOMPSON

Tenth Sunday After Pentecost

GOSPEL   Luke 11:1–13

Sermon Notes/Introduction

The Emphasis of the Day: On some Sundays the propers are more helpful than on others as one works to focus the emphasis of the day and seeks to develop a unified worship experience. On this Sunday the Introit brings us the essence of Psalm 119. It is a marvelous paean to the splendor of God's Word as it guides one's life and comforts with the sweet Gospel.

The Collect calls on God our Protector to multiply His mercy so that we "may so pass through things temporal that we lose not the things eternal."

The Gradual (from Psalm 145) leads us to praise the great works of our God, and the Verse elicits our intention not to depart from God because He has the words of eternal life.

The appointed Psalm for today (Psalm 138) is another exquisite expression of praise to God for all that He is and does for the believer.

The Old Testament Reading, Genesis 18:20–32, at first seems a bit jarring. It is the account of Abraham's "bargaining" with God to cancel His plan to destroy Sodom and Gomorrah. But it is a dramatic instance of God's listening patiently to the earnest intercessory prayer of a man of God.

The Epistle, Colossians 2:6–15, is an astounding exposition of Christology. Christ's deity, rulership, baptism, resurrection, converting power, forgiveness of sins, active and passive obedience, and triumph over the hosts of Satan are all laid out in one breathtaking paragraph. In this case, if one needs more explicit Gospel for the sermon, the Epistle provides it overwhelmingly.

Thus, we come to the Gospel reading, brought to a mood of wonder, praise, and love by the Gospel message with which we are saturated. Luke 11:1–13 has its subject right on the surface. It is about prayer. In response to their plea, Jesus teaches His disciples how to pray. First, He gives them the "Our Father" (somewhat abbreviated from Matthew's account), and then proceeds to emphasize the how of effective prayer with the parable of the importunate friend and concludes with an argument from the lesser to the greater about God's ability to out-parent human beings. The last sentence is startling. The last thing most people ask for in prayer is what Jesus considers the primary need—the Holy Spirit Himself.

Putting It Together: Let us try to pull all this richness of the day together in an outline that will guide a sermon so that the grandeur of all this Gospel revelation sends the congregation out of worship with singing hearts. One could take several approaches, but it seems that "how" is the most integrative line of direction. The malady is ineffective praying. The goal is effective praying. The content of the Gospel and of the other propers is the self-evident means.

Sermon Outline
IMPROVE YOUR PRAYING

I. Avoid the hindrances to effective praying.

   A. *Praying to the "wrong God."* Refer to Genesis 18 and

the residents of Sodom and Gomorrah. We as Christians do not always pray to the glorious, all-powerful God whose mercy is without end.

B. *Praying for the wrong things*. Read Psalm 138 to see what the psalmist did *not* pray for.

C. *Praying in the wrong way*. Luke 11 reminds us that timid prayer and lack of faith in our God are wrong.

II. Follow Jesus' directions for effective prayers.

A. *Praying to the right God*. Above all, the Colossians 2 reading sets us straight.

B. *Praying for the right things*. We pray for the spiritual gifts in the "Our Father" and for the Holy Spirit and offer intercessory prayer for others.

C. *Praying in the right way*. We pray as a child to a magnificent Father, confidently as Abraham and the importunate friend did.

RICHARD J. SCHULTZ

Eleventh Sunday After Pentecost

EPISTLE   Colossians 3:1–11

Sermon Notes/Introduction

A person's life has meaning only as one is united to Jesus Christ, His life and merit. The way in which the individual actually exercises that union in Christ will be seen in day-to-day conduct. One's spiritual vision should focus on the heavenly realm. The priorities of life should reflect this new higher relationship.

Last week we spoke of the significant life—we are "more than wanderers." We have a direction for our lives. Today we continue our consideration of the significant life, confident that we can be and are "Living in the Awareness of Our Destination."

Sermon Outline
LIVING IN THE AWARENESS
OF OUR DESTINATION

I. Our new life in Christ permits us a new view of living.

A. Our priorities for life and the resulting conduct reflect our understanding of the direction life should take.

     1. If life consists only in the current moment, then self-gratification is adequate to provide a fulfilling life.

     2. If we are to reach life's fulfillment by the acquisition of tangibles, then we should dedicate our energies toward building monuments that serve as milestones of our progress.

     3. Life's eventual fulfillment, correctly understood, is found in Jesus Christ alone. Therefore, if that is our understanding in faith, we should direct our energies toward fostering our relationship with the Savior.

  B. The conduct of those who have been granted new life in Christ should be a reflection of Him and His love active in them.

     1. New life in Jesus suggests that we would strive to put away thoughts, words, and actions that were associated with our former life, roadblocks to our destination.

     2. New life also suggests that we positively strive for the things that reinforce and better equip us for the life's journey we all must experience.

The journey to our final destination, God's eternal kingdom, may seem to be more than we can accomplish. The life of the believer has often been compared to walking the narrow path, while the path of the world seems to be wide and easy. But we must never forget that the path our Lord sets before us, though it be narrow, is clearly marked. He has promised us the energy to complete the journey and has Himself preceded us on the trail to remove the barriers and open the gates that we might arrive at our destination safe and sound.

 II. Christ Jesus does all that is necessary so that we can complete the journey.

  A. The Word shared with us through the prophets and apostles clearly defines the path God desires His people to walk.

     1. We see in the life of Jesus the love, commitment to His heavenly Father, and perfect obedience to the Father's will that should be the goal of each of us, although we recognize how imperfect our efforts will be.

     2. The Law, God's statements of yes and no, offer guidelines for our thoughts and actions, even as Paul records many in this pericope.

B. We live in the resurrection of Jesus. Our new life found in His life granted to us through faith is the energy source needed for us to prevail over all adversaries encountered in our travel.

1. Jesus imparts to us His merits as we are united to Him in Baptism, granting to us thereby the necessary energy through His Spirit to turn away from the easy path of destruction and choose the narrow path of life.

2. Jesus forgives our sin and removes our guilt. He lifts from us the heavy burden of our wrongdoing that we may not be detained or destroyed along the way.

3. Jesus reigns at the Father's right hand, still overseeing and remaining involved in our struggle, assuring us that we never travel alone.

C. The Lord Himself has made the path clear by His own death and resurrection.

1. Jesus has Himself walked the path. He has torn down the barrier of sin through His perfect life. He has opened the locked gate of death by His resurrection. He has cleared the way.

2. Jesus has done all that is necessary in order that, when the roll is called, you and I will be there to say, "By the grace of God I am here."

WM. G. THOMPSON

Eleventh Sunday After Pentecost

GOSPEL   Luke 12:13–21

Sermon Notes/Introduction

In the incident that forms the instruction to the parable of the rich fool, Jesus warns against "every form of covetousness," the greedy desire to have more. Knowing what is at the root of the brother's unreasonable request, He takes the opportunity to warn all against this prevalent and subtle sin. He makes the point that life's value depends on our relationship to God (from which flows the proper use of our possessions) and on the fact that our life is God's gift. The parable illustrates both of these points.

We note first the repeated use of the pronoun "my"— "my fruits," "my barn," "my goods," "my soul." This man never sees beyond himself. Furthermore, he never sees beyond this world. All his plans are based on life in this world. Jesus calls the man "senseless," "without reason," "without reflection or intelligence." He is without reason because this night his soul is to be demanded of him. To whom will his possessions belong then? He has said, "my fruits," "my goods." Now he is to be dispossessed at once. Life does not consist in having possessions but in having a right relationship with God.

Sermon Outline
IN WHAT DOES YOUR LIFE CONSIST?

I. Does life consist in the abundance of your possessions?
   A. God calls a person with such a life foolish.
      1. The man in the parable could not see beyond himself.
         a. He failed to thank God.
         b. He failed to accomplish anything good with his possessions.
      2. He never looked beyond this world.
         a. He neglected the truth that death might come at any time.
         b. He would be dispossessed immediately.
         c. He was oblivious of the fact that after death his possessions could render him no service.
   B. Jesus warns us to beware of covetousness.
      1. This is a subtle and prevalent sin.
      2. We often try to find meaning, security, contentment, and happiness in the abundance of things.
      3. To do so makes us senseless.
II. Or does life consist in being rich toward God?
   A. Christ became poor to make us rich.
   B. We are rich toward God when we can see beyond ourselves.
      1. We recognize God's claim on us.
      2. We use our possessions consistent with His will.
   C. We are rich toward God when we look beyond the world.
      1. We perceive the transient character of life.
      2. We perceive the limitations of earthly goods.
      3. We rejoice in the assurance of our eternal destiny.

NORBERT H. MUELLER

Twelfth Sunday After Pentecost

EPISTLE   Hebrews 11:1–3, 8–16 (KJV)

Sermon Notes/Introduction

The faith theme of Hebrews 11 really begins at 10:38, where it is shown that faith in Hebrews is the same as the faith stressed by Paul in Rom. 1:17 (Hab. 2:4) and Rom. 4:3 (Gen. 15:6). Faith is trust in the God who pronounced us righteous for Christ's sake. The examples in Hebrews 11 are encouragements and models for us to let faith have its way in us. Hebrews 11 is an illustration of what is taught beginning in 10:39 and continues in 12:1. Faith is defined as the "substance" or "confidence" behind our hope, the "assurance" or "conviction" of what cannot be seen with the naked eye. Hence, Moulton and Milligan suggest that 11:1 should be translated: "Faith is the *title-deed* of things hoped for" (*The Vocabulary of the Greek New Testament,* under *hupostasis,* p. 660). James Moffat (in Barclay) gives this definition: Faith is (1) belief in God against the world (cf. Shadrach, Meshach, and Abednego); (2) belief in the spirit against the senses (i.e., the real things are not material, but spiritual); and (3) belief in the future against the present (e.g., Fosdick once said that Nero condemned Paul to death years ago; as time passed, however, men called their sons Paul and their dogs Nero).

The heroes enumerated are those who refused the greatness of the world for the true greatness; they rejected the safety of earthly security and staked their lives on the promises of God. History proved them right. There are examples galore in current events and certainly in our immediate forefathers, who immigrated to America, built churches, schools and charities, and immediately proceeded to the foundation of missions. These records of old show that people can still live in the sunshine of God's favor and accomplish great deeds. Moreover, they show that our faith can be molded by the examples of others and that these others walked in the steps of the "pioneer and perfecter of our faith," Jesus Christ (12:2). An incidental but significant lesson is the epistemology in 11:3: By faith we can accept and "know" an *ex nihilo* creation, not because of scientific or empirical evidence but because faith accepts the Word of God.

Faith is the supreme characteristic of the Christian. Faith is not a passive thing nor a theoretical quantity, but it is a power that looks forward. As such it is called hope. But faith also looks back and recognizes the great deeds of God. And it looks at the present with trust and confidence. All three dimensions work together to give certainty; hope, trust, and knowledge are interchangeable. Such is Christian faith. We look to the faith of Abraham.

Sermon Outline
THE FAITH OF ABRAHAM

I. In Abraham we see how faith begins.
   A. God's grace always precedes faith.
      1. Archaeology supports the Biblical depiction of the idolatrous environment in which Abraham was raised and from which God called Him (cf. "Excavations in Ur, the City of Abraham" in *Halley's Bible Handbook* [23d ed.; Grand Rapids, Mich.: Zondervan Publishing House, 1962], pp. 90–91).
      2. God's grace, which called Abraham "to go out," is all the more amazing (v. 8).
   B. God's call to sinners is always accompanied by His grace.
      1. Jesus' words had the power to effect what is asked (e.g., Matt. 9:9; Luke 19:5; John 1:35–51).
      2. The call has always been to leave and to follow (cf. Ps. 45:10).
      3. God's grace has called and kept us in the faith (cf. Explanation of the Third Article, Luther's Small Catechism).
II. In Abraham we see the endurance of faith.
   A. Only the word of grace guided Abraham.
      1. He "obeyed and . . . went out, not knowing whither he went" (v. 8)—without maps, pictures, or surveys of the place that he was to inherit.
      2. Even when the senses call it folly, faith is confident in the Word (v. 1).
         a. True faith makes the sense captive and separates us from the earthly.
         b. True faith hearkens only to the "voice" of God. Such trust glorifies God.
   B. The "in-between times" are an adventure.
      1. Dangers and deprivations beset Abraham—only a portable tent in hostile territory.
      2. The inconsistencies were heightened for Abraham.

He was promised posterity, but his wife was sterile. Only faith could handle that situation (vv. 11–12).
   3. It is difficult to "wait" even when it is waiting on the Lord (Ps 27:14; 62:5; 69:3).
   4. Sarah conceived and hopes were realized.
 C. We are living in "in-between times" today.
   1. In the "security" of our comforts we need reminding that we are strangers and pilgrims in the diaspora (1 Peter 1:1–2).
   2. By not knowing where we are going and by following the Word, we remain open to God's guiding.
III. In Abraham we see the end of faith.
 A. Abraham saw the comforts of the world; besides, the two flights to Egypt and especially the command to sacrifice his own son tried his faith (Ps. 73:2–3).
 B. The chastening of the Lord is a purifying force (Heb. 12:3–11).
 C. The goal was always clear to Abraham: the City of God (11:10), the heavenly country (v. 16).
 D. All the saints of old "received the promises" (v. 13). Like a ship or airplane captain, Christians soon reach a "point of no return." As Christians we look only forward and upward, never back to the land we left. By faith we dare, and we finally win, by the grace that God supplies.

G. WALDEMAR DEGNER

Twelfth Sunday After Pentecost

GOSPEL   Luke 12:32–40

Sermon Notes/Introduction

In an age of increasing violence and sudden death heralding the last times, Christian watchful and faithful readiness is imperative. Our sinful instinct is to join crowds about us in a flight/fight response to mounting anxiety. Desperately we might seek to flee the pain of stark fear, hedonistically plunging into practices of instant pleasure (misuse of drugs and alcohol, entertainment to deny grim reality, growing immorality, and sexual abuse), or we can deliberately fight and angrily resist, denying the base sin in humanity that has unleashed the deadly and destructive forces now so apparent.

Sermon Outline
WATCH AND BE READY FOR HIS RETURN

I. How are Christians to watch?

    A. Disciples of Jesus are to establish priorities and value systems based on their citizenship in the kingdom of God. This great and gracious gift bestowed by the Holy Spirit through Christ's death and resurrection altered our lives and changed our perception of the world and life (v. 32). No longer driven by an accusing conscience or groaning under the burden of the Law, we are able to set aside earthly transient ambition and receive the timeless treasure of forgiveness won for us and all people by our Savior and committed to us through the Holy Spirit by faith. Thus renewed and equipped, we are able to discern accurately and comfortingly the difficult days we are traversing on our way to an eternity of joy and peace with our gracious God (vv. 33–34).

    B. Satan and the unregenerate world seek to engage and trouble us with the cares and worries of this life exclusively. Jesus is delaying His return, individually deferring that precious moment when He bids us set aside our earthly labor of love for Him and join Him in heaven, or collectively when the shattering trumpet of God announces the destruction of the universe we know and ushers us into a new earth and new heaven. In either case, the day of God's grace in Christ Jesus is drawing to a close. It is imperative that we work the works of Jesus who is coming soon.

    C. Our society has often deified science, idealized humanity, and in arrogance and self-righteousness sought to work out its own salvation. The bright hopes have dimmed, war and peace are seemingly beyond human control, and we are living in the weary hours of history (second and third watches—9 P.M. to 3 A.M., v. 38). Great deceptions and delusions are abroad both within and outside the church. The temptation to take our salvation with all its rich spiritual gifts for granted is strong as we wearily nod and sleep while evil enemies try to break in and steal our heavenly heritage (v. 39).

II. By what means are Christians to be ready?

    A. On the one hand, we are to examine critically and consider in the light of Scripture the full implications of modern, seemingly alluring philosophies popular in

our day (new morality, situation ethics, essential goodness and competence of human beings, the totally cyn-
ical existential dogma of despair) that either promise
fulfillment or actualization by our own power or plunge
us deeply into the *Angst* (pervasive anxiety) of despair
and disillusionment.

B. We know not the hour when the Son of Man will return.
Hence urgency accompanies the challenge of open
doors, inviting the saving Gospel and dawning hope
throughout our shrinking world. We are to "gird up
our loins" and get to work for Christ! Millions languish
in barren confusion, frightening violence, numbing
poverty, and starvation spiritually and physically. Our
Master is depending on us; may He find us busily engaged when He comes (v. 35).

C. Jesus uses the familiar customs of the marriage feast
to drive home another telling point. Bright lamps dec-
orating the banquet hall were brought and fueled by
the guests. Our lamps aglow with ample supplies of oil
(Word and sacraments), faithful servants will be ready
to open the door immediately when the Bridegroom
returns (vv. 35–36). Christians edified by the Holy
Spirit in family and congregational worship and Bible
study radiate heavenly hope and brightness in the
deepening darkness of our day.

Blessed are those who respond to the Savior's call. The
same Redeemer, who willingly placed His sinless body on the
altar of the cross as the all-sufficient sacrifice for humanity's sin
and rose triumphantly to endow us with new life, will serve us
graciously and personally (v. 37), either at the hour of death
or on the Last Day. He will invite us to partake of the eternal
banquet He has prepared for us. God grant that we may be
ever watchful and ready as we await joyously the coming of
our heavenly King! Amen.

MARTIN A. HAENDSCHKE

Thirteenth Sunday After Pentecost

EPISTLE   Hebrews 12:1–13 (NASB)

Sermon Notes/Introduction

"Therefore" (v. 1) connects the Epistle directly to the immediately preceding chapter, the great "cloud of witnesses" referring to the heroes of faith described in chapter 11. These witnesses are adduced to encourage the Hebrew Christians in their Christian race. In the Greek there is a distinction between "encumbrance" and "the sin which so easily entangles us." The only way to run the race with endurance is to fix one's eyes on Jesus, the author and perfecter of our faith. He makes faith possible, for by our baptism into Him, into His death and resurrection, we have been placed in the race that He has already pioneered and won. He will surely keep us to the glorious end. But Jesus is presented also as our example in the race; He endured dreadful hostility by sinners and yet, keeping the outcome before Him, His glorification at God's right hand, He persevered in carrying out His saving task. The Hebrew Christians had not yet had to resist to the point of martyrdom in their Christian race (v. 4). They were faltering, not only because they were failing to fix their eyes on Jesus, but also because they had forgotten the exhortation that explained God's purpose in disciplining His own (vv. 4–5). God is dealing with each of His children as a wise and loving Father, who must often discipline His child. The author compares our earthly fathers' discipline to what God meets out, reminding us that as we respected our fathers, so must we respect our heavenly Father (v. 9). Discipline is never joyful (v. 11). Only afterwards do we see how it yielded peaceful fruit of righteousness, righteousness manifested in firm reliance on the goodness of God, who spared not His own Son but delivered Him up for us all and who therefore will give us all things that are good for us, also in the way of discipline.

Scripture often compares the Christian life to a race (Gal. 5:7; Phil. 3:14; 2 Tim. 4:7). The Epistle uses the race image to remind us that "We Can Persevere in the Race."

Sermon Outline
WE CAN PERSEVERE IN THE RACE

I. We can persevere when we remember the witnesses.
 A. There are many witnesses.
  1. There are witnesses in both the Old and the New Testament (Heb. 11).
  2. We are not alone in the race. The number of Christian runners is large also today.
 B. Their witness is encouraging.

1. The witnesses of Hebrews 11 experienced some of the same encumbrances and sins as we (12:1).
2. By faith they were able to lay hindrances aside (v. 1; Heb. 11).
3. We can likewise lay hindrances aside through a faith that lets us distinguish between the permanent and the impermanent, the heavenly and earthly.

II. We can persevere when we submit to the Father's discipline.
   A. It is difficult to submit to discipline (12:11).
      1. When sickness and troubles come, we may begin to think like Job that God has become an enemy.
   B. It is important to accept the Father's discipline.
      1. Discipline testifies to the Father's deep love for His children (vv. 5–9).
      2. By His discipline God has our temporal and eternal good in view.
      3. Submission enables us to experience that good (vv. 10–11).

III. We can persevere when we fix our eyes on Jesus.
   A. He is the supreme example of endurance in the race.
      1. Christ endured much worse suffering than we will be required to endure (vv. 3–4).
      2. Yet He persevered for us by keeping the final joy in view (v. 2).
   B. Above all, He is faith's enabler.
      1. He authored our faith when in Baptism He started us in the race.
      2. He will perfect and finish what He has begun.

We can persevere in our Christian race when we remember the witnesses, submit to the Father's discipline, and fix our eyes on Jesus.

GERHARD AHO

Thirteenth Sunday After Pentecost

GOSPEL   Luke 12:49–53 (RSV)

Sermon Notes/Introduction

1. Christ came "to cast fire upon the earth" (v. 49). Verse 49, unique to Luke, is difficult. In light of the parallel in verses 51–53, "fire" apparently refers to the troubles and division

that He and His Word bring. The background to this phrase is probably found in Malachi 3–4. There the fire both refines and consumes. The Lord will come like a "refiner's fire" to refine and purify the sons of Levi (3:2–3). Such a fire distinguishes between the righteous and the wicked (3:18). Also the day of His coming will "burn like an oven" and consume the wicked (4:1). The fire that Jesus brings probably has this double nuance. On the one hand, the purpose of fiery trials is to purify believers (1 Peter 4:12—*purōsei*). "Through many tribulations we must enter the kingdom of God" (Acts 14:22; see Luke 6:22; 12:11; 21:12–19). In the present, this fire purifies believers and distinguishes between Jesus' disciples and the unbelievers (see Luke 8:13–15). On the other hand, at Jesus' Parousia the fire consumes the chaff (3:17).

The sentence *ti thelō ei ēdē anēphthē* in 12:49 is difficult. The most probable grammatical explanation is to understand it as a present contrary-to-fact condition without *an:* "How I would be glad if it were already kindled." Christ wants the fire to do its work. In dogmatic terms, Christ's *voluntas antecedens* is to save and purify all people (7:30; 19:10). His *voluntas consequens* is to condemn those who have rejected Him (3:17; 19:27).

2. Jesus did not arrive to "give peace on earth" but to bring "division." The parallel in Matt. 10:34 reads, "I have not come to bring peace, but a sword," where "sword" is used metaphorically (see Luke 22:36, 49–51). What a startling statement! Didn't Jesus come to bring "peace on earth" (2:14; 10:5–6)? Didn't He bring "peace" to Jerusalem (19:42)? Doesn't the resurrected Lord say to His disciples "Peace be to you" (24:36)? Isn't he the "Prince of Peace"? Yes, indeed He is; but it is God's "peace," not a worldly "peace," that He brings. It is not a millennial or utopian age on earth that Jesus brings. It is not a political and economic peace among nations that Jesus brings. This statement reveals as false all such political-liberation theologies and millennial theologies.

Jesus and His Word and work result in division among people, even division within the family. (12:53 alludes to Micah 7:6.) His call to discipleship is a call to follow Jesus above all else (Luke 9:23–26; 12:29–31; 16:13; 17:31–33; 21:34). It is a call to put Jesus above even the family (9:59–62; 14:25–33; 18:28–30). His disciples must be prepared to follow Him even if it means resistance from their families (21:16).

He is the "great divide." "This child is set for the fall and rising of many in Israel" (2:34). Whoever is not with Him is against Him and against you (9:50; 11:23). He is the "stone of offense" (20:17–18). As we read Luke-Acts, we see this tragic division throughout, culminating in Acts 28:24: "Some were convinced by what he said, while others disbelieved." It is the tragic saga of history that some "refused to love the truth and so be saved" (2 Thess. 2:10). His statement in today's Gospel reveals as a lie all forms of universalism, such as "anonymous Christians" or the automatic salvation of all Jewish people. Just as His garments were "divided" (Luke 23:34) while He was on the cross, so are people "divided" over Him and His cross. And the split in the family that His call can bring today will be consummated on the Last Day (17:34–35).

3. But Jesus does not want to create division. He "came to seek and to save the lost" (19:10). In 12:50 His saving purpose to die for all is revealed. This is His third prediction of His Passion in Luke (9:22, 44). If He came to bring fire for others, He Himself will be immersed in that fire. His "baptism" is the "baptism" of death (see Mark 10:38). The Old Testament provides the background of this phrase in which death is expressed in the imagery of drowning and being overwhelmed by water (see Ps. 42:7; 69:1–2).

There is a divine necessity in His death. "I have a baptism to be baptized with" (echō plus infinitive). Throughout Luke we see this "must" of His death (Luke 9:22; 13:33; 17:25; 22:37; 24:7, 26, 44—dei). And Jesus is constrained to accomplish it. "How hard pressed I am until it is accomplished." The verb sunechomai probably does not refer to a fear of death but to how totally gripped and governed He is by this. Beginning with 9:51, we see how determined He is to go to Jerusalem to die. His passion must "be accomplished" (teleō—see 18:31; 22:37; Acts 13:29).

This Good News empowers us to endure the resistance and the fiery trials that come to disciples. Christ's suffering in the fire for us enables us to endure the heat. As the Epistle says, He "endured the cross, despising the shame" (Heb. 12:2) for us. In the midst of our struggle and discipline, we are to "consider Him who endured from sinners such hostility against Himself" (v. 3), and then we will "not grow weary or fainthearted." In fact, He suffered "hell-fire" itself in our place when He was forsaken by His Father so that we will not be burned up like chaff (Luke 3:17). Our baptism into His "baptism" of death is the pledge that we will be with Him "in Paradise" (23:43). And now, as a loving father, He uses the fiery trials we experience as Christians to refine, purify, and discipline us (see Mal. 3). The cost of discipleship is great, but He paid the ultimate price in our place and now uses our trials for our benefit.

Sermon Outlines
TAKING THE HEAT
I. Goal: Christ calls you to take the heat.
II. Malady: Christ calls you to reject a heatless peace.
III. Means: Christ came to take the heat for you.

Another possible approach is the following:

THE PRINCE OF PEACE BRINGS RESISTANCE
I. The Prince of Peace brings not peace but resistance.
II. The Prince of Peace experienced not peace but resistance.

PAUL R. RAABE

Fourteenth Sunday After Pentecost

EPISTLE   Hebrews 12:18–24 (KJV)

Sermon Notes/Introduction

1. Ex. 19:12 makes clear that Mount Sinai was *not* to be touched. The Modern Language version translates Heb. 12:18 with "not touched" rather than the "touched" of many other versions. Although helpful, this is not really necessary since verse 18 does not suggest that it was *permissible* to touch Sinai. It implies that it was *possible* to touch it—with dire consequences ensuing.

2. It was not the specific command of verse 20 that could not be endured but the tone and implication of that command, the potentially terrifying relationship with God that it signified.

3. That even a beast was involved in the prohibitions and terrors of Sinai (v. 20) calls to mind Paul's discussion of the bondage of the creature in Rom. 8:19–22. It is interesting to note that throughout this pericope more than the world of human beings is discussed. Paralleling the allusion to the beast in Heb. 12:20 is the reference to angels in verse 22.

4. Mount Zion was a hill on which part of Jerusalem was built. Via synecdoche it came to be another word for Jerusalem, and via further synecdoche it has come to mean "the heavenly Jerusalem" (v. 22).

5. "Ye are come" (v. 22), translated "you *have* come"

in most modern versions, reminds us that the heavenly life begins here on earth already. "He that hath the Son hath life" (1 John 5:12). In a sense, to a degree, we *have* come to Mount Zion already.

6. Although "firstborn" (Heb. 12:23) is probably a compliment as well as a statement of fact, a reference to precedence in rank as well as in time, we need to caution ourselves that one does not come to the heavenly Jerusalem on the strength of one's own rank or merit. It is God who makes the imperfect perfect, as the latter part of verse 23 reminds us. The phrase "just men" in the same verse calls to mind the central truth of the Scriptures, that it is God who, because of Christ, *declares* people just (thereby saving them), and that it is God who thereafter begins to *make* them just through the same Christ (thereby initiating their sanctification, a process not completed till heaven).

7. Whether the reference in verse 24 is to the sacrifice of Abel or to the blood of Abel, in either case Christ is superior. His sacrifice on the cross far surpasses Abel's. And the blood Christ shed cried out for our forgiveness, not for vengeance as did Abel's blood.

8. Verse 24 is the climax, the high point, of the Epistle. It is Jesus, the Mediator, who makes all the difference between the Old Covenant and the New. The preacher must be careful in handling the contrast so as not to paint the Old Testament era as all Law and the New Testament era as all Gospel, or to make the God of the Old Testament merely "a consuming fire" and the God of the New Testament only a God who is love. Citizens of the Old Covenant had plenty of Gospel promises, and they were blissfully aware of the love of God. But the point is that Jesus changes our relationship with God from one of terror and separation to one of joy and intimacy and that He has *now come.* The delightful relationship with God is no longer *promise;* it is now *accomplished fact.* That is why the New Covenant is superior to the Old.

Let us today look at three mountains and what they tell us about our relationship with God.

Sermon Outline
FROM SINAI TO ZION VIA CALVARY

I. *Sinai*—the mountain that signifies what our relationship with God would be if it had not been for Jesus.

   A. Even as Mount Sinai was unapproachable because of

its fire and darkness (vv. 18–19), so our holy God, who "is a consuming fire" (v. 29), is unapproachable because of our sins.

B. Even as touching Mount Sinai led to dire consequences (v. 20), so our sin, our disobedience of God, results in death, both temporal and eternal.

C. Even as the prohibitions at Mount Sinai involved both man and beast, both the highest and the lowest (vv. 20–21), terrorizing them, so sin and God's condemnation of sin affect us all—there are no exceptions—and we are in the bondage of the fear of death (2:15).

II. *Calvary*—the mountain that makes the difference in our relationship with God.

A. The *Person* on that mountain makes the difference.
  1. He is better than Abel (12:24).
     a. Abel was a good man.
     b. But Christ is the God-Man (perfect, sinless).
  2. He is the Mediator between God and us (v. 24).

B. The *event* on that mountain makes the difference.
  1. Christ experienced death and damnation in our place.
  2. His sacrifice is better than Abel's (v. 24).
     a. Abel's blood called for vengeance.
     b. Christ's blood calls for forgiveness.

III. *Zion*—the mountain that signifies what our relationship with God now is, thanks to Jesus.

A. We are citizens of the heavenly Jerusalem.
  1. Already we enjoy this citizenship to a considerable degree ("you *have* come to Mount Zion," v. 22 RSV).
  2. After death we shall enjoy our citizenship even more fully (1 Cor. 13:12; Rev. 7:13–17).

B. We are united with a distinguished company.
  1. We are connected with the Church Triumphant (Heb. 12:23).
  2. We are linked with "an innumerable company of angels" (v. 22).
  3. We are in fellowship with God Himself, even the God who is "the Judge of all" (v. 23).

                                        FRANCIS C. ROSSOW

Fourteenth Sunday After Pentecost

GOSPEL   Luke 13:22–30 (RSV)

Sermon Notes/Introduction

1. The *sola gratia* of salvation needs to be emphasized with respect to this pericope. At first glance Jesus' statement "strive to enter" might appear to promote works-righteousness. This, of course, would contradict the rest of Luke's gospel. Christ and His work alone save. He "came to seek and to save the lost" (19:10). Sinners are forgiven by grace alone (chap. 15).

A works-righteous understanding would also contradict this pericope itself. Verse 22 states that Jesus was journeying "toward Jerusalem," Luke's second statement of the journey's goal (9:51 being the first). Jesus' trip to Jerusalem, mentioned repeatedly between 9:51 and 19:28–29 (13:33; 17:11; 18:31; 19:11), is for His atoning death. His atoning death is what saves.

Also those who are saved are those whom Jesus "knows" (*oida*, 13:25, 27). This usage of *oida* recalls the Old Testament's usage. There God has "known" and chosen by grace alone those who are His (Jer. 1:5; Hos. 13:5; Amos 3:2).

Finally, the reversal in Luke 13:30 illustrates this point. Luke expresses this reversal often and in various ways. "Whoever would save his life will lose it; and whoever loses his life for My sake, he will save it" (9:24; cf. 17:33). Those who exalt themselves will be humbled, but the humble will be exalted (14:11; 18:14). Those who receive the kingdom like a helpless infant will enter it (18:15–17). The point is not to do the good work of humility and therefore earn salvation. When the "last" become "first," it is by grace alone. Luke 18:13–14 demonstrates this. The publican who cries, "God, be merciful to me a sinner!" is "exalted" by God's mercy, not by his works.

2. Jesus does not give a speculative answer to the speculative question "Will those who are saved be few?" (13:23). Speculative questions and answers put off repentance and faith (see vv. 1–5). Instead, He answers with a present imperative: "Strive [and struggle continuously, *agōnizesthe*] to enter through the narrow door" (see 1 Tim. 6:12). It is a call to sanctification flowing from faith, not one of works-righteousness. It is a call to follow Jesus, though it be against the grain and in the face of the majority. It is a call to "repent" (Luke

13:1–5), to "acknowledge" Jesus before others (12:8), to be His disciple (14:25–33), and to "bear fruit" (13:6–9). And it is an urgent call to approach the narrow door now before that narrow door becomes a closed door. The closing of the door will come suddenly (see 12:40, 46; 21:34). The picture is of a traffic jam developing at the narrow door after it has been shut. (13:25 should be taken as a complete sentence, a future-more-vivid construction.) Once the door is shut, it is too late. There is no second chance, whether after the "rapture" or during a "millennium."

3. Today's Gospel illustrates the "scandal of particularity." As the Collect says, Christ is the Way and the only Way. He is not only the door (John 10:9) but also the doorkeeper who shuts the doors. He does not answer the previous question directly, but He does say that "many" will be locked out (see Matt. 7:13–14). Who are the "many"? Luke 13:28 indicates that they are the descendants of Abraham (see Matt. 8:11–12). They include those in Jerusalem who rejected Jesus (Luke 13:34). They include Jesus' contemporaries who "ate and drank" in his presence (see Matt. 7:21–23).

To be sure, Jesus did eat and drink with many (see Luke 5:30; 7:34, 36; 9:10–17; 11:37; 14:1). But mere casual acquaintance with Him and His Word is not the same as faith. Only those whom Jesus, the master of the house, "knows" will sit at the banquet table. As for those whom He does not "know," their works will accuse them as "workers of iniquity," a reference to Ps. 6:8. They will be cast down to Hades (Luke 10:15), where there will be "weeping and gnashing of teeth" (see Matt. 13:42, 50). But it needs to be emphasized that not all Jews are excluded. "Some are first who will be last," but not all the first ones (see Matt. 19:30; Mark 10:31). Luke-Acts reports of Jews who strove to enter through the narrow door, and that is still the case today.

4. Luke 13:29, an allusion to Ps. 107:3, highlights the inclusion of the Gentiles. They are the "last who will be first" in this context. Throughout the Old Testament we see the promise of the Gentiles' inclusion in the eschatological kingdom (see Gen. 12:3; Is. 11:10–12; 19:18–24; 42:1–7; Amos 9:11–12). Luke-Acts especially emphasizes this. From Luke 2:32 to Acts 28:28 one reads of the incorporation of the Gentiles into the kingdom, and it has been continuing ever since.

5. The narrow door leads into the kingdom of God. The kingdom is both a present (Luke 11:20; 17:20–21) and a future reality (as in this pericope). Usually the emphasis is on God's

gracious *rule* through Christ, but here the connotation is more that of a "kingdom," a house, the realm of salvation (see 14:15). There the faithful will enjoy the eschatological banquet promised in the Old Testament (Is. 25:6–8; 65:13–14). In the Lord's Supper Christ already gives us a pledge and foretaste of that banquet (Luke 22:16, 18, 29–30).

Sermon Outline
SHUT DOOR, OPEN DOOR, NARROW DOOR

I. The Law threatens us with the possibility of facing a "shut door" just like many of Jesus' contemporaries. It warns us against relying on a mere acquaintance with Christ and His Word or on a faithless participation in the Lord's Supper.

II. But when we confess our sins and flee to Christ, the Gospel comforts us with an "open door," open for us because Christ went to Jerusalem to die. It assures us that we who are "last" will be "first" because Jesus knows us and became "last" in our place. Our participation in the Sacrament in the kingdom now is a pledge that we will enjoy the kingdom's banquet then.

III. This then empowers us to strive continuously to enter through the "narrow door."

PAUL R. RAABE

Fifteenth Sunday After Pentecost

EPISTLE   Hebrews 13:1–8 (RSV)

Sermon Notes/Introduction

The Epistle encourages the hearer to develop a life-style in direct opposition to the cultural pattern of our modern society. "Independence" and "individuality" are the hallmarks of America today. The Biblical and secular understandings of these two words have little in common. The world views "independence" as freedom from something. God views it as freedom for something. The world views "individuality" as life for oneself; God views it as life for others.

Health devotees are a dime a dozen today. On almost every street one sees joggers. Health clubs are in every city. Prime bodies in prime minds is a national business. Why? Yes, health is a concern today, and God intends that our bodies be in shape, but there is a dark side to this national trend. The ancient Greeks had it in their games and art—the body beautiful and the philosophy of humanism, the exaltation of humanity and its reach for fulfillment to taste the limits of life. How does the Christian faith address the concerns for today's reach for independence and individuality?

Sermon Outline
INDEPENDENCE AND INDIVIDUALITY

I. Culture and Fulfillment.
   A. Independence from all restraint is the world's view of freedom.
      1. Human nature seeks to be free from control by God or others.
      2. Human nature in self-defined, self-chosen independence believes it is in touch with reality (v. 9). Our culture seeks fulfillment in license: "If it feels good, do it!" Morality in the Biblical sense is archaic, outdated, irrelevant. "I am 'god'; therefore I make my own moral standard, my own religious system."
   B. Individuality is the standard for fulfillment.
      1. Secular culture moves humanity into the center of the universe (Dan. 4). Human nature's perception of fulfillment finally centers on the individual's understanding of life.
      2. Modern individuality undermines relationships with God and neighbor (v. 4). Marriage for the pagan is no permanent bond; the marriage bond is only one of many relationships that are not necessary. The big "I" seeks gratification in new and expanding relationships. Trust and stability are useable only as they serve "me" (cf. Herod and Herodias, Matt. 14:3). Individuality without God undermines and distorts relationships.
   C. God condemns the world's perspective of reality.
      1. God's temporal judgment is often observed in the lives of immoral and self-centered people as the consequences of their behavior. The diseases of herpes and AIDS are two examples. People are not fulfilled by promiscuity. This is only one illustration relating to one area of life. There are countless others. Addiction to drugs, alcoholism, child abuse,

etc., become a way of life for frustrated and unful-
filled people. Unfulfillment is their fulfillment.

2. Judgment Day is the final announcement of reality,
God's heaven or hell. All must face judgment. God
is the final Judge (Jude 14–15). Eternal judgment
is everyone's "fulfillment."

II. Promise and Reality.

A. Jesus Christ is God's personal answer to the human
quest and need. True independence and individuality
are found only in Christ, the God-man (Heb. 13:8;
John 1:14).

B. Jesus Christ accepted the guilt of our sin and the death
that is our inheritance.

C. Jesus Christ and His salvation are apprehended only
by personal faith. Faith is not an academic exercise; it
is the repentant sinner's confidence in the cross of our
Lord.

III. Regeneration and Fulfillment.

A. Independence and individuality find expression in obedience to God's will. People are free in living under
Christ (John 8:31–32). God's Word produces fulfillment (Heb. 13:7).

B. The Epistle urges a specific life-style demonstrating the
independence and individuality of the new self (vv. 1–
6).

1. Christians continue in "brotherly love" (v. 1). This
is freedom for loving others, not freedom from service or love.

2. Christians entertain strangers. This is independence
for service to strangers. Hospitality is the outward
expression of love for the unexpected and uninvited
(v. 2).

3. Christians remember those in prison. This is an individuality that confuses the world because God's
people love the unlovable. It mirrors Christ's concern for the lost (v. 3).

4. Christians hold marriage in honor. Fulfillment is evident in the marriage bond. The Christian marriage
demonstrates the perfect balance between independence and individuality.

5. Christians are content with their possessions. Our
relationship to things in this world is important. It
reflects either fulfillment or frustration (1 Sam. 21).

Christians need a carefree attitude toward this world's goods (Heb. 13:5).

6. Christians remember those who rule over them. Here we see the proper order of things and people. Our faith is paramount in life (v. 6).

GEORGE KRAUS

Fifteenth Sunday After Pentecost

GOSPEL   Luke 14:1, 7–14

Sermon Notes/Introduction

V. 1: Meals on the Sabbath were often luxurious and costly. Only cold dishes were permitted. "They watched Him" explains the reason for the invitation. Jesus had just bitterly denounced the Pharisees (cf. Luke 11:39–52). In this pericope Jesus talks about seeking the lowest places at these feasts and about who ought to be the guests. *V. 7:* "Chief rooms": The first places, places of respect and honor. How the Lord—the essence of whose teaching is self-surrender and self-sacrifice—must have been disturbed by the self-seeking pride of the Pharisees. *V. 11:* This is a rule in Christ's Kingdom. Whoever takes pride in his own work and merit will be abased by being excluded from the Kingdom. Whoever humbles himself, acknowledging his own unworthiness and trusting alone in Christ, will be exalted by God's grace (Matt. 23:12; Luke 18:14). *V. 12:* This remark occurred some time later in the feast. Those attending the feast were from the upper ranks of Jewish society. "Not thy friends": Jesus did not mean to forbid our entertaining of those we love. He meant simply that, because of the life to come, we can do better (Neh. 8:10). "Lest they also bid thee": This is manifestly a selfish motive. This section of the pericope is a lesson in selfless service. The Law required service to the poor (Deut. 14:28–29; 16:11; 26:11–13). *V. 14:* Where there is no love, faith is missing. Hence, no recompense on the Last Day. The recompense is one of grace. God gives rewards to those who seek no rewards.

Our competitive life encourages self-seeking—grades in school, scrambling for a promotion, building a better mousetrap. But self-seeking can be self-destructive.

Sermon Outline
GUARD AGAINST SELF-SEEKING

I. Seek the lowest place.
   A. The Pharisees in their pride were concerned about their position.
      1. They scrambled for the place of honor at the table.
      2. In their pride they exalted themselves before God.
      3. Therefore they were abased by the world and by God.
   B. True humility seeks the lowest place.
      1. Jesus is our great exemplar (Phil. 2:7).
         a. He took on Himself the form of a servant.
         b. Therefore God also highly exalted Him (Phil. 2:9).
      2. We have so much to humble us.
         a. We daily sin (Ps. 51).
         b. Therefore in repentance and faith we come to God as beggars (Luke 15:18; 18:13).
      3. God exalts us.
         a. He gives us the righteousness Christ won (Rom. 4:5).
         b. He gives us everlasting life (John 10:27–28).

What we are, we are by grace. That should keep us humble (Phil. 2:3).

II. Be concerned about the poor.
   A. Self-seekers cater to their friends.
      1. They show them favors.
      2. They hope for favors in return.
   B. The humble act otherwise.
      1. They love their friends for their sake (Matt. 5:44).
      2. They are concerned also about the poor (Matt. 5:42; 7:12).
      3. They shall be recompensed (Luke 6:38).

Lord, help us to seek not self but the righteousness of Christ; help us not to use people but to serve them.

HENRY J. EGGOLD

Sixteenth Sunday After Pentecost

EPISTLE   Philemon 1 (2–9) 10–21 (RSV)

Sermon Notes/Introduction

People by nature are not inclined to forgive; they are inclined to seek revenge. How to get even, how to pay someone back for a wrong that has been done, either real or imagined, occupies many people's waking hours and fills the hours during which they toss sleeplessly in bed.

Christians know that God reserves vengeance for Himself or for the state, which He has established. They know that God expects them to forgive even as they are forgiven. But forgetting—that's a different thing. It's hard to put out of mind a wrong that has been committed against one personally. Common sense tells us not to trust the person who has wronged us even if we do forgive him or her. Yet forgive and forget is exactly what Paul asks of Philemon, and that's what God asks of each of us.

Sermon Outline
FORGIVE AND FORGET

I. The basis for the plea.
   A. Paul pleads "in Christ" (v. 8) and "in the Lord" (v. 16).
      1. Paul calls attention to the forgiveness Philemon receives from God through Christ.
      2. He thereby reminds Philemon of the wrong that Christ suffered even though innocent of any wrongdoing (cf. Luke 23:41).
   B. Paul pleads for his own sake (Philemon 9).
      1. We owe much to those who have been our fathers in the faith. Their example and their admonition are worthy of following (cf. Heb. 13:7).
      2. Paul had a special claim on Philemon.
         a. He was the aged apostle.
         b. He was a prisoner.
   C. Paul pleads in the light of Philemon's demonstration of his love (v. 7).
      1. He had provided hospitality for the church at Colossae that met in his home (v. 2).
      2. The fruits of faith were already evident; Paul was asking for an even greater fruit.

II. The plea to forgive.
   A. Onesimus had not lived up to his name. "Useful" in verse 11 is a play on his Greek name; he had not been faithful in service to Philemon.
   B. Onesimus had perhaps sinned against Philemon (v. 15). His flight was no doubt an effort to escape the consequences of his sin.
   C. Philemon is asked to put this sin behind him, to forgive it. He is to wipe out the account and not inflict even the minimum penalty (branding) usually inflicted on a runaway slave.
   D. We can apply the message today to spouse, parent, child, or fellow Christian.
III. The plea to forget.
   A. Philemon should receive Onesimus as Paul would have been received (v. 17).
   B. Philemon is to receive Onesimus as God received Philemon (v. 16).
      1. He is brother in the Lord.
      2. More than that, he is a brother in the flesh.
   C. This example can be applied in many ways today.

It was a hard request that Philemon received from the Lord through Paul. It's a hard request that you and I receive regarding those who have wronged and hurt us. Forgiving isn't so difficult, but forgetting is a different thing. God wipes our sins out of His memory, and we must do the same for others, especially for the brothers and sisters in the faith, who by ties of blood are nearest and dearest to us, those who are members of our own household. Forgive and forget—it's a tremendous challenge. But it's also a most precious fruit of Christian living.

JOHN W. KLOTZ

Sixteenth Sunday After Pentecost

GOSPEL   Luke 14:25–33

Sermon Notes/Introduction

Today's Gospel may revive an age-old question:

Sermon Outline
IS CHRISTIANITY HARD OR EASY?

I. *Confrontation of the text:*

I doubt that many of us debate this question in so many words, but I dare say that most of us confront the problem in our everyday life. In our past Christian experience, we may have expected certain things from our religion (in addition to heaven). Maybe we hoped it would break us of some bad habit like gossiping, overdrinking, or poor sportsmanship. And oh, how glad we were when we saw that it did! And right here most of us would like to rest on our oars. Now that the bad habit is broken, we expect things to go smoothly. But often they don't. Instead, we find ourselves bumping up against new situations requiring more love, more courage, more patience than ever before. Now that our goal is achieved, we'd be obliged to God if He'd leave us alone. Really, all we wanted to be was just an ordinary "regular guy." And God soon indicates that He wants more than an ordinary "regular guy."

Some of us may remember being reluctant in our childhood to tell our mother when we had a fever or a sore throat. It wasn't that we didn't want relief from our discomfort; we were pretty sure she'd come through with something to soothe the pain. But there was always the chance that the next day she'd bundle us off to the doctor. And we knew what to expect then. He'd not only take our temperature or look at the sore throat. He'd start examining a lot of other things. He wouldn't let sleeping dogs lie. He'd give us a general checkup, probably prescribe some bad-tasting medicine, maybe even administer a shot. At the very least, he'd ask a lot of embarrassing questions and insist that we change our life-style, like going to bed earlier or wearing a jacket outside. If we gave the doctor an inch, he'd take the proverbial mile. The point is: we couldn't get what we wanted from our mother, relief from discomfort, without also getting something we didn't want, a possible trip to the doctor's office.

It's something like that in our relationship to God. If we give Him an inch, He'll take a mile. If once we call Him in to cure something, a bad habit, for instance, He'll do it. But He won't stop with that. He'll give us the full treatment, and we end up getting more than we bargained for. God is delighted to have us claim by faith in Jesus that, in spite of what we know ourselves to be, we are children of God. In fact, as the Bible tells us, there is "joy in heaven over one sinner that repenteth." But in the long run God means to turn our claim into a fact, to effect in those He has declared to be His sons and daughters a character commensurate with this honor, and to get as far as possible with the transformation before our funeral and regardless of the cost to ourselves.

II. *Exposition of the text:*

Today's Gospel is one of those passages in the Bible that seems to make Christianity sound hard. It tells us that great multitudes accompanied Jesus (v. 25). It is probable that many in the crowd were thinking of becoming His disciples. So Jesus makes clear to them what discipleship involves: "If any man come to me, and hate not his father, and mother, and wife, and children, and brethren, and sisters, yea, and his own life also, he cannot be my disciple" (v. 26). Jesus, of course, isn't advocating hatred of our family in this passage. But He does mean that if things come to such a pass that it's a choice for us between Him and our family, we're to choose Him. Obviously, this isn't easy. Fortunately, most of us are spared this decision. But what is remarkable about the passage is this: If we dare not let even such reasonable excuses as family ties interfere with our discipleship, then certainly we dare not let our desire for money or pleasure or fame interfere. And most of us in our lifetime do face that decision.

Next Jesus says, "And whosoever doth not bear his cross, and come after me, cannot be my disciple" (v. 27). In common usage a cross is any trouble that comes our way. But in the strict sense of the word a cross is the trouble that comes our way precisely because we're Christians: for instance, experiencing ridicule for Christian behavior, losing a job because of commitment to Christian principle, being nagged by the sharpened conscience that Christianity inevitably develops. These are crosses, and these are the ones we must bear if we become Jesus' disciples.

Then Jesus tells a couple of stories (vv. 28–32). One is about a man intending to build a tower. Jesus advises him, before he begins construction, to consider whether he's got enough money to see the project through, lest failure to finish make him the laughingstock of the community. The other story is about a king with an army of 10,000 who plans to do battle with an enemy army twice that size. Jesus advises him also to sit down first and consider the odds. The point of both these stories is to count the cost of Christianity, to realize what it involves.

III. *Application of the text:*

It would be a mistake to interpret these sayings and stories of Jesus as an effort on His part to discourage discipleship.

Indeed, if anything is clear from the Bible it is that Jesus wants us to become His disciples. He yearns for us to build that tower called Christianity and to fight that enemy twice our size called Satan. We're sure of this because that's why Jesus lived, died, and rose again: so that we might become His disciples. But Jesus wants to make clear to us that becoming His disciples means more than joining an organization called the church as we would join a Kiwanis or Rotary Club. Christianity is more than having one's name on a membership list or one's picture in a congregational directory. It's more than getting baptized, confirmed, married, and buried under the aegis of the church. It's more than subscribing to a body of doctrine. No, Christianity is a life to take and live, and to live it one hundred percent under the sway of God. God doesn't want half; He wants all. As Jesus says in verse 33, "Whosoever . . . forsaketh not all that he hath . . . cannot be my disciple."

This sounds difficult. No matter what any preacher says, this world isn't too bad a place to live in. And with good luck we should be able to experience 70 or 80 years of it. Maybe we can enjoy all this and heaven too! Then along comes Jesus and pricks the bubble of our illusion. Discouraged, we cry out, "Lord, I can't build that tower. I can't fight that enemy. They're too much for me. I'm helpless!" Well, if that is our feeling, good! Of course, we can't build that tower and fight that enemy. That's exactly the feeling our Lord means to arouse in us, namely, "Lord, I'm helpless. You take over from here." That's exactly what God wants of us: to let Him take over through Jesus Christ. That is discipleship. That is what is meant by forsaking all that we have: giving up our self to God.

In a way Christianity is easy, so easy. We don't have to scrounge around for methods to get "in good" with God. We're "in good" with Him already (thanks to Jesus), and all we have to "do" is believe wholeheartedly that Jesus has taken care of everything, a faith that God Himself gives us through the Holy Spirit. But why, after all, are we to believe? To get to heaven? Yes, that's correct. That's the incredible thing about our God: He gave up His Son primarily in order that we, sinful wretches that we are, might, nevertheless, be with Him in heaven. But God has another goal in mind for us. He doesn't intend that we remain what we are, sinful wretches. He means to make us into dazzling, radiant creatures who in our own small way will be like God Himself. That we will be in heaven. But—and this is important to remember now—God begins this perfecting process already in this life, the minute we start, by

His power, believing in Jesus. And that's where Christianity may begin to seem difficult.

To sum up—and please note this carefully—the perfecting process doesn't have to take place in a person in this life as far as getting to heaven in concerned, but it will take place, or at least begin to take place, the moment the person becomes a Christian.

Imagine yourself as an old wreck of a car. God comes to salvage you from the junkyard—and to overhaul and repair you as well. At first, after you've been salvaged, you realize what He's up to. He's removing the rust, bumping out the dents, and patching up the holes. You knew all along that these jobs had to be done, and so you're not at all surprised. But suddenly He starts to tinker around in a way that may not make sense. He puts in a new motor, installs a larger transmission, adds on bigger fenders, and slaps on a lot of chrome. What on earth is He up to? Well, you thought you were going to be an ordinary compact. And instead God is making you into a luxury car. The King Himself means to occupy it!

Francis C. Rossow

Seventeenth Sunday After Pentecost

EPISTLE   1 Timothy 1:12–17

Sermon Notes/Introduction

The magnitude of the mercy for which Paul praises Christ is brought out in verse 13, where Paul describes himself as a former blasphemer, persecutor, and violent aggressor. These words describe both deeds and words of spitefulness, someone whose insolence and contempt burst forth in outrageous acts. Before his conversion Paul acted in the ignorance of sinful unbelief. The *hoti* clause does not seek to lessen his guilt through an excuse but is an explanation; he was not acting against his better knowledge. The same mercy Jesus asked for His murderers (Luke 23:34) He showed to Paul. 1 Tim. 1:16 makes clear that patience was behind Christ's mercy. Paul's experience is a model of what Christ does in general. Because Christ's patience will not undergo a more severe test than with Paul, no sinner ever needs to despair.

Paul could never get over what the mercy of Christ had done for him. His magnification of that mercy constitutes the theme of the Christian's life.

Sermon Outline
I OBTAINED MERCY

I. He received mercy despite his opposition to Christ.
  A. Paul's opposition was intense.
    1. He was injurious.
    2. He was a wanton persecutor.
  B. We are no different.
    1. Although we probably have not engaged in the persecution of which Paul was guilty, we are no better than Paul because we are born with a sinful heart.
    2. We fail to meet God's standard (Eccl. 7:20; James 2:10), and God has the right to punish us.
  C. But if God could extend mercy to Paul despite his sinfulness, nothing we have been or done or said can prevent Christ from extending that same mercy to us. But how is that possible?

II. Mercy comes through Christ Jesus.
  A. Christ came to save us.
    1. He kept God's law for us.
    2. He suffered on the cross the punishment for our sins. By His resurrection He testified to the completion of redemption. God is merciful through Christ, in whom alone is salvation (Acts 4:12).
  B. Christ's mercy comes to us individually.
    1. We received that mercy at our baptism.
    2. Our faith in Christ's mercy is strengthened through contact with the Word of the Gospel and participation in Holy Communion.

Before we reach the heaven that Christ's mercy has opened to us, we have a life to live. Mercy affects the way we live. It gives us purpose.

III. We received mercy for service to Christ.
  A. Christ strengthened Paul for service.
    1. Paul's apostleship was tremendously rich in accomplishments.
    2. The strength Paul received to do all this was evidence of God's mercy.
  B. We have obtained mercy so that whatever we do might be for Christ.
    1. Showing love and compassion to those around us, working at our job as well as we can, endeavoring to be faithful in whatever responsibility has been

given to us—these are all ways of expressing our faith and thereby serving Christ.

2. We can be faithful in our service because Christ will strengthen us for it, just as He did Paul.

The mercy of Christ comes to me in my sinfulness, it comes to me through Jesus Christ, it comes to me so that I can serve Him. I obtained mercy! What a fitting theme song for the Christian's life!

GERHARD AHO

Seventeenth Sunday After Pentecost

GOSPEL   Luke 15:1–10 (KJV)

Sermon Notes/Introduction

V. 1: Luke 15 is the golden center of the Gospel, revealing the love of the Savior for the lost. "Publicans and sinners": Taxgatherers and sinners about whom no one cared, much less the Pharisees, who regarded them as hopelessly lost. Christ's words, full of stern rebuke but also of hope, found the lost. The publicans and sinners came to hear Him, not simply to witness His miracles. V. 2: The Pharisees, who took pride in their holiness, and the scribes, learned doctors of the Law, were indignant. They cried: "He not only receives sinners; He eats with them." V. 3: The three parables are Christ's defense of His action. All have the same point of comparison: The joy in heaven over the repentant sinner. V. 4: "Wilderness": Wide, uncultivated plains that fringe portions of Palestine. Vv. 5–6: The diligent search, the tender care, and the later joy represent Christ's activities with publicans and sinners. Luther: "We can neither help nor counsel ourselves to come to quietness and peace of conscience, into escape from the devil, death, and hell, unless Christ Himself gets us and calls us to Him through His Word. And even if we come to Him and are in faith, we are not able to keep ourselves therein" (St. Louis [German] Edition, 11:1268). "He calls His friends": He looks for sympathy of feeling from His friends. Christ did not find that among the scribes and Pharisees. V. 7: What He looks for in vain on earth, Christ finds in heaven. The 99 just persons who had no repentance are the Pharisees, who mistakenly imagine that they need not repent (Matt. 9:12–13). Luther says that the 99 are the little flock of Christendom. Others refer the 99 to the angels. *V. 8:* A poor woman is presented, to whom the loss of a single coin is serious. God misses each lost soul and seeks its restoration. The worth of a single soul exceeds that of the whole world (Matt. 16:26; Mark 8:37; James 5:20). *Vv. 9–10:* God Himself with His angels rejoices over the sinner found and saved.

"This man receives sinners and eats with them." These words, meant to be a stinging jibe, were really a compliment. We rejoice and take comfort in the fact that Jesus is a friend of sinners.

Sermon Outline
THIS MAN RECEIVES SINNERS AND EATS WITH THEM

I. He seeks the lost.
  A. The lost are sought in the parables.
    1. Sheep get lost; in that condition they are the prey of wild animals.
    2. A woman loses a coin, something precious to her.
  B. Christ seeks the lost in real life.
    1. Publicans and sinners were lost.
      a. They lived in sin.
      b. They faced eternal death, the wages of sin.
    2. The Pharisees were lost.
      a. Their sin was pride, evidenced in their smugness and disdain for sinners and for Jesus (Luke 18:10–14).
      b. They were in the same lost condition as the publicans (Matt. 23).

We face the twin dangers of going astray by toying with sin or by sinful pride. We need to live in daily repentance over both.

II. Jesus seeks the lost.
  A. He came to seek and save what was lost.
    1. The shepherd leaves the 99 and seeks the one; the woman looks for the lost coin.
    2. Jesus came into the world to save.
      a. He could have left the world of sinners to their doom (Matt. 25:41).
      b. But He loved so much (John 3:14–17) that He came to fulfill God's law for us and to pay the world's debt of sin (Matt. 20:28; Gal. 4:4–5; Eph. 5:25–27).

    B. Through His Word He seeks the lost.
       1. He works through the Law.
         a. He reveals sin (Rom. 3:10–13).
         b. We are unable to save ourselves (Gal. 3:24).
       2. He works through the Gospel.
         a. He invites (Matt. 11:28).
         b. The Holy Spirit converts (2 Cor. 4:6).
         c. He gives us His righteousness (Rom. 1:16–17).
         d. He makes us His heirs (1 Peter 1:3–5; 1 John 3:1–2).

How good that Jesus has found us! Let no one think that he or she is beyond the reach of Christ's love.

    C. He continues to seek the lost through us (John 10:16).
       1. Two-thirds of the world is still in darkness.
       2. At times fellow church members become delinquent.
       3. We are to seek the lost.
         a. We have the command (Matt. 28:18–20).
         b. We have the means: the Law and the Gospel.
         c. We have the promise of the Spirit (John 16:8).

Let us learn from Jesus to be the friends of sinners, both the manifest sinners and the Pharisees.

III. He rejoices over the saved sinners.
    A. There is joy when a lost sheep is found or when a coin is found.
    B. The Pharisees did not rejoice.
       1. They held publicans and sinners in disdain.
       2. Church members may be tempted to deal that way with a fallen but penitent member (cf. Luke 15:25–32).
    C. There is joy in heaven.
       1. The whole purpose of God's mission of love is fulfilled (John 17:24).
       2. Every person is precious to God.
         a. Each is saved from death (Matt. 16:26).
         b. Each is saved for life (Matt. 25:34; John 10:10).

Let us join the angels praising God both for our own salvation and for the progress of the Gospel in the world.

HENRY J. EGGOLD

Eighteenth Sunday After Pentecost

EPISTLE   1 Timothy 2:1–8 (RSV)

Sermon Notes/Introduction

The church at Ephesus was a small, struggling congregation, and it could readily offer several good human reasons for being so. It was harassed by Roman officials, Jewish legalists, and pagan religious practitioners. It was undermined by Greek philosophers and shepherded by a young, inexperienced pastor named Timothy, who needed all the advice that Paul, his spiritual father, could give. Timothy's apparent indecisiveness had turned the Ephesian congregation into a timid group of souls. Like the disobedient King Saul (1 Sam. 15:17), the Ephesians thought too little of themselves, and their worship became, as it was in Isaiah's time (Is. 58), an outlet for wallowing in self-pity.

A church that looks only at itself will feel sorry for itself, but a church that looks to its gracious God and Mediator will look with love toward a world in need.

Sermon Outline
THINKING TOO LITTLE OF YOURSELF

I. A church that looks at itself.
   A. An introspective church feels sorry for itself.
      1. It sees only the sins and shortcomings of fellow members.
      2. There is anger, strife, and quarreling.
      3. It engages only in mere troubleshooting, taking an anemic and fatalistic approach to its internal affairs.
   B. An introspective church assumes a cowardly, defensive posture toward the world.
      1. It can only whine and complain about the "troubles in the world today."
      2. It becomes "apologetic" (in the negative sense) and feels the need periodically to resuscitate its God.
      3. It becomes selfish with the boundless blessings of God, limiting the scope of God's saving activity to its own backyard.
II. A church that looks at its God.
   A. It rejoices in the Savior-God.
      1. It believes in God's age-old plan for the salvation of the world.

    2. It makes no apologies for God's unilateral decision to love the human race.

B. It rejoices in the Mediator, sent by our Savior-God at the "proper time," who has reconciled God to the world (God-to-man aspect).

C. It worships the God and Savior who freely accepts our offerings of thanks (man-to-God aspect). Worship forms a bridge between what we believe and what we do.

II. A church that looks at the world.

A. A church that looks outward feels sorry for the world.

B. It proclaims the universality of God's grace.

C. It realizes that God's people are ambassadors of the King.

    1. It "goes on the offensive" with the grace of God.

    2. Its prayers testify that the human race, from the least to the greatest, in every corner of its existence, desperately needs the God we adore.

    3. It is mission-minded, accepting the challenge to relay God's love to the world.

Through the preaching of the Law we rightly admonish people not to think too highly of themselves, and in this way we prepare them for the hearing of the Gospel. But there is a proper time for stressing that through the forgiveness of sins God Himself has chosen us to be no less than His representatives to a fallen world, and therefore, we must not think too little of ourselves. The world needs what we have been given and what we have to offer.

JAMES BOLLHAGEN

Eighteenth Sunday After Pentecost

GOSPEL   Luke 16:1–13 (RSV)

Sermon Notes/Introduction

It is often observed that Luke 16 deals with the proper Christian attitude toward earthly wealth. Two parables (vv. 1–9, 19–31) and two sayings (vv. 10–13, 14–18) are said to urge the right use of wealth and warn against its wrong use (see William F. Arndt, *Luke*, Concordia Classic Commentary Series [1956; reprint, St. Louis: Concordia Publishing House, 1986], pp. 354–67).

Obviously, references to earthly wealth are common to each of this chapter's four pericopes. But two other candidates compete for consideration as the theme of the chapter: (1) The reversal of circumstances on a coming day of great change is of critical importance in both parables and in verses 10–13. (2) The transitoriness of mammon, which fails, is contrasted with the now available and eternally valid Word of God in the Scripture (vv. 9, 14–18, 19–31).

With these two thoughts the preacher might approach the readings for this Sunday and next from a slightly different angle and find homiletical alternatives to the life-goal stewardship sermons usually extracted from them. He might find the first parable as enjoining people to "Plan Ahead," with the second one pointing to the reliable basis on which to plan, our God-given "Planning Resource."

Verse 1: An absentee landlord leaving his affairs in the hands of an estate-manager was not uncommon (I. H. Marshall, *The Gospel of Luke,* New International Greek Testament Commentary Series [Grand Rapids, Mich.: Eerdmans, 1978], p. 617). It is unclear whether the steward was guilty of dishonesty or merely incompetence; *dieblēthē* connotes malice by the informants and *diaskorpizōn* makes no judgment about the cause of the waste.

Verse 2: It is clear, however, that he is going to lose his position: *ou gar dunē eti oikonomein.* This is the *critical* reality: a *day of greatly changed circumstances* is near. It is a day of reckoning (*apodos ton logon*).

Verse 3: And the steward knows it. His soliloquy muses on his dilemma.

Verse 4: Herein lies the point of the parable: the steward is (within the context of *his* knowledge and values) planning ahead. He must behave *now* in such a way that will benefit him when (after) he is "removed" (*metastathō*). For *this* he will be commended (v. 8) as *phronimōs,* far-sighted.

Verses 5–7: The steward's specific actions are here described. Some commentators (see Marshall, pp. 616–19) hold that the amounts by which the bills were reduced were the (perhaps excessive) *interest* owed and/or were the *steward's legal* (but perhaps exorbitant) *commissions.* This would mean that the steward was not hereby *cheating* his master but was merely using what was *legally* his to ensure his future position (and may even have been restoring his master's reputation as a fair landlord). In this case it would be an unqualified commendation that he wins in verse 8, and the steward could provide a good example for a "financial stewardship lesson" in accord with verses 9 and 10–13. But this approach is unconvincing because (1) if the steward truly had had legal claims to such commission, he would not have been reduced to digging and begging after his removal; (2) the master calls him "unjust, dishonest" (v. 8); and (3) the point of the parable is not simply about using the wealth entrusted to us but about planning ahead, beyond the *day of great change.* Therefore, we find it better to hold to the traditional picture, according to which these actions were an unscrupulous cheating of the master through the steward's abuse of his (now lame-duck) powers.

Verse 8: It is most natural to read verse 8a as part of the parable. *Ho kurios* (the master, not the Lord Jesus) praised the dishonest steward (the genitive is an adjectival phrase) not, of course, for his dishonesty, but (as it says) because he had acted wisely, with foresight, prudently. To *plan ahead* is the point. The words that follow in verse 8b are best taken as an observation by Jesus to the effect that this characteristic, foresight, is more common among worldly people as they deal in worldly matters (*eis tēn genean tēn heautōn,* loosely paraphrased: "in their own context") than among the "sons of light," those destined for life (and trusts, v. 11) in the age to come.

Verse 9: The direct application is in keeping with the central point. The meaning is clear, except for the difficult phrase *ek tou mamōna tēs adikias.* The noun phrase may mean just "worldly wealth" (Marshall, p. 621, with reference CD 6:15) rather than "ill-gotten gains." Thus it could mean *"by means of* [your use now of] worldly wealth [act prudently and] make friends for yourself" for your welfare in the age to come. Almsgiving is usually mentioned. But because mammon is said to "fail" (v. 9), it is attractive to consider the possibility that the prepositional phrase is a superliteral (misleading) translation of *mimamon* in which the *min* is *min*-privativum, yielding the meaning: "make friends for yourselves in *your own* context, that is *apart* from worldly wealth, which will fail."

You've heard of "financial planners"; they are not a new phenomenon!

Sermon Outline
PLAN AHEAD

I. This world knows the value of planning ahead.

    A. The steward knew that a rainy day of reckoning was soon to come.

    B. He acted with foresight to ensure his welfare beyond that day.

    C. But a day will surely come when that in which he has placed his trust will fail.

II. The sons of light have the light that enables them to plan for eternity.

    A. They have been transferred by grace from darkness into the kingdom of light.

    B. They know that a day of change is soon to come.

    C. They are given the things that will not fail on that day.

        1. The Word of the Gospel abides forever.

        2. The unshakable kingdom is the gift of God.

        3. The Holy Spirit is the down payment of life.

        4. Works of the new life will not be forgotten.

JONATHAN GROTHE

Nineteenth Sunday After Pentecost

EPISTLE   1 Timothy 6:6–16

Sermon Notes/Introduction

In the busy schedule of a pastor there is always the temptation to offer the hearers too little interpretation of too much text, since such a sermon requires far less preparation time. This temptation could become a reality in this pericope. The question explored here is this: What are the riches that are truly worth a fight? The first half of the pericope dismisses the ever-present wrong conclusion that material wealth is the grand prize for those who believe (vv. 6–10). There is gain (literally, "good business") in godliness, but Christ crucified and risen, as well as the life lived in Him (v. 11), is what the real "good business" is. Today, as in apostolic times, some say, in effect, that the resurrection is past already, that is, that "two chickens in every pot" are the object of Christian hope (e.g., the "happiness theologians"), but we move on to what the real fight is all about. Here is where the emphasis ought to be (vv. 11–16).

Sermon Outline
CLAIMING THE VICTORY

I. The losing battle.

    A. The sinful self is incapable of waging the battle.
       1. Our greatest enemy is our own flesh; it is the ground in which all manner of perverse seeds take root (v. 10).
       2. We stand as prisoners of war in our guilt; we are helpless against the Accuser and our own *opinio legis* (the rewards and punishments mindset).
       3. We have no vision of the prize of war to be won; we long only for what the eyes can see (Eccl. 5:11), for what does not satisfy (Is. 55:2).
II. Christ the Victor.
    A. Christ has faced all our enemies alone.
       1. He is the courageous warrior against Edom (Is. 63).
       2. He is the faithful witness who made the good confession for our sakes (Heb. 2:10–18; Rev. 1:5).
    B. Through His death and resurrection Christ has won the eternal victory over sin and death.
III. The good fight.
    A. The victory has already been won.
       1. We know that Christ has done the fighting for us.
       2. We lay hold of a life that has already been given to us.
       3. We fight for the faith that comprehends our Lord's entire gracious work on our behalf.
    B. Christ continues to do the fighting for us.
       1. He gives us the armor of salvation (Eph. 6:10–17).
       2. He supplies the needed weapon, the Word of God.
       3. The resources of our mighty Lord are limitless (1 Tim. 6:15–16).

The apostle Paul followed his own advice and won the crown of eternal life (2 Tim. 4:7). We see the "even now, not yet" aspect of Christ's victory by comparing the two letters of Timothy; Paul loved Christ's "epiphany" (His second coming, 1 Tim. 6:14).

JAMES BOLLHAGEN

Nineteenth Sunday After Pentecost

GOSPEL   Luke 16:19–31

Sermon Notes/Introduction

Here we are again dealing with worldly wealth and a *day*

of greatly changed circumstances. Not only does the story make evident the need to plan, but it also points to the testimony of Scripture as our God-given planning resource and the only reliable voice to guide such planning.

Verse 19: The variant readings that provide the rich man's name are to be rejected. Part of the art of the story is to leave this worldly egotist eternally anonymous.

Verses 20–21: But the account preserves into perpetuity the name of the "insignificant" beggar, Lazarus, whose poor estate is graphically portrayed. The rich man's neglect of Lazarus signals his failure to make friends for himself when the day of changed circumstances comes and worldly wealth shall fail (see v. 9).

Verse 22: Here we have the *critical* day, when circumstances change. The festive treatment of Lazarus contrasts with the stark description of the rich man's sad end: *apethanen . . . kai . . . etaphē.* Why Lazarus is carried to heaven (the unusual phrase "Abraham's bosom" must mean this) is not part of the concern of the narrative. Its point is to *warn* the self-centered and to point them to Scripture as their resource for planning ahead; it does not propose the equivalence of financial poverty and a state of grace. If *nomen est omen,* we might take a hint from the meaning of his name. Lazarus means "He (whom) God helps."

Verse 23: The plight of the rich man is described. We cannot press the details as a literal description of hell. The point (directing people now to heed the Scriptures) requires that the rich man and Lazarus be portrayed as separated but able to communicate.

Verse 24: The rich man now begs for what he did not give: mercy, care, relief from suffering. Ever the egotist, he still thinks Lazarus is there to serve him (I. H. Marshall, *The Gospel of Luke,* New International Greek Testament Commentary Series [Grand Rapids, Mich.: Eerdmans, 1978], p. 637).

Verses 25–26: If the parable were to end here, its point would indeed have to do only with wealth and charity, but it doesn't.

Verses 27–28: The rich man finally thinks of someone else (though he still reckons Lazarus must be there just to do his bidding). Here the real need comes out: "If only during my lifetime a voice had warned me and instructed me how to plan for this!"

Verse 29: The parable itself is an artistic way of letting such a "voice from the Beyond" point to the "planning resource" now available: the written Word of God, the Law and the Prophets. (The Writings are not meant to be excluded.)

Verses 30–31: This is a typical objection and its rebuttal. The man supposedly knows a better way: send someone back from the dead (not a new idea). But God's Word is *now* available; it calls for faith, but it will not fail. It is His testimony to the judgment and salvation that He will work.

Planning is not easy, but it's easier when you know the future.

Sermon Outline
OUR GOD-GIVEN PLANNING RESOURCE

I. "If I had only known!"
  A. The human dilemma is that people are ignorant of the "big picture."
  B. The rich man experienced a terrible plight after the day of change.
  C. Worldly wealth failed, showing the need for a better, more lasting basis of hope.
II. "Somebody's got to tell them!"
  A. The rich man sees people like himself heading for the same fate.
  B. His suggestion is unoriginal and unacceptable.
III. "Now hear this!"—the God-given planning resource.
  A. God's Word is special revelation from Beyond.
  B. His Word abides when all fails; it is eternal.
  C. His Word reveals His plan for eternity:
    1. He warns of judgment to produce repentance.
    2. He promises salvation to create faith.

JONATHAN GROTHE

Twentieth Sunday After Pentecost

EPISTLE   2 Timothy 1:3–14 (RSV)

Sermon Notes/Introduction

What makes a person like St. Paul? Most of us seem like such "soft mush" in comparison. Listen to him in the words of Frederick W. Myers' poem "St. Paul":

Oft, when the word is on me to deliver,
Lifts the illusion and the truth lies bare;
Desert or throng, the city or the river,
Melts in a lucid Paradise of air—

Only like souls I see the folk thereunder,
Bound who should conquer, slaves who should be kings—
Hearing their one hope with an empty wonder,
Sadly contented in a show of things;

Then with a rush the intolerable craving
Shivers throughout me like a trumpet-call
Oh, to save these! to perish for their saving,
Die for their life, be offered for them all.

How, I ask you, does one account for a love and a commitment like that? It must come from God, for only divine love can create such a response. The Epistle for this day picks out certain characteristics of greatness in the apostle. These will occupy our attention in our message.

Sermon Outline
CHARACTERISTICS OF PAUL'S GREATNESS

I. St. Paul had a clear conscience (v. 3). Nothing is so destructive of mental health and effective service to God as a conscience that condemns.

My conscience hath a thousand several tongues,
And every tongue brings in a several tale.
And every tale condemns me for a villain.
(Shakespeare)

Reality therapy, as practiced by William Glasser, as well as the integrity therapy of O. H. Mowrer and John Drakeford stress the important role that freedom from a sense of guilt plays in mental health. St. Paul knew the forgiveness of sins in Jesus Christ and was free to serve Him with a conscience as clear as newly fallen snow.

II. St. Paul was a man of prayer (v. 3). He was constantly remembering Timothy in prayer. One hallmark of people like St. Paul and Martin Luther was their regularity in prayer. St. Paul's word to the Thessalonians emphasizes the same idea: "Pray constantly" (1 Thess. 5:17). "The prayer of a righteous man has great power in its effects" (James 5:16). Of this, St. Paul, the man of God, was acutely aware.

III. St. Paul was a man of tender emotions (2 Tim. 1:4). He who longed night and day to see his beloved Timothy that he might be filled with joy sets an example for pure emotional expression in the Christian life. To stifle emotion, as we often do, is to deny expression to a vital facet of the human personality, not to mention virtually the entire list of the fruits of the Spirit found in Galatians 5. St. Paul felt and expressed deep emotion, just as our Lord Himself did on several occasions (cf. Matt. 9:36; 15:32; 20:34; Acts 20:19, 31, 37–38).

IV. St. Paul held deep theological convictions (2 Tim. 1:9–10, 13–14).

    A. Salvation derives from the purposes of God (v. 9).

    B. Salvation is based on the gracious work of Christ on our behalf (v. 10).

    C. The pattern of sound words is to be not only believed but also lived (v. 13).

    D. The truth of God is to be guarded (v. 14).

V. St. Paul had a profound sense of the call of God (v. 11). He knew that God had set him apart as preacher, teacher, and apostle. A sense of vocation (*vocatio*) is needed for the most effective Christian living, regardless of whether one is a member of the clergy or laity.

VI. St. Paul knew and trusted Jesus Christ (v. 12). The apostle knew Jesus Christ as Redeemer and Lord. He knew Christ as the constant companion with whom he could commune in prayer. He also knew Christ as One whom he could trust to preserve the Gospel by His power.

Christ was a living person to St. Paul—not some dim figure from the past but One who came to him in the sacraments and the Word as his contemporary. The complete devotion of the apostle to the person of Christ who dwelt within him (Gal. 2:20) was a notable facet of his life. The frequent use of the phrase *en Christo* in his writings is ample evidence for this.

Remarkable as St. Paul's life was, the same possibilities and resources for Christian maturity are open to all today. The Word, the sacraments, the privilege of prayer, the indwelling Holy Spirit with divine power—all are available to us today.

May God Himself enable us to say with the hymn writer:

My faith looks up to Thee,
Thou Lamb of Calvary,
Savior divine.
Now hear me while I pray;
Take all my guilt away;
Oh, let me from this day
Be wholly Thine! Amen.

RUDOLPH H. HARM

Twentieth Sunday After Pentecost

GOSPEL   Luke 17:1–10

Sermon Notes/Introduction

Verses 1–2 may contain an allusion to the rich man spoken of in the immediately preceding parable, who by his selfishness and worldliness dishonored God's name and offended believers whose faith was still weak and wavering. Better that such an offender's life be cut short, even by a horrible death, than that he entrap others so that they too end in hell. Christians are in danger of offending by treating others self-righteously and judging them harshly (v. 3). The Christian is to rebuke a sinning brother, to speak directly to him about his sin, and to forgive him as often as he indicates that he has repented. Any self-congratulation the apostles may have engaged in had now received a severe blow, and they felt their own weakness deeply. They also felt that a stronger faith would enable them to judge others more gently. They turned to the right source for an increase of faith (v. 5). The Lord reminds them (v. 6) that the amount of faith is not so important as the exercise of the faith they already have. Even a small faith enables Christians to do their duty toward fellow Christians. Faith is instrumental, for through faith the power of Christ becomes effective in the believer's life. Good works flow from faith. But these good works should not make Christians proud and lead them to expect recognition from others or from God. Faith is a gift of God, and so are the good deeds that spring from it. Christians succeed in forgiving and in not giving offense only by the grace of God. Why should they expect God to thank them? He does not owe us anything. Besides, our good works are still imperfect, and in doing them we are only doing our duty as God's servants (vv. 7–10).

The goal of the sermon is that the hearers would recognize that when they do good they are only doing their duty. The problem is that the hearers often expect both God and people to praise them for the good they do.

Introductory thought: The word "duty" has a dull, moralistic sound. We feel more comfortable with words like grace and love. Nor is "duty" a popular word. It refers to obligation, and many think they have no obligation to anyone. What Jesus says about duty in our text will help us in "Getting the Right Perspective on Duty."

Sermon Outline
GETTING THE RIGHT PERSPECTIVE ON DUTY

I. We are unworthy servants.
    A. Have we not sometimes caused offense?
        1. We have lived selfishly, without regard for the needs of those around us.
        2. We have lived immoderately (in the use of alcoholic beverages, money, language).

Little ones (weak Christians) may thereby have been led astray—a serious matter (v. 2). To cause offense is to be an unworthy servant.

    B. Have we not sometimes refused to deal lovingly with sinning brothers and sisters?
        1. We have failed to rebuke them personally for a sin we see them committing.
        2. We have failed to forgive them as often as they repent.

When we see our tendency at times to deal harshly and self-righteously with sinning brothers and sisters, we must confess our unworthiness. To know that we have not always done our duty is to have the right perspective on duty. But how, the disciples wondered, sensing their unworthiness, can we do our duty toward a fellow believer? They sensed that the fulfillment of duty was related to faith.

II. Faith makes it possible for us to do our duty.
    A. We need only to exercise the faith we have.
        1. What matters is not the amount of faith, or even faith itself, as though we were now obligated to get faith to do our duty. Rather, faith is instrumental.
        2. Faith joins us to Christ so that through faith we receive His power. Thus, even a little faith can do great things (v. 6).
        3. Wherever there is faith in Christ, Christians will deal lovingly with one another.
    B. We should not expect praise for doing our duty.
        1. Jesus gives faith and increases it (v. 5).
        2. He does not owe us a thing; it is by His grace alone that we have faith and are able to do our duty.

The right perspective on duty is to realize that we are unworthy servants. We have left undone what we should have done, and even when we have seemingly done our duty well, perfection has escaped us. But the right perspective on duty is also to know that with God all things are possible. Through the faith He gives us He enables us to do our duty and by His grace accepts the good that we do.

GERHARD AHO

Twenty-First Sunday After Pentecost

EPISTLE   2 Timothy 2:8–13 (RSV)

Sermon Notes/Introduction

The Good News that St. Paul shared with the world was rooted in history. It was not some vague, ephemeral thing that defied definition. Its roots caused it to be a *skandalon* or stumbling block to many and resulted in considerable suffering for those who espoused that Gospel of God's grace. As a matter of fact, in the Epistle St. Paul is nearing the hour in his life when he will be called on to make the supreme sacrifice for the "crime" of sharing the Good News with his contemporaries. A view of certain facets of that Gospel is provided in the Epistle for this Sunday.

Sermon Outline

GLORIOUS FACETS OF THE GLORIOUS GOSPEL

I. St. Paul's Gospel is the Good News about Jesus (v. 8). For St. Paul, everything centered in Jesus Christ. He was the hub of all things. But it is well to notice that St. Paul brings two specific details of the Good News to our attention today, each having great import regarding its reception by different groups of hearers. We are invited to remember two things in particular.

A. Jesus Christ is risen from the dead. Acts 17 contains a description of the apostle's ministry in Athens. People listened to him attentively, you will remember, until he mentioned the resurrection. At this some mocked, and the sermon was over. In spite of this, the resurrection remained the key to all St. Paul's preaching to the end, even though it may well have contributed to his imprisonment.

B. Jesus Christ is descended from David. The insistence that Jesus was indeed the Christ, the One promised to the fathers, was difficult enough for some people to take. But when St. Paul declared that Jesus was crucified for the sins of all humanity, it became a *skandalon* to the Jews (1 Cor. 1:23). It nonetheless was central to the Good News that St. Paul proclaimed, as it should be to our message.

II. St. Paul's Gospel was the Good News for which he was imprisoned (v. 9a). Essentially the apostle was imprisoned because he bravely and consistently preached a crucified and risen Christ. The proclamation of this Word of God through the ages has resulted in suffering of various kinds. St. Paul is one of the first in this glorious succession of martyrs. Our day is different only in the form the suffering takes.

III. St. Paul's Gospel is the Good News that cannot be bound (2 Tim. 2:9). Our Lord's words in Matt. 24:35 as well as the promise in 1 Peter 1:22–25 are of particular significance here. People may do their best (or worst) to stifle and bind the Word of God, even to the point of killing the one who enunciates it, but to no avail. Nothing can ultimately stifle the dynamic Good News of God's love in Jesus Christ. "God buries His workmen, but continues His work" (John Wesley).

IV. St. Paul's Gospel is the Good News of salvation and eternal glory (2 Tim. 2:10). All the forces of hell will be arrayed against a Word from God that has such powerful results. The Gospel is the "power of God for salvation to everyone who has faith, to the Jew first and also to the Greek" (Rom. 1:16). The same ones who resisted it were the ones for whom it was the best news in all the world. Jesus Christ had died for their sins. He was raised for their justification. The grace of God was available to them in the Word and sacraments. Salvation was theirs as a free gift. Eternal glory awaited them in heaven.

Thank God, what was theirs is also ours today. The Good News hasn't lost its power or its relevance. To sinful people of our day the promise comes afresh: "Whoever believes in Him should not perish but have eternal life."

> Lord Jesus, we give thanks to Thee
> That Thou hast died to set us free;
> Made righteous through Thy precious blood,
> We now are reconciled to God.
>
> By virtue of Thy wounds we pray,
> True God and Man, be Thou our Stay,
> Our Comfort when we yield our breath,

Our Rescue from eternal death. Amen.
(Christoph Fischer, 1597)
RUDOLPH H. HARM

Twenty-First Sunday After Pentecost

GOSPEL   Luke 17:11–19

Sermon Notes/Introduction

The concluding portion of last Sunday's Gospel raised the question, "Who bothers to thank a slave because he did what was commanded?" Today's Gospel reports the miracle of the healing of ten lepers. Ten men, afflicted with a disease that excluded them from normal society (Lev. 13:45–59) and inevitably brought death, sought help from Jesus. All ten were told to show themselves to the priest (Lev. 14:2–20). All ten were healed. But the fact that only one of ten returned to give thanks to Jesus raises interesting questions, among them: What happened to the nine?

Sermon Outline
WHO BOTHERS TO THANK GOD?

I. *Not* those whose only concern is to enjoy what has been given them.
  A. Ten met Jesus. Ten called Him "Master" (Luke 17:13). Ten were healed and undoubtedly rejoiced. Only one looked beyond the healing to the Healer (vv. 15–16). Giving thanks had greater priority for him than being certified as clean.
  B. Like the nine, we also often display a selfishness that is enamored of things that benefit us and that cares not at all for the God who supplies our every need.
  C. Beware! Such selfish myopia stifles thanksgiving. It sees no cause for gratitude unless we receive what we think is best, at the time we prefer, in the way we desire. When this attitude prevails, *who bothers to thank God?*

II. *Not* those who believe that God's good treatment is something they have earned for themselves.
  A. The text strongly emphasizes that the only man who returned to give thanks to Jesus was a Samaritan (v. 16), a foreigner (v. 18). He fell on his face at Jesus' feet, a symbolic act of complete subjection. He realized

that his healing was an act of pure mercy, not a payment that he deserved.

B. How much his views differed from those of the majority of people, both at Christ's time and still today! How easy it is, even for us, to pin our hope for God's favor on what we are or think or say or do. We desire and sometimes demand that God be kind to us and help us as a reward for our good church attendance or our righteous living or our delightful personalities.

C. Beware! Such self-righteous pride will not fall at Jesus' feet and give thanks to Him. It gives no glory to God for His marvelous works of mercy, for it sees God only as a paymaster who distributes benefits to those who have earned them. When this attitude prevails, *who bothers to thank God?*

III. *Only* those whom God has rescued from the dominion of sin and Satan by giving them faith in the saving work of Christ.

A. The event reported in the Gospel happened while Jesus was on the way to Jerusalem (v. 11) to lay down His life as the sacrifice for the sins of the world. The guilt of our selfishness and pride rested on His shoulders. The hands that in other cases healed with a touch were soon to be nailed to the cross in payment for our ingratitude and lovelessness. The voice that told the lepers to show themselves to the priest would soon cry out in pain and agony, "I thirst," and "My God, my God, why have You forsaken me?" as Jesus endured the full punishment of body and soul that we all deserve. But that same voice would sound forth again after His resurrection, announcing that forgiveness of sins should be preached in His name to Jews and Samaritans and all the nations of the earth.

B. Only the power of the resurrected Christ, received by us through faith, can purge our hearts of the spiritual maladies of selfishness and pride and ingratitude and sin. Only in the strength that He supplies are we able to overcome our natural inclination toward evil and truly give thanks and glory to God.

Through faith in Christ, the Samaritan leper received healing in his body (v. 19). Motivated by that faith, he returned to give thanks. For such as that leper, it is not at all a *bother* to thank God. The expression of heartfelt thanks to God with our lips and our lives is a joyous privilege that God provides for us here in time and hereafter in eternity.

JERROLD A. EICKMANN

Twenty-Second Sunday After Pentecost

EPISTLE   2 Timothy 3:14—4:5 (RSV)

Sermon Notes/Introduction

Having just finished a description of the lamentable spiritual decay to come in the last days, Paul's thoughts turn again to Timothy with a concern that he remain true to Christ even in the face of deception and opposition to Christ's words and ways. The entire emphasis of Paul in meeting and overcoming that challenge is the use of the Word of God. The "sacred writings" of 3:15 are the Old Testament, as Paul's use of the term "Scripture" in the next sentence indicates. The Scriptures are, therefore, useful in two significant ways—they instruct one for salvation (3:15), and they equip Christians to do "every good work" (3:17).

The only way in which Timothy can be sure to lead people in the true way, continues Paul, is with Scripture—the way in which Timothy was led to salvation in the first place. This is the central thought of the Epistle. The goal of this sermon is that the hearer seek the truth of God revealed in Scripture. The malady is that we too often want to have our ears tickled by the latest religious gurus and the most inventive theologians. The Scriptures alone are inspired and able to bring us the salvation of Jesus Christ.

What are we to do in the face of the smorgasbord of religious junk food available to us today? Our ears are indeed "tickled" by the many different teachings offered everywhere. What a blessing it is to have a guide through this maze of contradictory false teachings. The Bible is the guide. And it is much more. As we consider the blessings that God gives us through it we will "Thank God for His Great Book."

Sermon Outline
THANK GOD FOR HIS GREAT BOOK

I. This great book of God leads us to Jesus Christ and salvation.

A. Where does a teaching lead? is a significant question to ponder as we seek to know the truth.
  1. There are so many different teachers and teachings available to the religious mind, many even claiming to be Christian.
  2. Does a given teaching lead us to Jesus? This question can help us ascertain whether a teaching is true. If a teaching leads us to doubt our salvation by grace through faith in Christ, it is false.
B. God's book leads us to salvation through Christ.
  1. He is the focus of the Old and New Testaments. He lived and died for sinful humanity. He rose again from the dead. He will come again to judge the living and the dead.
  2. God's book leads us to trust Him. We learn of God's love, the forgiveness of sins, and the splendor of heaven through the Word of God.

II. This great book equips us to serve God.
A. If we are led to Christ, we are led to serve Him.
  1. He came and served fallen humanity.
  2. He calls us to serve Him. This portion of the Bible, for example, reminds Timothy of his duties as a pastor—preaching the Word, exhorting, instructing and training, and doing all these things with patience (3:16–17; 4:2).
B. God equips us to serve Him through His book.
  1. We are given the Holy Spirit and His fruits (one of these is patience) through the Word of God.
  2. Scriptural teaching, furthermore, corrects errors, guides us in righteous living, exhorts us to live for Christ, and always brings us back to Christ for forgiveness and strength. What a great blessing is our Bible!

The Bible is more than a literary classic or a coffee table ornament. It is God's Word. It leads us to Christ. It equips us to serve Him.

DAVID L. BAHN

Twenty-Second Sunday After Pentecost

GOSPEL   Luke 18:1–8a (RSV)

Sermon Notes/Introduction

The Gospels for today and next Sunday, both dealing with prayer, manifest Jesus' ability to use short stories about earthly life in teaching spiritual truths to His disciples and other hearers. As with most good short stories, these contain casts of only a few characters. Next week it will be the Pharisee and the tax collector. This week, let's examine what the importunate widow and the unjust judge teach us about "Persistence in Blessing, Persistence in Prayer."

Sermon Outline

PERSISTENCE IN BLESSING, PERSISTENCE IN PRAYER

I. What the widow in Christ's parable teaches us.
   A. About ourselves.
      1. Like the widow, we also experience injustice and evil at the hands of others. In her case, we don't know specifically what was involved. Similarly, we often don't know beforehand what people will do to us: malign us, impugn our motives, pilfer our homes and businesses, persecute us in overt or subtle ways.
      2. But we do know that our sin makes us deserve nothing but punishment from God. Not only do others sin against us, but we sin against them: thinking, speaking, and doing evil over and over again. Each of our sins against others is also a sin against God, a striving against Him that earns the disinheritance and death for which all sin calls.
      3. In the face of the evil done against us and the evil that we do, we are tempted to despair. We are virtually unable to help ourselves, and help from God appears to be unduly delayed. See Rev. 6:10.
      4. But God invites us to seek His help and blessing for Christ's sake. See Luke 11:9 (note the example of Jacob in the Old Testament Reading, Gen. 32:22–30). We are not unknown to God, as the widow was to the judge. We are "His elect" (Luke 18:7); that is, He has chosen us in Christ before the

foundation of the world. He has adopted us as His beloved children because of the vicarious work of His only-begotten Son.

B. About God.

   1. As the widow persisted in her pleas, so did our Lord persist in His work of winning for us His Father's good pleasure. He endured as our Substitute human injustice and wickednesses, drinking to its bitter dregs the cup of suffering that God administered to *Him* as the result of *our* transgressions. Never did He falter in carrying out His mission of salvation. He persisted, declaring, "It is finished," but also promising, "Lo, I am with you always."

   2. For the sake of His crucified and risen Son, God now persists in hearing our prayers and blessing us. Through Christ we have access to the throne of grace. See John 15:16 and Rom. 8:28.

II. What the judge in Christ's parable teaches us.

A. About ourselves.

   1. In stressing that the judge's decision was a selfish one, the parable reminds us that we also decide to do many things from a selfish desire to benefit ourselves, rather than a pure desire to praise God and benefit others. For example, our obedience to civil laws is sometimes motivated more by a fear of punishment than by a concern for the common good. Or a celebration of the Reformation can tend more toward self-aggrandizement than toward proclaiming with thankfulness and patience the glorious message that God has entrusted to us for the salvation of others.

   2. Such selfishness is unrighteousness, is contrary to God's will, and deserves condemnation. Yet it so thoroughly pervades all human thinking, also ours, that the parable is not at all absurd or unbelievable. The judge is a picture of how we by nature deal with one another.

B. About God.

   1. How different in this regard is God from sinful human nature. We can contrast the judge's forced and selfish decision with God's willing and selfless promises. God loved the world so much that He freely and selflessly gave His Son into death to save all sinners from death for life everlasting. Jesus did not

regard equality with God as a thing to be grasped but humbled Himself and became obedient even to death. The Holy Spirit deigns to enter even our frail and mortal bodies and build us into a holy temple in the Lord.

2. Unlike the judge, who in selfishness was capricious, God is altogether trustworthy. He wants us to hold Him to His promises of blessing. His answers to prayer do not always come according to our time-table. But He does answer—and always at the right time.

God wants us always to pray and not to despair. But only as we realize His faithfulness toward us for Christ's sake will we manifest the desired constancy in prayer. Only God's persistence in blessing leads to our persistence in prayer.

JERROLD A. EICKMANN

Twenty-Third Sunday After Pentecost

EPISTLE   2 Timothy 4:6–8, 16–18 (RSV)

Sermon Notes/Introduction

The 19th century American poet William Cullen Bryant, when viewing death, spoke of the moments

When thoughts of the last bitter hour come like a blight
Over thy spirit, and sad images
Of the stern agony, and shroud, and pall
And breathless darkness, and the narrow house
Make thee to shudder and grow sick at heart.

Even though everyone is not poetic, none escapes the thought of death, if for no other reason than that the life insurance salesman gently taps at the door with a reminder that you should provide adequately for the loved ones whom you will leave behind when you die. No one denies that there is a somberness and sternness about death. But the apostle Paul views a Christian's death from a more encouraging perspective. He speaks about "The Beauty of the Christian Death."

Sermon Outline
THE BEAUTY OF THE CHRISTIAN DEATH

I. It marks the end of the victorious life (vv. 6–7).

Paul's tireless missionary efforts for Christ resulted finally in imprisonment. The apostle entertains no hope that he will be freed. He expects death. But he has lived so that he can say that he has fought a good fight, has finished the race, and has kept the faith. Although sorely tempted by the devil, the world, and sinful flesh, the person who clings to Christ in the hour of death has won the battle against the big three. Life also has had a goal, and the race has been run to reach it. Sustained by Word and sacraments, the Christian remains in the faith. That's the victorious life that makes Christian death a thing of beauty.

II. It is an intimate moment with the Lord (vv. 16–18).

The verses omitted between the two portions of the Epistle show that, except for the companionship of Luke, Paul is alone. The first defense to which the apostle refers may well have been the first hearing of his case. At that occasion he was deserted, too. And yet the Christian is really never alone, for the Lord stands by even as He did at Paul's trial. Especially is this the case in the hour of death. There the Lord is the Christian's intimate companion. Using onomatopoetic forms (*errusthēn, rhusetai*) that sound escape, the apostle confidently asserts that as the Lord rescued him once from the lion's mouth, He will also rescue him from every evil at the moment of death. Others may leave, but the Lord is at hand to deliver. That's the beauty of a Christian death.

III. It opens the door to an eternal crown of righteousness (v. 8).

And what is the Christian hope in Bryant's "last bitter hour"? Coronation. A crown of righteousness is reserved in a heavenly kingdom. The crown is given by a judge who is just (*dikaios*). The crown belongs where He places it. It is a crown of righteousness—the *dikaiosunē* of last Sunday. Indeed, there is "no condemnation for those who are in Christ Jesus" (Rom. 8:1). "Be faithful unto death, and I will give you the crown of life" (Rev. 2:10). That's the beauty of the Christian death.

And thus I live in God contented
And die without a thought of fear;
My soul has to God's plans consented,
For through His Son my faith is clear.
My God, for Jesus' sake I pray
Thy peace may bless my dying day. (*TLH* 598:11)

WAYNE E. SCHMIDT

Twenty-Third Sunday After Pentecost

GOSPEL   Luke 18:9–14 (RSV)

Sermon Notes/Introduction

In the Gospel we hear a Pharisee saying, "I have done what Moses commanded. In fact, I did more than Moses commanded. So I am safe. Right?" But Jesus says: "No. You are all wrong. In my sight—and do not forget that I will be the Judge on the Last Day—you are not justified. That means I must send you to hell."

The Law has an important place in our lives. The Lord tells us and all His children in His holy law not to be extortioners, unjust, or adulterers. He tells us in His holy law to be liberal in giving. He urges us in His law to come to His "temple." But He makes it clear that He expects and is pleased with these works only when they are done by those whom He has already chosen and loved and brought to salvation. They are then proofs of His saving power in their lives.

The pharisee said: "My works are my own. See how much better I am than others." But his unbelief, his refusal to accept Jesus as the Savior, caused God to look at all his deeds as filthy in His sight. How different it was with the publican. Publicans were outcasts—the people whom the Jews had to excommunicate because they turned their backs on their own people, and thus on God Himself. There is no proof that the publicans as a class lived in open sin and shame, that they were adulterers, slanderers, or rebellious people. Their great sin—which is the greatest sin—is that they were unbelievers. They had undoubtedly been circumcised as infants and had gone to the temple and the synagogue as children. But they sold their heritage for a lucrative position with the Romans, proving that they had left the Lord.

Then Jesus came preaching repentance and salvation, as John the Baptist had done before Him. Jesus showed that He cared about publicans and sinners. He was their way back to the waiting arms of the heavenly Father. And many of them repented. They said with the publican in Jesus' story: "God, be merciful to me a sinner!" That was all they did. And even this they did only through the power of the Holy Spirit, who led them to contrition and faith in Jesus. He led them back to their merciful Father and sent them to their homes justified. Did they then, having been justified, love Him and serve Him?

Of course they did. But their works came as fruits of faith, as with Paul and Moses and believers of all times.

Sermon Outline
WORKS IN THEIR PROPER PLACE

I. The Pharisee and all works-righteous people with him think they can be saved by their works.
  A. They feel they are able of themselves to please God.
  B. But God condemns all their works.
    1. They are a denial of His saving work.
    2. They are therefore filthy rags in His sight.
II. The publicans and all who trust in Christ plead only for mercy.
  A. They recognize their unworthiness before God.
  B. They see their hope and salvation in Christ alone.
  C. They recognize that whatever good they do is itself a gift of God, a fruit of faith.
III. It is important that we learn our lesson well.
  A. Do not look for any part of your salvation in your works.
  B. Look for all your salvation in your merciful God.
    1. He saved you in Christ.
    2. He has brought you to faith in Him through His Word.
  C. Then keep on studying His Holy Word.
    1. His law will remind you of works that are pleasing to Him.
    2. His Gospel will give you strength to do these works in love to God and to people everywhere.

MARK J. STEEGE

Twenty-Fourth Sunday After Pentecost

EPISTLE   2 Thessalonians 1:1–5, 11–12 (RSV)

Sermon Notes/Introduction

Paul, writing from Corinth, sent a first letter to the Thessalonians that was filled with deep concern and warm affection for the recently established congregation. But it soon became apparent, as reports filtered back to the apostles, that a second letter was necessary. In it Paul would express his gratitude for the spiritual growth that the believers in Thessalonica were experiencing in spite of persecution. It would go on to calm those who were becoming confused or excited with respect to Christ's second coming. Finally, the apostle would exhort the congregation to keep clinging to the traditions that they had been taught, whether by the spoken or the written Word.

We all like compliments. For purposes of an introduction the preacher could begin by sketching a music recital, a school play, a staff meeting, or some related setting. In this setting an authority figure (teacher, director, supervisor, foreman) compliments those who have demonstrated progress in their training or who have performed well on the job. This statement could provide a connecting link into the Epistle. "Permit Me to Compliment You" could provide a useful summary of this text. In effect, Paul was complimenting the Thessalonian congregation. For application, the preacher could ask whether Paul's criteria for complimenting the Thessalonians have been met by the congregation to which he is preaching. "Permit Me to Compliment You" captures the attention of the listeners. The force of the words will hinge on the identity of the one who compliments and the substance of the compliment. Both of these should encourage the listeners to accentuate the qualities that have elicited the compliment.

Sermon Outline
PERMIT ME TO COMPLIMENT YOU

I. Paul was complimenting the Thessalonian congregation.
   A. The authority of Paul's apostolic office ensured the significance of the compliment. (These were no casual words from an unknown passer-by.)
      1. The Thessalonians were "in God our Father and the Lord Jesus Christ" (v. 1).
      2. The Thessalonians had received Paul's Gospel preaching: "Grace to you and peace from God the Father and the Lord Jesus Christ" (v. 2).
   B. There was substance to Paul's compliment ("We are bound to give thanks. . . . We ourselves boast of you"; vv. 3–4).
      1. The Thessalonians gave evidence of a growing faith.
      2. The Thessalonians expressed a mutual love for one another.
      3. The Thessalonians were a steadfast congregation in the midst of persecution and affliction.

II. Paul's compliment was a message of encouragement to the Thessalonians.
   A. God had been—and Paul implies that He would continue to be—at work in the Thessalonians.
      1. He works so that the Thessalonians might "be made worthy of the kingdom of God" (v. 5).
      2. He works so that the Thessalonians might be made "worthy of [God's] call" (v. 11).
      3. He works so that the name of the Lord Jesus might be glorified in the Thessalonians (v. 12).
   B. God's grace in Christ Jesus was the source of this encouragement.
III. Paul's compliment is a message of encouragement to us today also.
   A. There is substance that deserves compliment in this congregation. (Or the preacher could take an examination approach: Is there substance that deserves compliment?)
      1. There is faith.
      2. There is love for one another.
      3. There is steadfastness.
   B. Such compliments should generate encouragement.
      1. In Christ, we have been made worthy to take seriously living in His kingdom.
      2. In Christ, we have been made worthy to take seriously our call.
      3. In Christ, we have been made worthy to bring glory to His name.

Let us focus then, on God's criteria of compliment. Let us be a congregation so encouraged by His compliments that others may desire to be part of our fellowship. It is the Lord's great pleasure to extend words of compliment to us.

RANDALL W. SHIELDS

Twenty-Fourth Sunday After Pentecost

GOSPEL   Luke 19:1–10 (RSV)

Sermon Notes/Introduction

Zacchaeus wanted to get a good view of Jesus as He was passing through Jericho, but because of his small stature and the large crowd in his way, he climbed a sycamore tree to get a better look. People today struggle to get a good view, too—of who they are, of where they are going, of what lies around the many corners of their lives. But like Zacchaeus, they are thwarted from having a clear view by a host of factors stemming from their sinful natures.

Sermon Outline
SEEKING AND SAVING THE LOST

I. In our attempts to see Jesus or in trying to make sense out of life, "climbing trees" avails little.
   A. Zacchaeus wanted to see who Jesus was, but he was kept from doing so by two considerations.
      1. Physically he was not a large man, and the groups of people clustering around Jesus made it next to impossible for him to get a satisfactory view.
      2. Far more important was the spiritual consideration. Zacchaeus was a rich man (v. 2) and an overseer of the hated tax collectors. Verse 8 hints that he had not gained his riches by entirely honest means (his restitution exceeded the Law's penalty for extortion; cf. Lev. 5:16; Num. 5:7), and naturally he would have been despised by his fellow Jews, who would have scorned him whose name meant "righteous" or "pure" one. Certainly Christ would have no time for him; after all, Jesus had warned that wealth could be a hazard in entering the kingdom (Luke 18:25).
   B. People today also long for a better view, but are foiled both by who they are and by the outside forces threatening them.
      1. We are bombarded by "crowds" of material, psychological, and spiritual concerns that block our view of Jesus and impel us to climb personal "sycamore trees" in the hope of spotting the one clue that will make sense out of life, assure us of how things will turn out in the end, or perhaps even give us an empirical "sign" that our timid faith is not in vain.
      2. We are irreversibly inclined to sin and operating with a confused standard of righteousness. We fail to understand why our most strenuous efforts to please God bring us no closer to Him and leave us with a profound sense of emptiness and failure.

  3. Indeed, the exercise of scaling a tree did not prompt Jesus' call to Zacchaeus, nor does it prompt Him to speak words of forgiveness and consolation to us. In and of itself, "climbing trees," that is, running on the treadmill of the Law, will only exhaust us and lead us to despair.

II. In spite of our failure and shortcomings, Jesus calls to Zacchaeus and to us and *invites Himself* into our houses.

  A. It was not necessary for Zacchaeus to elevate himself, for Jesus knew who he was and called to him without having inquired about his identity. There was no good reason for Jesus to lodge with Zacchaeus, for everyone knew and observed that he was a "sinner" (19:7). The reason is simply stated in verse 10: "The Son of Man came to seek and to save the lost."

  B. This same undeserved favor calls to us and says: "Hurry and come down, for today I must stay in your house." Jesus Christ lives in and among us—in grace (i.e., the kingdom of God)—through His Gospel Word and His sacraments.

   1. Through the announcement of His death and resurrection, the barriers that block our view and communion with Him are broken down, and from the vantage point of the open tomb life's most pressing questions find their final resolution. ("Salvation" in Luke includes deliverance from the anxieties that hinder one's appreciation of God's outreaching love; cf. v. 9.)

   2. Through the washing of Baptism He calls each of us by name (cf. v. 5) and makes us true children of Abraham (v. 9). The grace shown a fallen Israelite in the Gospel is extended to all people: the church becomes the New Israel (Luke 7:1–10; Acts 10–11; Rom. 9–11).

   3. Through the sacramental meal that He instituted shortly after this event, we receive the body and blood of Christ and the forgiveness He purchased on the cross by offering His body and blood there.

Having come down from our sycamore trees, the sons of Abraham and heirs of the promise live penitently, sacrificially, and joyfully. Zacchaeus received his Lord gladly, pledging to clean up his business and to use his gifts to aid people who did not share his good fortune. We have similar opportunities.

Finally, when one is assured of life's outcome by virtue of Baptism (Rom. 6:3–5), the challenges, cares, and frustrations of this age will never be able to overpower us. By God's grace we know how things will turn out in the end, and meanwhile nothing will divert us from or alter that assured result.

DAVID A. LUMPP

Twenty-Fifth Sunday After Pentecost

EPISTLE   2 Thessalonians 2:13–3:5 (NKJV)

Sermon Notes/Introduction

1. In his first letter to the Thessalonians, Paul had said much about Christ's second coming. Some of his readers apparently had misunderstood two of his emphases. One was that people should be "blameless in holiness . . . at the coming of our Lord Jesus Christ" (1 Thess. 3:13; 5:23). This frightened some of Paul's readers. How could anyone possibly be blameless when Christ returned? Paul's other emphasis was on the certainty of Christ's return in judgment, and some of his readers inferred from the frequency of this emphasis in Paul's letter that Christ's return would occur in the immediate future. As a result, they decided to quit working and idly await that event.

Paul addresses both of these concerns in his second letter. The opening two verses of this Epistle reading assure the first group that salvation is all God's doing—that blamelessness is His gift, not their achievement. The rest of the reading urges the second group to refrain from idleness and to be busy in the Lord's work, and the verses after the Epistle urge people to be busy even in their respective everyday vocations. The Lord's return would not be *that* immediate; first "the man of sin" had to be "revealed" (2 Thess. 2:2–3).

2. Reference to this "man of sin" in the preceding verses and to the turmoil accompanying his appearance suggests that Paul wants to address one more concern: that people in the face of tribulation remain courageous in their attitude and activity. The Epistle is riddled with exhortations to "hang in there" and "keep plugging."

3. Verse 13 virtually explodes with major doctrines: election, salvation by grace, the Holy Spirit, the Gospel, faith. Although it would not be homiletically expedient to devote considerable pulpit time to all these doctrines in a sermon on this text, it is imperative that the preacher recognize—and pro-

claim—their role in this pericope, namely, that they are the foundation, the power, for the numerous exhortations to Christian living that follow.

4. Note the direction or shape of the Epistle reading: from general to particular, from large to small, from doctrine to practice, from justification to sanctification, from faith to good works. It begins with a brief review of basic Christian doctrine (vv. 13–14), then turns to the area of Christian behavior (vv. 15–17), then urges a specific Christian action, prayer (3:1–2), rounding out the appeal with God's help in Christ as the means to Paul's expressed goals (vv. 3–5). The passage is shaped like a funnel or an inverted pyramid (see outline).

5. A few translations appropriately highlight the sharp contrast between the faithlessness of the wicked men described in verse 2 and the faithfulness of the Lord described in verse 3.

6. The New King James's rendition "the evil one" (v. 3) is an improvement on the King James's "evil," not only because its presentation of evil as a person rather than a principle parallels the "wicked men" of the previous verse but also because it reminds us of "the man of sin," "the son of perdition" discussed in the preceding context. Even more relevant is the suggestion that in our battle with evil we are always dealing with *specific* evils emanating ultimately from a *personal* devil.

7. The modifier "in the Lord" (v. 4) is a "squinting" construction, pointing simultaneously to both what precedes it and what follows it. Unlike most squinting constructions, however, this one is symptomatic not of carelessness in writing but of richness in meaning. It suggests that the Lord is the source both of Paul's feeling of confidence (described in what precedes the modifier) and of the goodness in his readers about which he is confident (described in what follows the modifier). Wherever the virtue is, in Paul or in his readers, Jesus is the power for that virtue.

8. The King James Version translates verse 5, "The Lord direct your hearts . . . *into the patient waiting for Christ."* This rendition has the virtue of connecting our text with the immediate and broad contexts of discussion about Christ's second coming. The New King James Version (together with most other versions) translates it, "The Lord direct your hearts . . . *into the patience of Christ,"* establishing a parallelism between "the patience of Christ" and "the love of God" in the same verse (both subjective genitives) and strengthening the Gospel thrust of the text: God's love enables our love and Christ's patience enables our patience.

Sermon Outline
THE BLESSED INVERTED PYRAMID
OF CHRISTIAN LIVING

I. The foundation of the pyramid.

(Here present the cardinal doctrines of 2:13–15 as the basis and impetus for the directives of the two remaining parts of the sermon outline—a foundation, incidentally, reinforced by the closing verses, 3:3–5.)

II. The bulk of the pyramid.

(Here present the discussion of Christian behavior in general supplied in 2:15–17, behavior based on and flowing from Part I.)

III. The apex of the pyramid.

(Here present Paul's plea in 3:1–2 for the specific virtue of prayer for the ministers and ministry of the Gospel.)

FRANCIS C. ROSSOW

Twenty-Fifth Sunday After Pentecost

GOSPEL   Luke 20:27–38 (RSV)

Sermon Notes/Introduction

1. As we near the end of another church year, a sermon on the resurrection of the dead is timely. In fact, this doctrine is always timely.

2. This pericope is one of several accounts in this portion of Luke's gospel that record the efforts of the "chief priests and scribes and the principal men of the people . . . to destroy Him; but they did not find anything they could do, for all the people hung upon His words" (19:47–48). Since others had been silenced, the Sadducees were now ready to give it a try.

3. The Sadducees were in the priestly class but not identical with it and were powerful politically. Normally they were foes of the Pharisees, "for the Sadducees say there is no resurrection, nor angel, nor spirit; but the Pharisees acknowledge them all" (Acts 23:8). The Sadducees belonged to the "death ends it all" school; human beings are only material and have no spirit.

4. The Sadducees, with the story of the woman who married the seven brothers, hoped that Jesus would say something that would contradict the law of Moses about successive mar-

riages; the implication was that the resurrection was inconsistent with the law of Moses.

5. Jesus responds by pointing out that the resurrection is regulated by larger laws than the Levirate laws. Marriage is necessary for this life because people die, and for the human family to survive there must be births. In eternity there is no death and therefore no need for the marriage relationship to continue—no need for births.

6. In the Matthew and Mark accounts, Jesus is more severe with the Sadducees: "You are wrong. . . . You know neither the Scriptures nor the power of God." This is a strong rebuke of their spiritual ignorance.

7. Moses believed in the resurrection. Jesus quotes the passage in the burning bush incident when God identified Himself as the God of Abraham and Isaac and Jacob, and points out that God is not a God of the dead, but of the living. "God of the dead" is a contradiction in terms; it is inconsistent with the nature of God.

8. Every use of "I am God" not only implies the resurrection but also a covenant relationship with God, the relationship that grew out of the covenant in which God provided the promise of salvation and in which the people, with God's help, provided the response of faith in God's promise and obedience to God's will. The living God has living people who have a covenant relationship with Him. They live to Him.

9. The phrase "sons of God" describes the relationship of the converted, the regenerate who come to faith in our Redeemer Jesus Christ. By nature we are not members of God's family; in Christ we are (Rom. 9:26). Believers are also called "sons of the resurrection," which is part of being "sons of God."

10. Note that Luke 20:36 says "equal to angels," not "same as angels." In heaven the children of God are like angels in this respect that they do not die nor do they marry.

11. Jesus' words about our resurrection from the dead remind us of His resurrection, which is the cornerstone of our faith. The Christian's daily life is lived and expressed through resurrection power. This pericope provides opportunities for applying that truth to our life as well.

12. Belief in the resurrection gives life an aim, purpose, and goal. The trouble with not having a goal is that you can spend your life running up and down the field, but you never score a point.

Sermon Outline
I BELIEVE IN THE RESURRECTION

I. The Old Testament teaches it.
   A. The Sadducees try to use the Old Testament to disprove the resurrection (vv. 28–33).
   B. Jesus uses the Old Testament to prove the resurrection (vv. 34–38).
   C. Other Old Testament passages support this: Job 19:25–27; Is. 26:19; Dan. 12:2.

II. The New Testament teaches it.
   A. Jesus is "the resurrection and the life" (John 11:25).
   B. The resurrection consists of
      1. the restoration and glorification of the body (1 Cor. 15:42–49); and
      2. the reunion of body and soul.
   C. Our resurrection has its basis in Christ's redemption of the human family and in His resurrection (Rom. 10:9; 1 Cor. 15:17; 1 Thess. 4:14).
   D. *Application:* Jesus' resurrection has significance for us not only on Judgment Day but also right now, for already in this life it effects in us a spiritual resurrection, empowering us to live ever more and more in harmony with God's will.

III. It is consistent with the nature of God.
   A. God created human beings for life, not death (Luke 20:37–38).
   B. The Father sent His Son to rescue fallen humanity.
      1. He buys us back, redeems us (Mark 10:45).
      2. He gives us new life (2 Cor. 5:17).
   C. This gives power, purpose, and meaning to our life (Luke 20:38, "for all live to him"; 2 Cor. 5:15; Eph. 2:10; 1 Thess. 4:3).

ELMER W. MATTHIAS

Third-Last Sunday in the Church Year

EPISTLE   2 Thessalonians 3:1–5 (RSV)

Sermon Notes/Introduction

The Introit intones pure Gospel. God is the subject for each of the five verses from Psalm 85. The Collect speaks of absolution and deliverance. Though now unrevealed to empirical observation, Jesus is alive and active, according to the implication of *apokaluptetai* in Luke 17:30. The world exhorts the exhausted to draw on their own limited resources. Christianity looks to God, absolving and delivering, alive and active in the person of Jesus Christ. We wait for this revealing, and we "keep watch" according to the imperative of the Alleluia Verse (Matt. 24:42). "May the Lord direct your hearts"—your weary, burdened, burned-out hearts—into this blessed reality!

The experts in time management posit "concentration of power" as a key to purposeful, productive living. This concentration of power consists, simply stated, in direction. The apostle Paul understands the even greater importance of direction in our relationship with God. And so the Epistle this day contains Paul's prayerful desire that our Lord give us "Direction for the Heart."

Sermon Outline
DIRECTION FOR THE HEART

I. Our Lord is the Path-Opener, the Obstacle-Remover (2 Thess. 3:5; here a word study of "direct"—*kateuthunai*—yields valuable results.)
   A. Obstacles do stand in the path.
      1. Spiritual apathy and lack of discipline plagued the Thessalonian Christians (vv. 6–15).
      2. "Wicked and evil men" dogged the missionary efforts of Paul (v. 2).
      3. We can find "the Way" blocked by internal (Rom. 7:23–24) and external (Eph. 6:12) obstacles.
   B. The Holy Spirit turns us to the Lord for direction (2 Thess. 3:5).
      1. He takes the initiative to seek the lost (Luke 19:10).
      2. He keeps safe those who have been found and gives them growth.

Christ calls us (Matt. 4:19; John 21:19) and by His call enables us to follow. But where?

II. Our Lord leads us.
   A. "Into the love of God" (2 Thess. 3:5 NASB, a subjective genitive, i.e., "God's love").
      1. God's love moved Him to give us life at the cost of a great sacrifice (John 3:16).
      2. The blood of that sacrifice (Jesus Christ) opens the path and removes the obstacles (Eph. 2:13–14) to God's love (v. 19).

3. God's love, shared with us through His Word and His Son's precious body and blood, now empowers us to live with direction—His direction (see 2 Cor. 5:15).

B. "Into the steadfastness of Christ" (2 Thess. 3:5 NASB, a subjective genitive, i.e., "Christ's steadfastness").

1. Christ's steadfastness took Him to Calvary (Heb. 12:2).

2. Christ endured our problems and sufferings, giving us hope in their place.

3. Christ's steadfastness, communicated to us through the life-giving Gospel, sustains us in our weariness and restores our joy for life. What an antidote for burdened, stressed hearts!

If you have ever been lost (or had a child lost), you know the stress that besets a person, the gratitude felt toward someone who gives direction, and the relief and joy experienced when one's destination is reached. Our Lord wants to give us that same relief and joy. May He direct our hearts into the love of God and steadfastness of Christ!

THOMAS R. AHLERSMEYER

Third-Last Sunday in the Church Year

GOSPEL   Luke 17:20–30 (KJV)

Sermon Notes/Introduction

Introductory thoughts: In *Foolishness to the Greeks* (Grand Rapids, Mich.: Eerdmans, 1986), Lesslie Newbigin discusses what would be involved were there to be a "genuine missionary encounter between the Gospel and the culture that is shared by the peoples of Europe and North America." He stresses that modern Western culture is "the most widespread, powerful and persuasive" among all contemporary cultures, that it is really a pagan society, and that its paganism, "having been born out of the rejection of Christianity, is far more resistant to the Gospel than the pre-Christian paganism with which cross-cultural mission has been familiar."

This pericope has much to contribute to a genuine missionary encounter with people of modern Western culture who, with their secular humanism and "scientific" orientation, cannot (or will not) believe in a kingdom that "cometh not with observation," whose apathy and indifference to things divine and materialistic, worldly pursuits are indeed like those of the people living at the times of Noah and of Lot. It likewise has much to contribute to that missionary encounter in terms of preparing today's disciples of Christ for their difficult task.

Textual notes: Verse 21: entos humōn—By these words does the Savior mean to say "within you" or "among you"? We agree with Paul Bretscher that the meaning of *entos* in this case must and can best be determined by the context and related passages. The miracles of Jesus, His preaching of the Gospel of the kingdom, His announcements that the kingdom of God had come, and the agreement of His words and works with the Old Testament Scripture all give ample evidence that in Him the kingdom had made its appearance. Mark 11:9–10 and similar references show a close relation between the King and His kingdom. Jesus told the Pharisees: "The kingdom of God is here, it is among you, in your midst, but you do not see it, you do not recognize Me as the King nor the operations of the kingdom." Compare Mark 4:26–27; John 3:3; Rom. 14:17. (For a more complete discussion see Paul M. Bretscher, "Luke 17:21," *Concordia Theological Monthly* 15 [1944]: 730–36.)

Verse 22: Ylvisaker considers it reasonable to believe that the discourse to the disciples was occasioned by the question of the Pharisees and has both a logical and a historical connection. There will be days of persecution and distress of such severity that the disciples would earnestly desire to experience a day of the coming kingdom of glory—yet even that relief would not be possible.

Verses 23: Impostors and false teachers will come. The disciples are warned not to follow their direction or to run after them.

Verse 24: The reason: everyone will know it when He returns.

Verse 25: But first it is necessary that He suffer many things, including death (Luke 24:7, 26, 46). He tells them this in advance to prepare them. He informs them also that He would be rejected by the Jews.

Verse 27: Indifferent, worldly minded, deaf to the word of warning sent through Noah, not some or most but all were overwhelmed (*kataklusmos*), inundated, dashed, and swept away.

Verse 29: "The day that Lot went out" restates "the day that Noah entered." Only so long does God's patience wait

(1 Peter 3:20). That the day of grace can and does end in the lifetime of many needs to be taught. Not to do so is to remove much urgency from mission.

Verse 30: That it will be the same on the day that the Son of Man is revealed means that God Himself says that the vast majority will perish. The disciples will have some but not much success. This must be preached! *Apokaluptetai* implies that the Son of Man has been living and reigning, although not visibly. He is the One who assures His little flock in Luke 12:32 that they have no cause for fear.

Sermon Outline
THAT FEWER PEOPLE MIGHT BE LOST

I. People need to receive the instruction given the Pharisees on the kingdom of God.
   A. It does not come with observation.
   B. Yet it is in their midst.
II. The disciples of Christ need to be instructed, warned, and prepared for their mission.
   A. They must be instructed regarding the severe trials and persecutions they will experience.
   B. They must be warned about impostors and false teachers.
   C. They must be prepared by learning well:
      1. Christ's suffering and rejection were necessary.
      2. The vast majority of humanity (especially those living in the end of times) will perish.

The picture the Lord presents of the days preceding His second coming tells us honestly, not gruesomely, that we will not experience much success. It is presented as part of His "whole counsel," which we must faithfully proclaim so that fewer might be lost—that fewer people continue to live in apathy, widespread indifference, and the worldly pursuits that characterize modern Western culture.

HARLEY L. KOPITSKE

Second-Last Sunday in the Church Year

EPISTLE 2 Corinthians 5:1–10 (NKJV)

Sermon Notes/Introduction

The approaching end of the church year calls the Christian's attention to Christ's return in judgment and the end of all things. It also reminds us of our own end—the death of our body. Some of us, afflicted with sickness this past year, have been made particularly aware of the body's frailty. And we all in varying degrees have been painfully reminded of the body's proclivity for wrongdoing. We long to be free of the body's weaknesses and limitations. Still we do not wish for a bodiless existence in eternity. We thrill to God's promise of a resurrected body in heaven—free of sin and sickness—and we look forward to the fulfillment of His promise. In the meantime, we learn that God has a use, a purpose, for our mortal body here on earth as we today consider "A Christian's Perspective on the Human Body."

Sermon Outline

A CHRISTIAN'S PERSPECTIVE ON THE HUMAN BODY

I. Christians recognize the limitations of their present bodies.
   A. They clearly see the evidence of these limitations.
      1. The body is an "earthen vessel," much inferior to the treasures of Christ that it contains and conveys in Christian ministry (4:7).
      2. The body is subject to numerous weaknesses and hardships (vv. 8–12, 16).
      3. The body is ultimately mortal, subject to destruction and dissolution (5:1).
   B. They understand the purpose of these limitations.
      1. One purpose is to show "that the excellence of the power [of the Christians' ministry] may be of God and not of us" (4:7).
      2. Another purpose is that Christians might continually "lift up [their] eyes to the hills—From whence comes [their] help" and realize that their "help comes from the Lord, Who made heaven and earth" (Ps. 121:1–2).
II. So Christians yearn for the resurrected body of heaven.

A. Despite the limitations of the body, they do not wish for a bodiless existence in heaven.
   1. Phillips paraphrases 2 Cor. 5:3: "We do not want to face utter nakedness when death destroys our present dwelling—these bodies of ours."
   2. The *Good News Bible* translates part of verse 4: "It is not that we want to get rid of our earthly body."
B. In fact, they yearn for the resurrected body of heaven.
   1. Verse 2: "earnestly desiring to be clothed with our habitation which is from heaven."
   2. Verse 4: "not because we want to be unclothed, but further clothed, that mortality may be swallowed up by life."
C. God assures them that their yearning for such a body will be realized.
   1. Christ's own bodily resurrection is the precedent for the Christians' resurrection (1 Cor. 15:20).
   2. The Holy Spirit's presence in the Christians' earthly bodies is the guarantee ("deposit") of their future resurrection (2 Cor. 5:5).
   3. Hence, Christians *know* that if their "earthly house . . . is destroyed," they have "a building from God, a house not made with hands, eternal in the heavens" (v. 1).
D. They experience this assurance not by sight but by faith (v. 7), a faith that, like the Holy Spirit, is also God's gift (Eph. 2:8).
III. Nevertheless, Christians see usefulness for their present bodies in the program of God.
A. True, they prefer "to be absent from the body and to be present with the Lord" (v. 8).
B. Nevertheless, their aim, "whether present or absent," is "to be well pleasing to [God]" (v. 9). Christians abound in the work of the Lord. (Materials from the Old Testament Reading, Jer. 8:4–7, and especially from the Gospel, Luke 19:11–27, will prove useful here.)
C. They recognize that how they use their present bodies in the service of the Lord and His people will constitute the evidence to Jesus, their Judge on the Last Day, of the presence of saving faith (2 Cor. 5:10; see also Matt. 25:31–46).

FRANCIS C. ROSSOW

Second-Last Sunday in the Church Year

GOSPEL   Luke 19:11–27 (KJV)

Sermon Notes/Introduction

The parable in the Gospel for the day is similar in several respects to the parable of the talents in Matt. 25:14–30. This makes it easy to confuse the two parables and to make applications, especially in the Luke story, that might not be warranted. It is helpful, therefore, when preparing a sermon on the parable from Luke to note the differences between it and the story in Matthew. The two are separate parables with two distinct interpretations.

An investment is involved in both parables, and each one has the aspect of accountability. But it should be noted that the parable of the pounds or minas in Luke has the nobleman distribute the same capital to each servant. In Matthew the distribution is unequal and made because of the natural endowments of the recipients. A faithful use of native gifts and abilities is the emphasis in the Matthean parable. The Luke narrative, on the other hand, deals with the productive use of an identical gift. Although there are other differences between the two illustrations, this is perhaps the most significant for homiletical purposes.

Financial planning is a major business in contemporary American life. Investment firms regularly invite people to presentations on how to make the best use of whatever money they have available after meeting life's daily essentials. The business is not new. In Jesus' day, too, investment opportunities were available and familiar even to the common people. Our Lord was able, therefore, to speak about the kingdom of God in terms of "Investment Opportunities."

Sermon Outline
INVESTMENT OPPORTUNITIES

I. Capital.

According to the parable a nobleman was preparing to go into a far country to receive a kingdom. That was a familiar occurrence in Jesus' day. It was not unusual under the Roman government for local puppet rulers to go to Rome to receive their political commissions. In fact, King Herod's son Archelaus had to do that and was unwanted as ruler by some whom he was to govern.

Before the nobleman left to get his kingdom, he distributed a mina (perhaps about three months' salary) to each of 10 servants. Each recipient had the same amount with which to work and was given the specific instruction to do business with the capital.

Since verse 11 makes clear that Jesus' audience was expecting to see Him, now near Jerusalem, establish a visible kingdom, the interpretation of the opening details of the parable is obvious. Jesus will establish no such kingdom. Instead, He will be going into a far country to receive His kingdom. There will be His death and resurrection, His ascension and session at the right hand of God before He returns visibly a second time.

But Jesus will not leave His servants without something to do and without a commodity with which to work. He has given His church capital, the message of the Gospel of salvation and the divinely instituted sacraments. These means of grace are the mina that each servant received.

II. Gain.

The parable becomes succinct as the gain of the servants is reported. Only three servants are mentioned, two who had done the wise thing and invested and one who had done nothing but tie up his master's working capital in a facial sweat towel.

Very significant is the comment of the two financially astute servants. They do not say, "I have gained this amount of profit for you." They report instead, "*Your* mina has earned . . ." (vv. 16, 18). They did merely what they had been commanded to do and discovered that the money had the power to accomplish things.

That is surely the way it is in the kingdom of God. We have been given the Word to proclaim and the sacraments to use. Of His means of grace the Lord has said, "My word . . . shall not return unto Me void, but . . . it shall prosper in the thing whereto I sent it" (Is. 55:10). It is for us to invest; the Lord's gifts have the power within themselves to produce the gains.

And what kinds of spiritual investment opportunities are available? We might think first of the Lord's commission to make disciples of all nations. When we proclaim the Gospel, we are investing among those who do not know Christ and are not part of the Christian community. But that is not the only place where investments are made. Every worship service is a time when the Gospel is doing business, for with our proclamation we exhort, strengthen, and build up God's people. Every pastoral call at a sickbed is an investment opportunity for God's mina. Every pastoral counseling session, every layperson's testimony to Christ in word and deed, every class in religious instruction, every baptism and service of the Lord's Supper is a place where God's mina is making spiritual gains. It is our task to promote that host of spiritual ventures where God's capital can work.

III. Accountability.

The conclusion of the parable makes it an especially appropriate sermon text for the Second-Last Sunday in the Church Year. The focus at the close of the church year is on end things. Among these is our Lord's second coming and judgment. The Lord is serious about the work that He has given His servants to do, and there will be accountability.

The seriousness and inevitability of the Lord's final accounting receive special emphasis with the double judgment reference in the Gospel. The citizens who had not wanted the nobleman to rule over them were executed in his presence. Moreover, the servant who had not invested showed disloyalty to his lord and lost everything. God's judgment is real and severe.

On the other hand, there was also a reward of grace. It was generous beyond measure. Faithfulness in just a little received the most undeserving recompense.

So it is in the kingdom of God. "Well done" is the word to the faithful. But what did they do? The Lord chose them and provided them with capital to invest. God's Word and sacraments that they shared were the means that sustained them and kept them faithful to Christ. But let there be no mistake. The eternal blessings that come as a result of such faithfulness are sure and secure because they rest on the work and merit of Him who is the nobleman of the kingdom, Jesus Christ, the Son of God and Redeemer of the world.

WAYNE E. SCHMIDT

Last Sunday in the Church Year: Sunday of the Fulfillment

EPISTLE   Colossians 1:13–20

Sermon Notes/Introduction

Our world is far more like the people quoted in Luke 23:35–39 than like Paul in Colossians 1:13–20. Instead of the powerful, pounding, insistent words of the epistle—"He, He, He, He, in Him, in Him, in Him"—we hear the taunting words, "If you . . ." That is the world in which the congregation lives, filled mostly with taunts and only occasionally, mostly on Sunday mornings, with a few triumphs. The Epistle, then, must confront the taunts with the triumph of Him who is Conqueror and Savior, Lord and Brother. That is the preaching task.

The end of the church year is so different from the end of the calendar year. Newspapers carry articles on the 10 most important news stories of the year. The last calendar page is torn off, and we have to remember to write the new year on our checks. The year may end with some meaningless parties, but that is no surprise, because the end of a year really is no big deal at all. But the end of the church year is a big deal. It signals the end of the narration of the greatest story in all history and the new beginning of the recitation of that story for people of faith. In majestic words the Epistle tells us about Him who is the subject of the story and the object of our praise, Jesus Christ. "Here is your King!" it declares boldly. But did you listen to the Gospel? Most of those whom it quotes taunt Him and us with His humiliation: "This is your King, nailed to a cross and dying?" Both the triumph and the taunt go together. The crown without the cross is self-crowning. The cross without the crown is defeat. A cross and a crown—that is salvation. So we look to King Jesus, for in Him we see both "Taunt and Triumph."

Sermon Outline
TAUNT AND TRIUMPH

I. The taunt and the triumph of Jesus Christ, the image of God (v. 15).
   A. The taunt:
      1. Herod's taunt and the slaughter of the innocents.
      2. Satan's taunt: "If you are the Son of God . . ."

       3. The taunt of those under the cross: "If he be Christ, the Chosen One . . ."

       4. The ignorant taunt of the disciples: "Now, Lord? Now the kingdom of glory?" (Acts 1:6).

   B. The triumph: the obedience of the perfect one to the Father.

       1. Jesus' words: God is like a Shepherd seeking His sheep and laying down His life for them, like a father welcoming home a prodigal.

       2. Scripture's word (1 John 1:1–3).

   C. Taunt and triumph for the Christian.

       1. The taunt:

          a. "Grab the crown! You deserve it!"

          b. "Stay on your knees! You'll never be good enough!"

       2. The triumph (Col. 1:13–14).

          a. The restoration of the divine image.

          b. The manifestation of the divine image in us ("light," "salt").

II. The taunt and the triumph of Jesus Christ, the first-born of all creation (v. 16).

   A. The taunt: Where is the majesty?

       1. Every power on earth and in heaven was created through and for Him.

       2. Yet Pilate struts Rome's power, soldiers offer mere vinegar, a crowd mocks, and even thieves cry, "Do something, then!"

   B. The triumph:

       1. Isaiah described the purpose of Christ's humiliation (Is. 53:5).

       2. Christ achieved His triumph not as Judge but as Substitute.

       3. Christ became subject to created powers that they might no longer imprison us.

   C. Taunt and triumph for the Christian.

       1. Many created things beckon us to crown them as king.

          a. Such things include one's work, family, bank account, possessions, and insurance policy.

          b. Who is the king of the life of each of us here? Who wears the crown?

       2. The triumph of King Jesus is grasped by believing in Him (John 1:10–13).

          a. The thief received the crown from the cross.

      b. At the end of the church year, Christians should unclutter life to see their eternal appointment and the waiting crown.

III. The taunt and the triumph of Jesus Christ, the head of the church and all things (Col. 1:19–20).
    A. The taunt: Look at the body hanging on the cross!
    B. The triumph:
      1. His physical body rose from death.
      2. His spiritual body, the church, lives and moves and grows.
    C. Taunt and triumph for the Christian.
      1. The weakness of the church and our weakness taunt us.
      2. The power of Christ in us is our triumph.

We live daily with the taunts of the devil, the world, and our flesh. But the Christ of cross and crown is moving us toward the final Last Day of the Church Year when "every knee shall bow and every tongue confess that Jesus Christ is Lord!" As we wait in anticipation for that day, our Lord of cross and crown says: "Be thou faithful unto death, and I will give thee a crown of life."

RICHARD G. KAPFER

Last Sunday in the Church Year: Sunday of the Fulfillment

GOSPEL   Luke 12:42–48 (RSV)

Sermon Notes/Introduction

1. The last Sundays of the church year have a character distinct from the others of the Pentecost cycle. The mood is of Christ's second coming and of His judgment, along with the end of our own earthly life. In the Gospel, appropriately enough, Luke turns to the matter of being prepared for the Parousia. It is the third in a series of parables and sayings on the theme of watchfulness and faithfulness for the time of judgment.

2. Prefacing the pericope is Peter's question, "Lord, are you telling this parable for us or for all?" (v. 41). This query may have been posed to provide the opportunity for warnings about the abuse of their positions by church leaders. But Jesus does not answer the question directly. Instead, He draws at-

tention to the responsibility of all servants.

3. The parable deals with the conduct of a steward (who was a slave; he is called *doulos* in v. 43), whom his master would place in charge of his whole estate while he himself was absent on a long journey. If the steward were to prove faithful, he would be richly rewarded, but if he abused his authority, he would be severely punished when the master had returned and taken him by surprise. At verse 46b the parable has been allegorized. It is no longer an earthly master who stands before the steward but the Son of Man, who has come as Judge. That Christ is thinking of His followers is intimated in placing the offender "with the unfaithful."

4. An interesting gradation of punishments is given in verses 47–48a: for active tyranny the punishment is death (*dichotomēsei* in v. 46 means "to cut in two," the dismemberment of a condemned person); for conscious and deliberate neglect, the punishment is a severe beating; for unintentional neglect, a light beating. The verses suggest that the punishment of disobedience will be in proportion to knowledge of the master's will. In large measure, this reflects notions of Jesus' day about sins that were unconscious and less culpable than those that were deliberate (Num. 15:27–31; Deut. 17:12).

5. The preacher may find that some of his hearers will be troubled by the thought that a person who sinned in ignorance will be punished. Our nation's judicial system, as well as contemporary ethical thought, tends to relieve the individual who "unknowingly" commits an indiscretion of guilt. The preacher may need to emphasize Paul's point in Romans 1 to the effect that there is no such thing as absolute moral ignorance. The emphasis is on the fact that the beating is *light*. But in the words of Leon Morris, "We should not minimize the importance of doing God's will. God's servant must make every effort to find out what God's will is and do it. We are all accountable" (*The Gospel According to St. Luke,* Tyndale New Testament Commentaries Series [Grand Rapids, Mich.: Eerdmans, 1974], p. 219).

6. The Gospel concludes with the Lord's declaration that responsibility rests on those who have received much. The passive and the impersonal forms stand for the divine name, and the verse might be translated: "Of every one to whom God has given much will He require much, and of him to whom God has entrusted much will He demand the more." The saying can readily be applied to Christian leaders. They, even more than disciples generally, need to be prepared for the

Parousia. For them readiness means their faithfulness in fulfilling the commission given them by Christ.

7. As the foregoing observations would suggest, this pericope is rich and multifaceted, as are most of the parables the Lord told. The homiletician might focus on verse 48b and expound on "Our Blessings and Responsibilities." But for the Last Sunday in the Church Year one should bring to the fore the themes most consistent with the propers. The following outline is but one suggestion:

Sermon Outline
FAITHFUL TO THE END

I. Called to Faithfulness.
II. The Consequences of Unfaithfulness.
III. The Way to Faithfulness.
    A. Spirit and Word.
    B. The Sacraments.

JOHN F. JOHNSON

Reformation Day

EPISTLE   Romans 3:19–28

Sermon Notes/Introduction

"Not guilty!" Those words lift an immense burden from the anxious heart of the accused person in a human court. The announcement is a powerful peal of liberty, even when fallible human courts have erred in pronouncing the verdict.

Quite in contrast to erring human courts are the infallible judgments of the Lord God. No mistakes occur at His bar of justice, and when the Lord says, "Not guilty!" the proclamation stands immutable and forever true. Part of God's gift through the Lutheran Reformation was the reassertion with unmistakable clarity of this truth.

Sermon Outline
NOT GUILTY IN GOD'S INFALLIBLE COURT

I. Crime was indeed committed (Rom. 3:19–20, 23).

It is often a double challenge to present an effective sermon on texts from Romans. First of all, the pastor must himself thoroughly understand both the concepts and the argument of the apostle Paul. Second, there is the demanding task of presenting doctrine in both a clear and a listenable way.

In the Epistle reading several key words should arrest the homiletician's attention. Having quoted from both Psalms and Isaiah in the words immediately preceding the text, Paul speaks about what the Law (*ho nomos*) says. His reference is to the preceding quotations, and thus he uses the term *nomos* to refer to the Old Testament. But the apostle continues with specific references to works of Law, thus focusing on God's code of perfection for His creatures. Looking into the mirror of this law of God, all humanity finds itself hopelessly stained. Note the universality of those who have committed crimes against God—*pan stoma, pas ho kosmos, pasa sarx.* All have been prosecuted and found guilty. Every possibility of refuting charges has been exhausted.

II. Just freedom, however, has been secured (vv. 21, 24–26).

Under those conditions the God of justice Himself acts. He brings forth what is both holy and just. It is called the *dikaiosunē theou,* another key phrase in Pauline theology. This righteousness of God is a revelation made known not only in the New Testament but in the Old as well, for "the law and the prophets bear witness to it." It is the righteousness of God that effects the verdict of "Not guilty!" This verdict does not in any way set aside justice, as if God were like a judge who recognized guilt but whimsically pardoned it. The excellence required by God's law was in truth brought to the courtroom. God made His own Son the *hilastērion,* a word that in the context of these verses clearly indicates expiation. God's justice was satisfied. Humanity had to be declared not guilty.

The act of Jesus Christ that brought acquittal is spoken of as *apolutrōsis.* Although this word does not always include the idea of ransom, its stem was commonly associated in the Greek-speaking world with the ransom of slaves, prisoners of war, and criminals condemned to death. Such ransom connotations are inescapable in the present context. In the words of Jesus, "the Son of Man came . . . to give His life a ransom (*lutron*) for many" (Matt. 20:28).

Not to be overlooked are two other words, *dōrean* and *charis.* No act of accused humanity accomplished the lawful acquittal. Grace bestowed freely brought it about that humanity could be declared *dikaios,* in the age before as well as after Christ (Rom. 3:26).

III. Faith apprehends the gift (vv. 22, 27–28).

How does the gratuitous verdict become the sinner's personal possession? Paul concludes in verse 28 that it is not because of works of Law but on the principle of faith. Faith, of course, is not the cause of the *dikaiosunē theou,* for then faith itself would become a work. Instead, faith is the hand that appropriates the gift. Paul's final statement summarizes the role of faith, but *pistis* has really been a binding thread throughout the argument (see verses 22, 25–26).

How do people become right before God? That was the issue at the time of the Lutheran Reformation. Rom. 3:19–28 provides the answer. For an effective reinforcement of this answer, all stanzas of "Salvation unto Us Has Come" (*Lutheran Worship* 355) might be sung. This Reformation era hymn has been called the "poetical counterpart of Luther's preface to the Romans."

WAYNE E. SCHMIDT

Reformation Day

GOSPEL   John 8:31–36 (NKJV)

Sermon Notes/Introduction

1. "Continue in My Word" (v. 31)—what does this mean? Remain loyal to a set of true doctrines? Use the Scriptures diligently? Cling to the Gospel? Do what God commands? A quick comparison of various translations will turn up all the possibilities just suggested. (For example, check the NIV, *Good News Bible,* Modern Language, and *Living Bible* versions.) So the best answer to the preceding questions seems to be yes or "All of the above." It is better to be all-inclusive than parochial in our application of verse 31. Let the doctrinally orthodox not overlook the implications for everyday Christian behavior in Jesus' directive "Continue in My Word." Let the social activists not ignore its implications for doctrinal purity.

2. "The truth" (v. 32)—what is it? The truth of the Scriptures in general? Or more specifically, the truth of the Gospel? Or is "the truth" a "who" rather than a "what," a person rather than a teaching, in short, the Lord Jesus Himself? (Compare "the *truth* shall make you free" of verse 32 with "the *Son* makes you free" of verse 36.) Again, the best answer seems to be yes or "All of the above." Interpreting Scripture with Scripture, we learn that "the truth" is both a "what" and a "who," both the written Word (the Bible) and the incarnate

Word (the Lord Jesus). (Compare John 17:17 with 14:6.) Although it is valid, even desirable, for purposes of definition to differentiate between the written Word and the incarnate Word, between the Bible and the Gospel, between formal principle and material principle, the experience of the church demonstrates the necessity of keeping the two meanings of "the truth" together in public proclamation. To minimize the written Word will ultimately affect the authority and purity of our proclamation of the incarnate Word. To minimize the incarnate Word will ultimately lead to a Law-oriented, Gospel-less bibliolatry.

3. A crux arises in verse 33: Who is the antecedent of "they"? The believing Jews of verses 30–31? (If so, the faith ascribed to them there seems to have deteriorated considerably by verses 33–34.) The hostile Jews of verses 19, 22, 25, and 27? (If so, we have a classic instance in verse 33 of remote and/or ambiguous antecedent.) Commentators divide on the issue. For the preacher to air the matter in the pulpit is to flirt with pedanticism and irrelevance. But he will need to resolve the question in his study, for whichever answer he arrives at will determine the thrust of his sermon. If he identifies the antecedent of "they" as the believing Jews, the preacher will likely address his sermon to the fluctuations, the ups and downs of everyday Christian faith. But if he identifies the antecedent of "they" as the hostile Jews of the context, the preacher may address his sermon to the sharply contrasting outcomes of belief and unbelief.

4. The "son" of verse 35 is translated generically in most versions ("a son"), whereas the "Son" of verse 36 is identified more specifically as Jesus ("*the* Son") in all versions. In any case the logic of verses 35–36 is mildly elliptic. The full progress of thought is spelled out below. (Note especially step "d.")

    a. A slave does not abide in his master's house forever; he is not free.
    b. A son does abide in his master's house forever; he is free.
    c. Jesus, because he is the Son of God, abides in His Father's house forever; He is "free indeed."
    d. Jesus changes us from slaves (of sin) to sons (of God).
    e. Therefore, we abide in His Father's house forever; we are "free indeed."

5. The outline below relies heavily on the immediate context as well as on the Gospel reading itself. Although generic in form, the outline can easily be adapted to a Reformation

observance by using the popular Reformation themes of religious liberty or faithfulness to God's Word as an introduction.

Sermon Outline
LIKE FATHER, LIKE SON

I. Jesus: a genuine case of "like Father, like Son."
   A. In verse 19, He says, "If you had known Me, you would have known My Father also." "I and My Father are one," Jesus claims in John 10:30. (See also 8:16, 18–19, 26–27, 54–55; as well as 14:9.)
   B. Review appropriate sections from the Apostles', Nicene, and Athanasian creeds that describe the equality of Jesus with God, His Father.
   C. Jesus' deity—"like Father, like Son"—is a cardinal doctrine of our Christian faith.

II. Unregenerate sinners: an ironic case of "like father, like son."
   A. Jesus' enemies claimed to be descendants of Abraham (8:33)—"like father, like son" in that respect.
   B. Although Jesus concedes that they were physically descended from Abraham (v. 37), He points out that their behavior is unlike that of their ancestor (vv. 39–40).
   C. Ultimately, Jesus demonstrates that their lies and deeds (and those of all unregenerate sinners today) prove them to be children of the devil (v. 44)—ironically, "like father, like son" in that respect!

III. Saved sinners: a blessed case of "like Father, like son."
   A. "Whoever commits sin is a slave of sin" (v. 34). This, alas, includes us.
   B. Slaves are "in bondage" (v. 33). They are not free. They cannot abide in God's house forever (v. 35).
   C. Jesus is not a slave but the Son of God (cf. part I of this outline). He is "free indeed."
   D. But taking on Himself the form of a servant and becoming obedient to death, even the death of the cross (Phil. 2:7–8), Jesus has changed us from slaves of sin to sons of God (Rom. 8:14–17). We share His status— "like Son, like son"!
   E. Being sons of God, we are now "free indeed" (John 8:36), sure of abiding in God's house forever (v. 35). Already in this life, we begin to share God our Father's freedom, His presence, and His likeness.
   F. Thus, by God's grace, we too are now—in a sense—

a case of "like Father, like son"!

Let us maintain this blessed "like Father, like son" status that God has conferred on us through Jesus by continuing in God's Word (v. 31). Then we will be "disciples indeed" (v. 31). Then we "shall know the truth, and the truth shall [keep] us free" (v. 32).

FRANCIS C. ROSSOW

Thanksgiving Day

EPISTLE   1 Timothy 2:1–4

Sermon Notes/Introduction

In 1:12–17 St. Paul exalts the marvelous mercy of God that moved Him to deal patiently with the obnoxious blasphemer Paul was before his conversion. Instead of destroying Paul, God convinced him of forgiveness in Christ and gave him faith in and love for Christ. But not only did God save Paul; God appointed him to the apostleship. What marvelous mercy it was to take an implacable enemy of Christ and transform him into a faithful proclaimer of the love of Christ! Paul had reason to thank God. Thanksgiving is both the subject and broader context of the Epistle.

In 1:18–20 St. Paul points out that by taking seriously the prophetic utterances spoken to Timothy (possibly at his ordination) regarding his role as a pastor, Timothy would be able to hold on to faith that expresses itself in thankfulness. Faith accompanied by thankfulness and a good conscience has not been easy to maintain. Paul refers to Hymenaeus and Alexander, who had let the evil around them shipwreck their faith and good conscience. The church disciplined Hymenaeus and Alexander in the hope that they would return to faith and to its fruit, thankfulness.

In the Epistle reading Paul now goes on to show that this thankfulness relates not only to what God has done for us but also to what God has done and continues to do for us through others. He emphasizes intercessory prayer. In view of the difficulties Christians experienced from heathen rulers, Paul singles out kings and all those in authority as individuals for whom Christians ought to pray so that Christians would be able to live quiet and peaceable lives that please God, who is the Savior of all and who wishes all to be saved.

It's hard for us in the U.S. to imagine what it would be like to be persecuted because of our Christian commitment. Persecution by heathen authorities was a reality for Paul, for Timothy, and for the Christians they served. Similar persecutions continue today under Communist and other oppressive regimes in the world.

Although our government may not discriminate against us overtly, we find it difficult to persevere in faith because of no less real persecution from unbelieving family members and business associates. It is appropriate on this Thanksgiving Day to pray for others, also for our county's leaders and for all who are in authority.

Sermon Outline
PRAY FOR OTHERS ON THIS THANKSGIVING DAY

I. We pray that we might persevere in faith.
   A. Living out our faith according to Christian principles has never been easy.
      1. Timothy felt threatened.
      2. So do we when we are hindered from following Christian principles in our jobs or elsewhere.
      3. The result is that we can make shipwreck of faith and a good conscience.
   B. On this Thanksgiving Day we have reason to pray for those who cause us difficulty in living out our Christian faith.
      1. God hears those prayers. What a gift of God it is when He directs life's circumstances so that we can live godly lives in quietness and peace.
      2. We have reason to thank God for those who have helped us by their example and encouragement to live a godly life.

Today let us pray for others so that they might help us to preserve our faith by a faithful use of the means of grace.

II. We pray that God might bring more people to a knowledge of the truth.
   A. God can accomplish His saving will despite difficult circumstances.
      1. Who would ever have thought of Paul as good salvation material? None of us deserves salvation any more than he did. Our sin condemns us all.
      2. Yet God saved us through what Jesus did for us, no matter how great our sin or how difficult our life

circumstances. God has brought us to know the truth about our sin and our Savior.

B. God wants us to pray for others on this Thanksgiving Day so that any threats on their part to Christianity may come to naught and God's gracious will would be done.

1. There is a continuous battle going on in our world between the forces of Satan and of God. The powers of evil do not wish God's saving purposes to be realized in this world.

2. We can thank God for those who have been His instruments in thwarting evil purposes and in bringing more people to a knowledge of the truth.

Let us pray for others on this Thanksgiving Day so that they might help us to persevere in faith and so that God might bring more people to a knowledge of the truth.

GERHARD AHO

Thanksgiving Day

GOSPEL   Luke 17:11–19 (NKJV)

Sermon Notes/Introduction

1. The gratitude of the one healed leper and the thoughtlessness of the remaining nine healed lepers make this pericope a "natural" for a Thanksgiving Day sermon. Yet the preacher must be careful not to accent the human responses described in the reading at the expense of the intense divine activity portrayed throughout the account. Even more important, the preacher, if he is to preach a full Gospel, must clarify in his sermon that a proper human response is utterly dependent on the activity of God. The latter is cause; the former is result.

2. To see a parallel between the dread disease of leprosy and the dread disease of sin and to recognize an analogy between the way in which leprosy ostracized its victims from society and the way in which sin severs us from God and people are not necessarily "allegorizing" or "spiritualizing" the incident, if in making the association the preacher neither negates nor minimizes the miracle of healing that actually occurred. Meaning dare not nullify historicity and facticity; on the other hand, historicity and facticity need not preclude meaning.

3. A number of profound applications can be inferred from

the simple directive of Jesus in verse 14: "Go, show yourselves to the priests." (a) An urgent, poignant appeal for help receives a simple, immediate response. The instruction to the lepers to be examined by the priests assumes the prior healing; it begs the question in a sense. Jesus talks as if the miracle had already occurred; He takes the healing for granted. The incident reminds us of God's words in Is. 65:24: "It shall come to pass that before they call, I will answer; and while they are still speaking, I will hear." (b) The miracle is low-key, utterly devoid of fanfare and razzle-dazzle. There are no elaborate preparations for the healing. No spectators are summoned to witness the miracle. No attempt is made to arouse the curiosity of the lepers about the details of the healing process. The author of the miracle Himself does not wait around to see its completion. Jesus is a miracle worker but never a magician. Once again we are reminded that God's ways are not our ways. (c) The directive requires a considerable degree of faith by the 10 lepers. They had to set out for their examination by the priests without any immediate empirical evidence that there was any healing to examine. For them to have asked for healing and then to be told to go to the priests, assured that by the time they arrive, the requested miracle will have occurred, took some doing on their part—ultimately God's doing! Only God, the author of faith, could bestow such a faith (Eph. 2:8–9). All of the lepers, even the nine who later proved ungrateful, pass this test of faith with flying colors. So far, so good. (d) In executing the miracle, Jesus does not ignore the Levitical requirement that a healed leper should be examined by a priest to be declared free of disease officially. Here we see one more indication that Jesus came not to destroy the Law and the Prophets but to fulfill them (Matt. 5:17). (e) Even as the healed lepers were directed (and empowered) to fulfill the requirement of Levitical law, so we, healed of the leprosy of sin, are directed (and empowered) to fulfill God's moral law. In short, given the input of God's power through Jesus, faith acts, faith responds, faith does things.

4. Although Jesus' words to the grateful leper, "Go your way" (Luke 17:19) may be regarded as a general dismissal to return to the normal routines of life, it is more likely a specific reminder to complete the earlier directive of seeing the priests for clearance. The spontaneous outburst of gratitude from the Samaritan was not a substitute for his obedience but a supplement to it. Nor were the other nine at fault for carrying out Jesus' directive. Their mistake lay in stopping at that point, not

expressing their thanks at some interval to the author of their healing. The lesson seems clear: Like the Samaritan we are to keep the spirit of the Law as well as its letter. Spontaneity, as well as duty, is to characterize Christian behavior.

5. "Your faith has made you well" is Jesus' final pronouncement to the healed Samaritan. Does this statement refer merely to the healing of his leprosy? If it does, then we must remember that the healing is God's doing, not the Samaritan's; his faith is not the *cause* of the healing but the *instrument* through which God does the healing (not *causa efficiens* but *causa instrumentalis*). More likely, though, Jesus' pronouncement means that the Samaritan's faith is full, complete; it is a faith that sees in Jesus not only a miracle worker but also a Savior from sin. Hence his faith becomes a vehicle through which God not only gives physical healing but also provides eternal salvation. (After all, the other nine were also healed of their physical ailment!) The King James Version allows for this expanded meaning with its more inclusive rendition: "Thy faith hath made thee *whole*," and Modern Language says it unambiguously, "Your faith has *saved* you" (emphasis mine).

Sermon Outline
"HIS LOVE—OUR RESPONSE"

I. His love (God's doing).
   A. The Epistle displays in graphic detail Jesus' love to a group of lepers.
   B. Thanksgiving Day reminds us in numerous ways of God's love to us through Jesus.
II. Our response (also God's doing).
   A. The Epistle shows Jesus bestowing the faith that empowers the responses of obedience *and* gratitude.
   B. Thanksgiving Day once more exposes us to the Good News of salvation in Christ, through which God gifts us with the faith that will empower us to do His will and to pour out our hearts in thanksgiving to Him for all His mercies.

FRANCIS C. ROSSOW

SCRIPTURE INDEX

Studies marked CTQ originally appeared in *Concordia Theological Quarterly;* those marked CJ originally appeared in *Concordia Journal.* Studies designated "New" were written for this volume.